This Day in U.S. Military History

Paul Brandus

WEST WING
REPORTS

Bernan Press
Lanham · Boulder · New York · London

Thank you to *Chase's Calendar of Events* for permission to use some material for this book.

Published by Bernan Press
An imprint of The Rowman & Littlefield Publishing Group, Inc.
4501 Forbes Boulevard, Suite 200, Lanham, Maryland 20706
www.rowman.com
800-462-6420

6 Tinworth Street, London SE11 5AL, United Kingdom

Names: Brandus, Paul, author.
Title: This day in U.S. military history / Paul Brandus.
Description: Lanham : Bernan Press, [2020] | Includes index. | Summary: "For each day of the year, Paul Brandus (West Wing Reports), author of the acclaimed This Day in Presidential History, offers milestone events, dramatic stories, and arresting quotes from the storied history of the U.S. armed forces."— Provided by publisher.
Identifiers: LCCN 2019045885 (print) | LCCN 2019045886 (ebook) | ISBN 9781641433853 (cloth) | ISBN 9781641433860 (epub)
Subjects: LCSH: United States—History, Military—Anecdotes. | Chronology, Historical.
Classification: LCC E181 .B796 2020 (print) | LCC E181 (ebook) | DDC 355.00973—dc23
LC record available at https://lccn.loc.gov/2019045885
LC ebook record available at https://lccn.loc.gov/2019045886

♾ ™ The paper used in this publication meets the minimum requirements of American National Standard for Information Sciences—Permanence of Paper for Printed Library Materials, ANSI/NISO Z39.48-1992.

Table of Contents

Mount Suribachi, February 1945. National Archives.

Preface

From Lexington and Concord to Tora Bora, Fallujah—and everything in between. On land, at sea, in the air, the brave men and women of the United States Armed Forces have served our country with valor for nearly 250 years.

This book covers the events, the leaders, the individual acts of heroism that tell the story of our military—and by extension, the story of America itself. Beginning on New Year's Day and ending on New Year's Eve, each day contains facts, figures, and insights that tell that story. You'll visit Gettysburg and Belleau Wood. Midway, Normandy, and Iwo Jima. The skies over Germany and Japan. Pusan and the Chosin Reservoir. Khe Sanh, Da Nang. Baghdad. And so much more. Every branch, every war, every major chapter in our military's rich and proud history.

The development of America's military has also been powered by scientific and technological advances—the product of entrepreneurial vision and risk-taking that is so emblematic of what can be called "the American way." This kind of vision helped give birth to everything from the first ironclads, to airplanes, radar, "smart bombs," and more. This too, is part of our story.

We've also included photos, some of which you've probably never seen before, and a quote for each day.

We hope you enjoy it, and if you have any suggestions for future revisions, please write to me personally: ThisDayMilitaryHistory@gmail.com

Paul Brandus

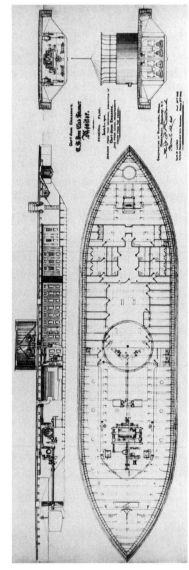

USS *Monitor* plans, 1862. NH 50954 courtesy of Naval History & Heritage Command.

January

January 1

1815: Under the command of General Andrew Jackson, the U.S. artillery repulsed an attack against American fortifications around New Orleans. The British were forced to withdraw.

1862: U.S. warships attacked Confederate emplacements along the Potomac River. Only one U.S. vessel, the *Yankee*, was damaged. Attacks by the so-called Potomac Flotilla helped force the withdrawal of Confederate gun batteries along the river.

1863: In a surprise attack, Confederate warships defeated Union forces at Galveston, Texas. The U.S. defeat resulted in the capture of the Northern Army Company stationed there.

1883: William "Wild Bill" Donovan, director of the Office of Strategic Services (OSS), was born in Buffalo, New York. A World War I hero, he was appointed head of the newly created OSS in 1942—precursor to today's Central Intelligence Agency, which was created five years later. Donovan gained legendary status within the American intelligence community for his emphasis on covert and paramilitary operations. Among other honors, he was the recipient of the Medal of Honor, the Distinguished Service Cross, the Distinguished Service Medal and the National Security Medal.

1942: President Franklin D. Roosevelt and Prime Minister Winston Churchill issued a declaration, later signed by 26 countries, which vowed to create what is now known as the United Nations. The group vowed that the future United Nations would work for global peace and emphasize "life, liberty, independence, and religious freedom, and to preserve the rights of man and justice."

1947: The U.S. and British occupation zones in Germany merged to form the "Bizone," that later became West Germany.

1951: As the Korean War raged, nearly half a million Chinese and North Korean troops launched a huge offensive, seizing Inchon and Kimpo Airfield. The U.S. Fifth Air Force launched heavy counterattacks.

1955: Lt. General John W. O'Daniel was assigned to assist the South Vietnamese government in organizing and training the South Vietnamese army. The United States began sending aid to South Vietnam.

1962: The first Navy Sea, Air, and Land (SEAL) teams were established. The guerrilla and counter-guerrilla units are drawn from the naval Underwater Demolition Teams.

1966: 1st Marine Division advance forces arrived in South Vietnam, to be followed in March by the entire division—20,000 Marines. The 1st Marine Division would remain in Vietnam until spring 1971. Twenty Marines from the 1st Division would be awarded the Medal of Honor for conspicuous bravery.

1967: Operation Sam Houston began, aimed at stopping the movement of North Vietnamese troops and equipment into South Vietnam from communist sanctuaries in Cambodia and Laos.

2002: The Treaty on Open Skies, a mutual aerial surveillance agreement, entered into force on this day. An early version of this idea was proposed by President Dwight Eisenhower to the Soviets in 1955, who rejected it. But George H.W. Bush revisited the idea in 1989, resulting in a signed agreement on March 24, 1992, between NATO and Warsaw Pact members. Thirty-four nations have ratified the treaty, which allows for unarmed aerial surveillance flights over participant regions.

2003: U.S. and British warplanes attacked an Iraqi mobile radar system after it entered the southern no-fly zone.

2009: The United States handed control of Baghdad's "Green Zone" to the Iraqi government. It was seen as a symbolizing the restoration of Iraqi sovereignty, nearly six years after an American-led invasion of the country then controlled by Saddam Hussein.

★ QUOTE OF THE DAY

"If I remember [an old Hawaiian phrase] correctly, it is *hoomanawanui,* which, freely translated, means, 'Time will take care of that.'"

Fleet Admiral Chester W. Nimitz, answering press inquiries about future war efforts on January 1, 1942

January 2

1863: The Battle of Stones River, Tennessee, ended with a Union victory. In heavy fighting, 42,000 U.S. troops withstood an assault by 35,000 Confederate forces, leaving approximately one-third of troops on both sides dead, wounded, or missing—some of the highest casualty rates of the entire Civil War. The victory left Union forces in control of central Tennessee, and President Abraham Lincoln, in a letter to Major General William "Old Rosy" Rosecrans said, "…you gave us a hard victory which, had there been a defeat instead, the nation could scarcely have lived over."

1918: The U.S. Army's Distinguished Service Medal was created. It is awarded "by the President to any person who, while serving in any capacity with the Army shall hereafter distinguish himself or herself, or who, since 04-06-1917, has distinguished himself or herself by exceptionally meritorious service to the Government in a duty of great responsibility in time of war or in connection with military operations against an armed enemy of the United States."

1941: Preparing for a possible war, Franklin D. Roosevelt said the United States would mass-produce 7,500-ton freighters—which would soon be known as "Liberty Ships."

1942: Under the command of General Douglas MacArthur, U.S. forces retreated in the Philippines. Manila and the U.S. naval base at Cavite had fallen to Japan, prompting the defensive maneuver.

1945: Roughly 1,000 U.S. Army Air Force bombers attacked targets in western Germany while about 1,000 Royal Air Force bombers hit other German targets. The city of Nuremberg was destroyed in one hour.

1966: American ground troops moved into Vietnam's Mekong Delta for the first time.

1967: Operation Bolo: In what was called the largest air battle of the Vietnam War, F-4 Phantom pilots shot down seven North Vietnamese MiG-21s. U.S. forces used tactical deception to draw the MiGs out where they were gunned down. Colonel Robin Olds, the 8th Tactical Fighter Wing Commander, shot down a MiG and became the only American ace with aerial victories in World War II and the Vietnam War.

★ QUOTE OF THE DAY

"Brave men die in battle."

William Rosecrans

January 3

1777: U.S. troops defeated British troops in Princeton, New Jersey. General George Washington, who had moved his forces overnight from Trenton, surrounded British forces, who were led by General Cornwallis. It was the third major British defeat in ten days.

1945: Ahead of planned invasions of Iwo Jima, Okinawa, and Japan itself, General Douglas MacArthur and Admiral Chester Nimitz were given key commands. MacArthur was placed in command of all U.S. ground forces and Nimitz in command of all U.S. naval forces. Later in 1945, both men would accept the formal Japanese surrender ending World War II (see September 2).

1951: The Eighth Army evacuated Seoul as Chinese troops crossed the Han River east and west of the South Korean capital. Meantime, in one of the largest air raids of the war to date, more than 60 B-29s dropped 650 tons of incendiary bombs on the North Korean capital of Pyongyang.

George Washington at Trenton. Library of Congress.

1990: Panamanian dictator Manuel Noriega surrendered to the U.S. Army's Delta Force. The United States had invaded the Central American nation two weeks earlier in Operation Just Cause (see December 20). He was taken to Florida and arraigned on drug-trafficking charges.

1993: The strategic arms reduction treaty—START II—was signed by President George H.W. Bush and President Boris Yeltsin in Moscow, Russia. Together each country had about 20,000 nuclear warheads; the pact called for a reduction of nearly 75 percent by 2003. The treaty was approved by the U.S. Senate in 1996 but the Russian government did not agree to START II's terms until 2000, and the pact was eventually abandoned.

✶ QUOTE OF THE DAY

"I shall constantly bear in Mind, that as the Sword was the last Resort for the preservation of our Liberties, so it ought to be the first thing laid aside, when those Liberties are firmly established."

George Washington

January 4

1910: The first U.S. battleship—the *Michigan*—was commissioned. The "dreadnought" ship was faster, was more lethal, and had more armor than prior warships. It was used as a training vessel during World War I.

1944: Operation Carpetbagger: U.S. Army Air Force aircraft began dropping supplies to guerrilla forces across Nazi-held western Europe. Resistance fighters played a significant role in opposing and tying down German forces; by summer 1944, for example, they tied down eight of 26 German divisions in northern Italy. The French Resistance also played a large role, notably in the months ahead of the Allied invasion of Normandy (see June 6).

1945: General George Patton's Third Army repulsed German forces near Bastogne, Belgium. As their offensive in the Ardennes began to stall, the Nazis withdrew tank units from the front and moved them to the Eastern Front, where Soviet forces were rapidly advancing.

1965: Lyndon Johnson links American security to that of Vietnam's. In his State of the Union address, the president said continued U.S. support for

South Vietnam was essential because, "Our own security is tied to the peace of Asia."

1989: Libyan shootdown: two U.S. Navy F-14 Tomcats downed two Soviet-made MiG-23s over the Gulf of Sidra. The Americans believed the Libyan aircraft were attempting to engage them.

2007: Iraq shakeup: George W. Bush named Navy Admiral William J. Fallon as commander of U.S. Central Command (CENTCOM) and General David Petraeus as Commander of Multinational Force Iraq. The moves came as the president prepared to order a surge of U.S. forces to tamp down sectarian violence in Iraq (see January 10).

★ QUOTE OF THE DAY

"The end is in sight."

Richard Nixon, discussing American involvement
in Vietnam on January 4, 1971

January 5

Captain Charles E. Yeager (left), Major Gus Lundquist, and Captain James Fitzgerald with the Bell XS-1. Library of Congress.

1781: Richmond, Virginia, was attacked by Brigadier General Benedict Arnold. Arnold, formerly a major general in the Continental Army, had switched to the British side in 1780. Commanding a British naval expedition, he had the city burned and ransacked on January 6. Approximately 200 men responded to Virginia governor Thomas Jefferson's call to defend the city; the insufficient response caused Jefferson to flee. But it was one of Britain's final Revolutionary War triumphs; it would surrender at nearby Yorktown that fall.

1914: U.S. Marine pilots and ground forces acted in coordination for the first time during Atlantic Fleet maneuvers near Puerto Rico.

1949: Captain Charles E. "Chuck" Yeager flew the Bell X-1 to an altitude of 23,000 feet at a record ascent of 13,000 feet per minute.

1951: The United States staged a heavy air attack on Pyongyang. Fifty-nine B-29s dropped 672 tons of incendiary bombs on the North Korean capital.

1967: U.S. Marines conducted amphibious operations in the Mekong Delta. It was the first time that U.S. combat troops were used there; the objective was to destroy communist ammunition dumps, ordinance and engineering workshops, and other facilities.

1991: President George H.W. Bush warned Iraq that the deadline to meet Allied demands for a withdrawal from Kuwait was approaching. Iraq had invaded Kuwait the previous August, a provocative move that Bush vowed "would not stand."

★ QUOTE OF THE DAY

"Time is running out."

George H.W. Bush, warning Iraqi leader Saddam Hussein

January 6

1777: George Washington established winter quarters for the Continental Army in hills near Morristown, New Jersey. After major victories over the British in Trenton and Princeton, the general's army was exhausted. Rather than endure another long winter without proper supplies, some soldiers deserted; others refused to reenlist. As he rebuilt his army, Washington kept an eye on the British army, which was stationed across the

Hudson River in New York City. Morristown's hills also allowed Washington to guard roads leading north to New England and south to Philadelphia.

1838: Alfred Vail demonstrated a telegraph system using dots and dashes—a precursor to Morse code. Along with Samuel F. B. Morse, Vail was instrumental in developing and commercializing the telegraph, which proved to have significant military operations in the Mexican-American-War, the Civil War, and beyond.

1942: A month after Pearl Harbor (see December 7), Franklin D. Roosevelt authorized the biggest arms buildup in U.S. history. The president said that in the next year the United States would build 45,000 planes, 45,000 tanks, 20,000 antiaircraft guns, and 8 million tons in new ships.

★ QUOTE OF THE DAY

"These figures and similar figures for a multitude of other implements of war will give the Japanese and Nazis a little idea of just what they accomplished."

Franklin D. Roosevelt, announcing a massive
U.S. military buildup

January 7

1782: The Bank of North America, the first U.S. commercial bank, opened. One of its principal purposes was to help finance the army.

1865: Cheyenne, Arapaho, and Lakota Sioux attacked Julesburg, Colorado, in retaliation for the Sand Creek Massacre (see November 29). Dozens of Americans were killed and the town of Julesburg was plundered.

1918: The Supreme Court ruled that conscription was constitutional. In *Arver v. United States*, the court determined that conscription during wartime was authorized by the Constitution, which gave Congress the power "to declare war…to raise and support armies."

1942: The siege of Bataan began. Following Japan's invasion of the Philippines, American and Filipino troops were forced to withdraw to the Bataan peninsula near Manila. Despite being outnumbered and short on supplies, they held out for three months (see April 9).

1942: Design was finalized for the first U.S.-produced jet-fighter. The Bell P-59 Airacomet, featuring an engine built by General Electric, was completed in mid-1942 and made its first test flight in October 1942 at Muroc Dry Lake (now Edwards Air Force Base), California. One year later, the airplane was ordered into production, but never saw combat. Still, the P-59 provided valuable data for the development of future jet aircraft.

1953: Harry Truman revealed that the United States had developed a hydrogen bomb, three years after ordering the new Atomic Energy Commission to develop one.

1960: The first Polaris missile was launched. A two-stage solid-fueled nuclear-armed submarine-launched ballistic missile, the Polaris was the U.S. Navy's first sea-launched ballistic missile (SLBM), and a key part of the U.S. nuclear triad from 1961 to 1996.

★ QUOTE OF THE DAY

"Science and technology have worked so fast that war's new meaning may not yet be grasped by all the peoples who would be its victims."

Harry Truman

January 8

1815: General Andrew Jackson defeated a larger British force in the Battle of New Orleans—the final battle of the War of 1812. Jackson, working with French pirate Jean Lafitte, commanded 5,700 men against 8,000 British troops. Yet the Americans prevailed, losing an estimated 55 men, to Britain's 385, and 185 casualties to Britain's 2,000. Ironically, the clash came 12 days after a peace treaty was signed between the United States and Britain (see December 24).

1877: Crazy Horse's last stand. Outnumbered and with inferior weaponry, the Lakota leader and his warriors fought their final battle against U.S. cavalry at Wolf Mountain, Montana. Their defeat came six months after the killings of General George Armstrong Custer and 200 of his men near Montana's Little Bighorn River.

1951: The Fifth Air Force blasted Kimpo Airfield west of Seoul, to keep communist aircraft from using it. Meantime, the U.S. 2nd Infantry

Division, with the help of French and Dutch battalions, stopped a Chinese advance south of Wonju.

1967: Operation Cedar Falls began when 16,000 U.S. soldiers linked up with 14,000 South Vietnamese troops in what was the largest American offensive to date in Vietnam. The operation's primary goal was to locate and destroy the so-called "Iron Triangle" near Saigon that had been used as a communist staging area for attacks on Saigon.

2008: Operation Phantom Phoenix began when U.S. forces across Iraq launched a mission to further reduce sectarian violence and better secure Iraq's population, notably in Baghdad. One particular goal was to root out and destroy al Qaeda car, truck, and suicide bomb networks.

☆ QUOTE OF THE DAY

"Peace, above all things, is to be desired, but blood must sometimes be spilled to obtain it on equable and lasting terms."

Andrew Jackson

January 9

1793: The first manned U.S. balloon flight was conducted by Jean-Pierre Blanchard. He carried landing clearance orders signed by President George Washington (and a small black dog as a passenger) during the 46-minute trip between Philadelphia and Debtford Township, New Jersey.

1861: A Union ship was attacked as it approached Fort Sumter in Charleston harbor. The shots fired on the *Star of the West*, a merchant vessel, were the first exchanged between North and South. South Carolina had seceded from the Union two weeks earlier, and rebels immediately demanded that federal troops at Fort Sumter leave. President James Buchanan refused. Fort Sumter itself would soon be attacked (see April 12), a date regarded as the beginning of the Civil War.

1862: David Farragut was given command of Western Gulf Blockading Squadron, flagship *Hartford*. Farragut—who before he was even a teenager served in the War of 1812 under the guidance of his adoptive father—commanded an area extending from Western Florida to the Rio

Grande. He became the first rear admiral, vice admiral, and admiral in the United States Navy and would be remembered for his order at the Battle of Mobile Bay: "Damn the torpedoes, full speed ahead" (see August 5).

1918: The final battle against Native Americans took place in Bear Valley, Arizona, when U.S. troops engaged with 30 Yaquis. A short firefight left one Yaqui commander dead and nine others were captured.

1945: The Sixth Army landed on the Lingayen Gulf of Luzon, another step in General Douglas MacArthur's campaign to rid the Philippines of Japanese invaders.

As he had done before (see October 20), MacArthur had himself filmed wading ashore; this time he was met by cheering Filipinos. Luzon saw the introduction of a deadly new Japanese tactic: kamikaze boats, which were loaded with explosives and rammed into U.S. warships.

1951: Douglas MacArthur called for a major expansion of the Korean War. He said greater reinforcements were needed and he also proposed attacking communist China, which had entered the war two months earlier. But President Harry Truman, through the Joint Chiefs of Staff, told him that fighting would be limited to Korea itself.

1952: Harry S. Truman warned Americans of a "perilous time," and called for robust action to thwart communism. In his State of the Union, the president said the United States was threatened by both the Soviet Union and China, which had been seized by communists in 1949—and said, ominously, that the world was walking "in the shadow of another world war."

1976: The first operational F-15A Eagle for combat use was assigned to the 1st Tactical Fighter Wing at Langley AFB, Virginia.

1991: Peace talks with Iraq collapsed. After meeting with Iraq's foreign minister for six hours in Geneva, Secretary of State James A. Baker III said they had failed to resolve the Persian Gulf crisis. The United States had demanded that Iraq withdraw from Kuwait, which it had seized five months earlier.

★ QUOTE OF THE DAY

"The United States and the whole free world are passing through a period of grave danger. Every action you take here in Congress, and every action that I take as President, must be measured against the test of whether it helps to meet that danger."

Harry Truman

January 10

1941: "An Act to Promote the Defense of the United States" (HR 1776) was introduced in the US House of Representatives. This was the Lend-Lease policy that President Franklin D. Roosevelt had proposed in his State of the Union (January 6). Lend-Lease gave FDR the authority power to "sell, transfer title to, exchange, lease, lend, or otherwise dispose of" anything he considered useful to any American ally—thus enhancing the defense of the United States itself. The bill was enacted March 11, 1941. By the end of World War II, supplies worth close to $700 billion in 2018 dollars were distributed to dozens of countries.

1942: The Ford Motor Company began to make Jeeps. The name came from the acronym "G.P.," which stood for "General Purpose" vehicles. A smaller company, Willys-Overland, won the original contract to build Jeeps, but demand was so great that Ford, with much greater production capacity, stepped in.

1943: A massive offensive on Guadalcanal began. Heavy air and artillery bombardment backed the 50,000 U.S. troops.

1944: Congress passed the GI Bill of Rights. The bill, which was swiftly signed by President Franklin D. Roosevelt, was designed to smooth the transition to civilian life for the nearly 16 million men and women in uniform. The bill provided for education and housing benefits—which would prove to be a huge long-term boost for the U.S. economy.

1946: The U.S. Navy established its first nuclear power school at Submarine Base, New London, Connecticut. Known as the "home of the submarine force," New London today is the base to 15 attack-class submarines, the largest single contingent of subs in the fleet.

2007: George W. Bush announced a "surge" of U.S. troops in Iraq. The president said an additional 20,000 troops would be used to tamp down sectarian violence to protect individual neighborhoods in the Iraqi capital of Baghdad.

★ QUOTE OF THE DAY

"I don't think we could continue the war without the jeep. It does everything. It goes everywhere. It's as faithful as a dog, as strong as a mule, and as agile as a goat."

War correspondent Ernie Pyle in a 1943 column

January 11

1863: Union forces captured Arkansas Post, a Confederate stronghold on the Arkansas River. The huge post was 25 miles from the confluence of the Arkansas and Mississippi rivers and had been built to maintain Confederate control of the White and Arkansas rivers and to protect Vicksburg, a major Confederate-held city on the Mississippi River. Led by General John McClernand and Admiral David Porter, the victory (also known as the Battle of Fort Hindman) gave the Union control of central Arkansas and lifted morale one month after the North's crushing defeat in the Battle of Fredericksburg (see December 11).

1944: The Eighth Air Force carried out a daylight raid on Oschersleben, Germany, hitting three Nazi aviation targets. Major damage was inflicted but fierce German resistance—in the form of 500 Luftwaffe planes—resulted in the loss of 60 bombers and five escort fighters.

1962: A B-52 completed a record flight from Kadena Air Base, Japan, to the Torrejón Air Base, Madrid, Spain, without refueling—a distance of 12,532 miles—topping its December 14, 1960, record of more than 10,000 miles.

1963: President John F. Kennedy was warned of a long and costly war in Vietnam. Michael Forrestal, an aide to National Security Advisor McGeorge Bundy, told Kennedy that Viet Cong recruitment in South Vietnam was effective enough to continue the war without any infiltration from the North.

1965: The USAF's XC-142A Vertical/Short Takeoff and Landing (V/STOL) transport aircraft successfully took off like a helicopter, then adjusted its wings for conventional forward flight, and finally made a vertical landing. Only five were built.

2002: Detainees arrive at Naval Station Guantanamo Bay, Guantánamo Bay, Cuba. The 20 men, captured during the new U.S. war on terror, arrived at the hastily constructed Camp X-Ray.

★ QUOTE OF THE DAY

"We pass the brink at midnight January 15."

> Secretary of State James A. Baker III, telling U.S. Air Force pilots in
> Saudi Arabia to be prepared for war with Iraq.

January 12

1918: The Distinguished Service Cross and Distinguished Service Medal were established. Acting on a recommendation from General John J. Pershing, Commander-in-Chief of the Expeditionary Forces in France, Congress passed, and President Woodrow Wilson signed, bills allowing for the awarding of these medals.

1939: The "changing world conditions outside of the American Hemisphere . . . make it imperative that we take immediate steps for the protection of our liberties." President Franklin D. Roosevelt asked Congress for a minimum of 3,000 new planes in addition to increases in funding to all the armed forces branches.

1951: B-29s dropped what came to be known as cluster bombs for the first time on communist forces in Korea. The 500-pound bombs were fused to burst in the air and shower the enemy with thousands of steel fragments.

1954: Secretary of State John Foster Dulles said the United States would protect its allies with the "deterrent of massive retaliatory power." It reflected the Eisenhower administration's decision to rely on America's nuclear arsenal as the primary means of defense against communist aggression. President Dwight D. Eisenhower, fiscally conservative, believed that the United States could not afford gigantic defense budgets; thus reliance on nuclear weapons would both intimidate potential American enemies and save the government money.

1962: Operation Chopper, the first American combat mission in the Vietnam War, took place. Dozens of U.S. Army Piasecki H-21s transported over 1,000 South Vietnamese paratroopers for an assault on a suspected Viet Cong stronghold ten miles west of Saigon.

1962: Operation Ranch Hand—the first use of what came to be known as "Agent Orange" in Vietnam. U.S. forces dropped the first of 19 million gallons of defoliating herbicides that would be dropped over 10 to 15 percent of Vietnam and parts of Laos between 1962 and 1971. Designed to destroy vegetation that hid communist troops, the Agent Orange—named for the color of its metal containers—did just that, but generally failed to stop enemy operations. This chemical warfare on the part of the United States remains controversial today, and is linked to everything from skin rashes to birth defects and cancer among Vietnamese civilians and American service members who were exposed to it.

1991: Congress voted for war with Iraq. Although not a formal declaration of war, the House of Representatives, by a 250-183 margin, gave President George H.W. Bush the authority he wanted to attack Iraq. The vote followed a narrow 52-47 margin in the Senate.

★ QUOTE OF THE DAY

"[It would be unwise to] permanently commit U.S. land forces to Asia," or to "become permanently committed to military expenditures so vast that they lead to 'practical bankrutcy.'"

Secretary of State John Foster Dulles

January 13

1846: James Polk dispatched 4,000 troops to the Mexican border as war with that country loomed. Mexico and the United States had cut diplomatic relations nine months earlier, following the American annexation of Texas. The troops would occupy the disputed area between the Nueces and the Rio Grande rivers.

1972: Richard Nixon announced more troop withdrawals from Vietnam. Nixon, accelerating his efforts to get the United States out of Vietnam, said 70,000 Americans would come home by May, reducing troop strength to about 69,000. When Nixon became president in January 1969, there were some 540,000 Americans in Vietnam; he would wind down the war by spring 1973.

1997: Seven black soldiers received the Medal of Honor for World War II valor. The lone living survivor, former Lt. Vernon Baker, received his medal on this day from President Bill Clinton at the White House.

2004: A U.S. soldier at Abu Ghraib prison in Iraq reported abuse of the prisoners held there. Criminal charges were lodged against six soldiers on March 20.

★ QUOTE OF THE DAY

"America is profoundly thankful for the patriotism and the nobility of these men and for the example they set, which helped us to find the way to become a more just, more free nation. They helped America to become more worthy of them and more true to its ideals."

Bill Clinton, January 13, 1997

January 14

1891: General Nelson Miles, commander of U.S. Army troops in South Dakota, reported that rebellious Sioux were returning to their reservation. It signified the last major Native American uprising, and came two weeks after the massacre of 150 to 300 men, women, and children of the Miniconjou Lakota and Hunkpapa Lakota at Wounded Knee, South Dakota (see December 29).

1911: The battleship *Arkansas* was launched. A 26,000-ton Wyoming-class ship, the Arkansas would see battle in World War I, was later modernized and saw action in World War II, in both the European theater—supporting the Normandy invasion—and Pacific theater—supporting the invasions of Iwo Jima and Okinawa. In 1946, the *Arkansas* was deliberately sunk after being anchored near an atomic bomb test in Bikini Atoll.

1943: "The Big Three"—U.S. president Franklin Roosevelt, British prime minister Winston Churchill and Soviet premier Joseph Stalin—met to discuss World War II strategy. At their conference in Casablanca, Morocco, the leaders decided to demand that the Axis powers (Germany, Italy, and Japan) surrender unconditionally.

1969: Twenty-eight crew members of the U.S. aircraft carrier *Enterprise* were killed and 314 were injured in a series of explosions that ripped through the ship—the first nuclear-powered aircraft carrier—as it sailed to Vietnam. The *Enterprise* was retired in 2012.

2005: Army SPC Charles Graner Jr. was convicted at Fort Hood, Texas, of abusing Iraqi detainees at Baghdad's Abu Ghraib prison. He was later sentenced to ten years in prison.

★ QUOTE OF THE DAY

"Looking at the purpose of our government toward the Indians, we find that after subjugating them it has been our policy to collect the different tribes on reservations and support them at the expense of our people."

Nelson Miles

January 15

1865: Fort Fisher, North Carolina, fell to Union forces, and Wilmington, the Confederacy's most important blockade-running port, was closed. The victory came after a three-day bombardment—a continuation of President Abraham Lincoln's strategic decision in 1861 to blockade all major southern ports.

1929: The Senate ratified the Kellogg-Briand pact, a global treaty in which signatories pledged not to use war to resolve their differences. Sixty-two nations signed the pact, including Germany and Japan. In ratifying the treaty with only one dissenting vote, the Senate insisted that it would not limit America's right of self-defense, and that the United States was not compelled to take action against any other nation that violated it.

1943: Construction of the Pentagon, headquarters of the U.S. Department of Defense, was completed at Arlington, Virginia. Built in 16 months (starting on September 11, 1941), it remains to this day the world's largest office building, covering 6.34 million square feet. Yet the pentagonal shape helped reduce walking distances within.

1973: Richard Nixon ordered an end to the bombing of North Vietnam as peace talks between the United States and Hanoi accelerated. A peace treaty would be announced two weeks later (see January 27), bringing the war—at the time the longest in American history—to an end. In terms of duration, the war in Vietnam would be exceeded by two wars that the United States fought simultaneously—in Afghanistan and Iraq.

2002: Operation Enduring Freedom—Philippines (OEF-P) began: an effort by the United States to help the Philippines combat terrorism. Within OEF-P was another project—Operation Smiles—that built schools, medical clinics, and fresh water wells for civilians.

★ QUOTE OF THE DAY

"A pentagonal has never worked out well and great confusion is apt to result in the circulation of the building,"

William H. Lamb, architect on the Commission on
Fine Arts, opposing the shape of the Pentagon

January 16

1944: General Dwight D. Eisenhower assumed supreme command of the Allied Expeditionary Force in Europe. He would soon oversee Operation Overlord—the allied invasion of Normandy, in German-controlled France.

1991: George H.W. Bush announced the start of Operation Desert Storm—a U.S.-led military coalition (28 countries) to push Iraq out of Kuwait. Iraqi leader Saddam Hussein had invaded Kuwait the previous August; Bush quickly said "This will not stand." After a five-week bombing campaign and a 100-hour ground war, the president ordered an end to hostilities. One hundred and twenty-five American soldiers were killed in the Persian Gulf War, with another 21 declared missing in action.

2001: Bill Clinton awarded former president Theodore Roosevelt a posthumous Medal of Honor for his service in the Spanish-American War.

★ QUOTE OF THE DAY

"I am convinced not only that we will prevail but that out of the horror of combat will come the recognition that no nation can stand against a world united, no nation will be permitted to brutally assault its neighbor."

George H.W. Bush

January 17

1781: The Battle of Cowpens took place in the colony of South Carolina. American forces were victorious; it was considered a turning point of the war in the south. It compelled British general Lord Cornwallis to pursue the main southern American army into North Carolina; he would eventually surrender to U.S. forces (commanded by General George Washington) and French forces at Yorktown, Virginia (see October 19), ending the Revolutionary War.

1944: Operation Panther, the Allied invasion of Cassino, in central Italy, was launched. Allied forces had been fighting their way up the Italian peninsula for six months, following their invasion of Sicily—and while Italy, once allied with Germany and Japan in World War II, had surrendered four months before (see September 18), German forces still occupied the country.

1955: *Nautilus* (SSN-571), the first nuclear-powered submarine began its first voyage and sent the message that it was "underway on nuclear power."

1961: Dwight D. Eisenhower warned of the "military-industrial complex." In his farewell address to the nation, the president, a five-star general who led the Allied invasion of Nazi-occupied France on D-Day, told Americans that the U.S. defense establishment was too big, too costly and, ironically, posed a threat to America's liberty. He said the U.S. defense industry was profiting off Americans' national security paranoia; and warned of the danger of "misplaced power."

★ QUOTE OF THE DAY

"You and I, and our government—must avoid the impulse to live only for today, plundering, for our own ease and convenience, the precious resources of tomorrow. We cannot mortgage the material assets of our grandchildren without risking the loss also of their political and spiritual heritage. We want democracy to survive for all generations to come, not to become the insolvent phantom of tomorrow."

Dwight D. Eisenhower

January 18

1911: The birth of naval aviation continued, when Eugene B. Ely made the first successful airline landing on a warship, piloting his Curtiss aircraft safely onto the deck of the *Pennsylvania*, which was anchored in San Francisco Harbor. It was also the first use of the tailhook system, which was designed and built by circus performer and aviator Hugh Robinson. Ely had demonstrated the first takeoff from a warship the previous fall. The Navy soon developed sites for naval aircraft operations in Annapolis, Maryland, and San Diego, California.

1961: Operation Chrome Dome began a Cold War strategy of having thermonuclear-nuclear-bomb-laden B-52 Stratofortresses on continuous airborne alert missions on the perimeter of Soviet borders. The operation ended when a B-52 crashed near Thule AFB in Greenland (see January 21).

★ QUOTE OF THE DAY

"It was easy enough. I think the trick could be successfully turned nine times out of ten."

Eugene Ely

January 19

1770: Colonial rebels, led by Alexander McDougall, fought with British soldiers in New York. The skirmish between British forces and the so-called Sons of Liberty was one of the early incidents that eventually turned into the Revolutionary War itself. McDougall was a major general in the Continental Army and a delegate to the Continental Congress. George Washington called him a "pillar of the revolution."

1946: The first demonstration of long-rage navigation (LORAN). The joint Navy-Coast Guard system was originally developed to improve radio navigation for U.S. coastal waters, but was later expanded to include the entire continental United States and Alaska.

1946: General Douglas MacArthur established an International Military Tribunal to try Japanese war criminals. As with the Nuremberg trials, which prosecuted former Nazis in Germany, the Tokyo War Crimes Tribunal charged officials with three types of crimes: "Class A" crimes for those who conspired to wage war, "Class B" crimes for those who committed "conventional" atrocities or crimes against humanity, and "Class C" crimes for those who planned, ordered, or failed to stop "such transgressions at higher levels in the command structure." Twenty-eight Japanese military and political leaders were charged with Class A crimes; more than 5,700 were charged with Class B and C crimes. China—which had been invaded and brutally occupied by Japan—held 13 tribunals of its own, resulting in 504 convictions and 149 executions.

1960: The United States and Japan signed a mutual defense treaty. Protests in Tokyo erupted, forcing President Eisenhower to cancel a planned visit.

2003: The United States offered Saddam Hussein immunity from prosecution if he left Iraq. With a second war in the Persian Gulf looming, U.S. defense secretary Donald Rumsfeld made the offer in a TV interview; the Iraqi leader did not take the United States up on it. An American-led invasion was launched two months later (see March 20).

★ QUOTE OF THE DAY

"If to avoid a war, I would…recommend that some provision be made so that the senior leadership in that country [Iraq] and their families could be provided haven in some other country."

Donald Rumsfeld, US Secretary of Defense

January 20

1887: Pearl Harbor was first leased as a U.S. naval base. The navy began using it as a refueling and repair base; it would eventually become the headquarters of the U.S. Pacific Fleet. In 1941, a surprise attack on Pearl Harbor by Japan thrust the United States into World War II (see December 7).

1903: The Midway Islands were placed under jurisdiction of the Navy Department. They are located 1,150 miles west-northwest of Hawaii—approximately "midway" between California and Japan. An air and submarine base was built in 1940, just before the United States entered World War II.

1914: The Navy began an aviation training station at Pensacola, Florida. The first aviation unit consisted of nine officers, 23 enlisted men, and seven aircraft.

This Day in U.S. Military History

★ QUOTE OF THE DAY

"A good Navy is not a provocation to war. It is the surest guaranty of peace."

Theodore Roosevelt

January 21

1911: The first air-to-ground radio message was sent by Lt. Paul W. Beck. He had designed a transmitter to send telegraph signals and used Phillip O. Parmalee's Wright plane flying at 500 feet for his demonstration.

1943: The Casablanca Directive was issued, establishing priorities for the U.S. and British bombing of German targets for the remainder of World War II. Targets were initially prioritized in the following order: 1) submarine construction yards, 2) German aircraft industry, 3) transportation, 4) oil plants, then 5) other targets in enemy war industry.

1954: The first nuclear submarine—the *Nautilus*—was launched at Groton, Connecticut. The ship's nuclear propulsion system allowed *Nautilus* to remain submerged for extended periods, allowing it to break numerous operational records. In 1958, it became the first submarine to complete a submerged transit of the North Pole (see August 3).

1968: One of the biggest battles of the Vietnam War—the siege of Khe Sanh—began. Taken by Marines a year earlier, the base was used as a staging area for forward patrols and launch point for operations to cut the Ho Chi Minh Trail (a communist supply line) in Laos. The battle began with 6,000 Marines and South Vietnamese soldiers defending their base against 20,000 North Vietnamese soldiers. At its peak, up to 45,000 American soldiers and up to 100,000 North Vietnamese troops would square off. American aircraft dropped 100,000 tons of bombs while communist forces fired over 10,000 rockets, mortar, and artillery rounds. Before the 77-day siege was lifted by U.S. forces in July, at least 274 Americans were killed and 2,541 wounded; the U.S. estimated (in public) that North Vietnamese losses were 10,000 to 15,000, but private estimates said that perhaps 5,500 enemy were killed.

1968: A B-52 loaded with four hydrogen bombs crashed at North Star Bay, Greenland, near Thule Air Base. The crash caused conventional explosives aboard to detonate and the nuclear payload to rupture and disperse. Six crew members ejected safely before the crash, but a seventh was killed. The dispersion of radioactive material sparked a massive—and quiet—decontamination effort. It is believed that parts of at least one of the nuclear weapons has never been recovered. The catastrophe ended Operation Chrome Dome.

★ QUOTE OF THE DAY

"Caution: Being a Marine in Khe Sanh may be hazardous to your health."

Written on the back of a U.S. Marine's flak jacket,
from an article in *Newsweek* magazine

January 22

1879: U.S. troops effectively crushed the so-called "Dull Knife Outbreak," killing or capturing warriors associated with Cheyenne chief Dull Knife. Dull Knife himself escaped and found refuge with Chief Red Cloud on the Sioux reservation in Nebraska. Dull Knife (sometimes called Morning Star) had long favored peaceful relations with Americans—even as they encroached upon Cheyenne homelands in what are today Wyoming and Montana. But an 1864 massacre of more than 200 peaceful Cheyenne Indians by Colorado militiamen led Dull Knife to question whether the Americans could ever be trusted.

1953: The Air Force withdrew its remaining F-51 Mustangs from combat in Korea as it prepared to transition to Sabre jets—thus ending the use of American single engine, propeller-driven aircraft for offensive combat operations in the Korean War.

2015: The United States said 6,000 ISIS fighters had been killed by U.S. and coalition troops in Iraq and Syria. The estimate, which was made public by the U.S. ambassador to Iraq, said the dead included half of the command structure of the terror group—which called itself the "Islamic State."

★ QUOTE OF THE DAY

"All we ask is to be allowed to live, and live in peace."

Chief Dull Knife of the Cheyenne

January 23

1960: The bathyscaphe *Trieste* descended to the bottom of Challenger Deep in the Pacific Ocean. With a crew of two, Jacques Piccard and Don Walsh, the deep-diving research vessel—purchased by the U.S. Navy in 1958—reached 35,797 feet in the Mariana Trench near Guam.

1968: A U.S. Navy intelligence ship was seized by North Korea, sparking a yearlong crisis for President Lyndon Johnson. The *Pueblo*—which the United States averred was in international waters—was fired upon, wounding the commander and two crewmen, before being captured and taken to a North Korean port. The 83-man crew was bound and blindfolded, charged with espionage, and held captive for 11 months (see December 23). During their time in captivity, they were regularly beaten and tortured; one American died during the ordeal.

1973: President Nixon announced an end to the Vietnam War. The president said a peace agreement with North Vietnam would bring "peace with honor" to what was then the longest war in U.S. history, in which 58,209 Americans died. The war has since been eclipsed in length by U.S. wars in Afghanistan and Iraq, launched in 2001 and 2003, respectively.

1991: Allied forces achieved air superiority in Iraq. General Colin Powell, Joint Chiefs of Staff Chairman, announced that 12,000 sorties had been flown. He said the focus of Operation Desert Storm would shift to attacking Iraqi ground forces around Kuwait.

2013: A ban on women serving in combat was reversed. The move potentially cleared the way for women to serve in front-line units and elite commando forces.

★ QUOTE OF THE DAY

"Our strategy to go after this [Iraqi] army is very, very simple. First, we're going to cut it off, and then we're going to kill it."

General Colin Powell

January 24

1942: Two U.S. commanders were blamed for the Japanese attack on Pearl Harbor. A special court of inquiry determined that Navy Rear Admiral

Husband E. Kimmel and Army Lt. General Walter C. Short were guilty of dereliction of duty and for the base's lack of preparedness before the surprise attack by Japan on December 7, 1941.

1943: President Roosevelt and Prime Minister Churchill wrapped up a wartime summit in Morocco. The two leaders said that the top priorities for the war in Europe would be to combat Nazi U-boats—which were sinking Allied supply ships at a rapid rate—and to aid the Soviet Union, which was fighting the Germans on the Eastern Front. Roosevelt and Churchill said they would demand nothing less than the "unconditional surrender" of the Axis powers—Germany, Italy, and Japan.

1966: Defense Secretary Robert McNamara recommended increasing U.S. troop levels in Vietnam to more than 400,000. Yet in a memo to President Johnson, he warned that even this, along with increased bombing, might not be enough to ensure military success. U.S. troop strength in Vietnam would ultimately peak in 1968 at some 538,000 personnel.

⭐ QUOTE OF THE DAY

"I don't think that it has ever been put down on paper by the prime minister and myself, and that is the determination that peace can come to the world only by the total elimination of German and Japanese war power."

Franklin D. Roosevelt

January 25

1863: Union general Ambrose Burnside was removed as commander of the Army of the Potomac. Burnside had only been commander for two months, following the sacking, by President Lincoln, of General George B. McClellan (see November 5). Lincoln was displeased with Burnside's inability to sufficiently take the fight to Robert E. Lee's Confederate Army of Northern Virginia. Ironically, when Burnside was first appointed to the job, he hesitated in accepting, unsure that he was up to the job.

⭐ QUOTE OF THE DAY

"I was deeply mortified by the escape of Lee across the Potomac, because the substantial destruction of his army would have ended the war."

Abraham Lincoln, in a July 21, 1863, letter to Oliver O. Howard

January 26

General Douglas MacArthur, August 1945. Library of Congress.

1863: General Joseph Hooker assumed command of the Army of the Potomac. A West Point graduate and veteran of the Seminole War and the Mexican War, Hooker—nicknamed "Fighting Joe"—was the latest in a string of Union commanders. But Hooker wound up disappointing President Lincoln just as his predecessor, Ambrose Burnside, had: In May 1863, Hooker's army was thrashed by Confederate forces in the Battle of Chancellorsville (see April 30), and he was replaced by General George Meade.

1880: Douglas MacArthur was born in Little Rock, Arkansas. The West Point graduate (first in the class of 1903) went on to become a five-star general during World War II. In 1944 he became one of just five men to receive the title of General of the Army (with George C. Marshall, Dwight D. Eisenhower, Henry H. Arnold, and Omar Bradley). He received the Medal of Honor among many awards and honors.

1943: The first OSS (Office of Strategic Services) agent parachuted behind Japanese lines in Burma. The aggressive nature of the OSS's "Detachment 101" reflected the vision of OSS chief General William "Wild Bill" Donovan, who believed that such clandestine missions would prove immensely valuable in supporting regular combat operations. The OSS was the precursor to the Central Intelligence Agency, and today, a statue of Donovan stands in the lobby of CIA headquarters in Virginia.

1953: The last F4U Corsair was produced. The Chance Vought Aircraft Company made more than 12,000 Corsairs, renowned for their roles in both World War II and Korea.

2005: A U.S. helicopter crashed in Iraq's western desert killing 31 people. Bad weather, and not enemy fire, was blamed.

✯ QUOTE OF THE DAY

"Beware of rashness. Beware of rashness, but with energy, and sleepless vigilance, go forward, and give us victories."

Abraham Lincoln, in a letter to General Joseph Hooker

January 27

Vice Admiral Hyman G. Rickover standing on the *Scorpion*'s sailplanes with another officer during builder's trials, June 27, 1960. NH 97215 courtesy of Naval History & Heritage Command.

This Day in U.S. Military History

1862: Abraham Lincoln ordered Union forces to take the offensive against the Confederate Army. The president's General War Order No. 1 was a reflection of Lincoln's frustration that his army and navy commanders weren't acting boldly enough in taking the battle to the enemy.

1900: Hyman Rickover, known as the "father of the Nuclear Navy," was born in Russian Poland. Immigrating to the United States in 1906, Rickover, who rose to the rank of four-star admiral, would serve in the navy for 63 years—making him the longest serving member of any of the U.S. armed forces. Rickover, a two-time recipient of the Congressional Gold Medal, was instrumental in helping to build the navy's nuclear surface and submarine force.

1939: The Lockheed P-38 Lightning made its first flight. The P-38, known for its distinctive twin booms and a single, central nacelle containing the cockpit and armament, was nicknamed the "fork-tailed devil" by the Luftwaffe and "two planes, one pilot" by the Japanese during World War II. It was the only American fighter aircraft in production throughout World War II.

1943: The first U.S. bombing raid of Germany was conducted, when Eighth Air Force bombers attacked the German port of Wilhelmshaven. Of 64 planes participating in the raid, 53 reached their target and managed to shoot down 22 German planes, losing three planes in return.

1967: Three astronauts were killed after their Apollo 1 command module caught fire during a rehearsal for an upcoming space mission. They were USAF lieutenant colonels Virgil I. "Gus" Grissom and Edward White, and Navy lieutenant commander Roger B. Chaffee.

1973: The Paris Peace Accords officially ended U.S. involvement in the Vietnam War. The war cost the United States dearly in both blood and treasure: an estimated 58,220 Americans were killed, another 153,303 were wounded and, as of 2018, 1,643 were still missing. In terms of direct war costs, the government spent some $1.06 trillion in 2018 dollars, and another $33 billion in aid to South Vietnam. This does not include decades' worth of veterans' benefits and medical care. South Vietnam would be taken over by North Vietnam in the spring of 1975.

1973: End of the draft: Secretary of Defense Melvin Laird said that the United States would switch to an all-volunteer force, negating the need for the military draft.

★ QUOTE OF THE DAY

"Success teaches us nothing; only failure teaches."

Hyman G. Rickover

January 28

1909: A decade after the Spanish-American War, U.S. troops left Cuba, ending direct American control of that country. The United States did maintain—and continues to maintain—Guantanamo Bay Naval Base, which is today America's oldest overseas military base.

1915: President Woodrow Wilson signed a bill creating the U.S. Coast Guard. It brought five different federal agencies under one roof: the Revenue Cutter Service, the Lighthouse Service, the Steamboat Inspection Service, the Bureau of Navigation, and the Lifesaving Service.

1938: With war clouds gathering over Europe and Asia, Franklin Roosevelt called for the construction of a two-ocean navy. "We cannot assume that our defense would be limited to one ocean and one coast and that the other ocean and the other coast would with certainty be safe," FDR said. In 1940, the Two-Ocean Navy Act would be approved by Congress, providing funds for a massive expansion of the fleet.

1966: Operation Double Eagle—the largest U.S. amphibious landing since Inchon, during the Korea War—began when more than 5,000 Marines came ashore at Quang Ngai Province, South Vietnam.

1986: The space shuttle *Challenger* exploded 73 seconds after launch. Astronauts Francis R. Scobee, Navy Cmdr Michael J. Smith, Dr. Judith Resnik, Dr. Ronald E. McNair, Air Force Lt Col Ellison S. Onizuka, Gregory Jarvis of Hughes Aircraft Corp., and schoolteacher Christa McAuliffe were killed. This tragedy delayed America's manned space program for more than two years.

★ QUOTE OF THE DAY

"We lived in the dirt, slept in holes if we were lucky (we had no tents or sleeping bags, and sleeping in a hole provided some protection from enemy mortars), or slept *on* the ground, fearfully. We marched without apparent purpose in chilling northeast monsoon rains, suffered heatstroke with the arrival of the southwest monsoon, pulled leeches from our legs, ate little but field rations, and fought rust on our weapons and fungus on our bodies."

Bob Ingraham, USMC, retired

January 29

1756: Henry "Light-Horse Harry" Lee III was born at Dumfries, Virginia. A cavalry officer in the Continental Army during the Revolutionary War, he commanded highly mobile light cavalry groups which were not only effective in battle, but also in conducting reconnaissance, disrupting enemy supply chains, and making raids behind enemy lines. Such tactics—which earned Lee the nickname "Light-Horse Harry"—are early examples of what is today called guerrilla warfare. Lee, who also served as governor of Virginia and a representative in Congress, was also the father of Robert E. Lee, who commanded the Confederate army during the Civil War. He died March 25, 1818, at Cumberland, Georgia.

1834: Andrew Jackson became the first president to use federal troops to put down labor unrest. Workers building the Chesapeake & Ohio canal were angry over working conditions and low pay.

1968: Lyndon Johnson's war tax: with the cost of the Vietnam War mounting, President Johnson asked for the 2018 equivalent of $145 billion to continue fighting. Congress would soon pass a 10 percent surcharge on individual and corporate income.

2002: The phrase "Axis of Evil" was used by George W. Bush in his State of the Union to describe nations that the United States considered terrorist states: Iraq, Iran, and North Korea.

★ QUOTE OF THE DAY

"I am absolutely certain that, whereas in 1965 the enemy was winning, today he is certainly losing. The enemy's hopes are bankrupt."

General William Westmoreland,
commander of U.S. forces in Vietnam

January 30

1862: The *Monitor*, the Union's first sea-going ironclad vessel, launched at Greenpoint, New York.

1945: The "Great Raid": In a daring raid, Army Rangers and Filipino guerrillas rescued 486 Allied prisoners of war from a Japanese prison camp near Manila. Many of the POWs had been held for years since their surrender during the Battle of Bataan (see April 9).

1968: The Tet Offensive began. In their biggest offensive of the entire Vietnamese war, communist forces launched attacks across South Vietnam, striking dozens of cities, military bases, and the U.S. embassy in the heart of Saigon itself. Historians say Tet wound up as a U.S. military victory, but at home it shattered American confidence that the war was proceeding well and would soon end. Politically, it would fuel the growing antiwar movement in the United States and led to President Lyndon's decision to not seek re-election that year.

★ QUOTE OF THE DAY

"We have been too often disappointed by the optimism of the American leaders, both in Vietnam and Washington, to have faith any longer in the silver linings they find in the darkest clouds... For it seems now more certain than ever that the bloody experience of Vietnam is to end in stalemate."

Walter Cronkite, CBS News journalist, discussing Vietnam during a
February 1968 visit

January 31

1944: U.S. troops begin landing on the islands of Kwajalein Atoll. The atoll, part of the present-day Republic of the Marshall Islands, was a key Japanese stronghold, and became the target of one of the most concentrated bombardments of the Pacific War.

1945: Private Eddie Slovik became the first American soldier since the Civil War to be executed for desertion. Slovik, a draftee, was trained to be a rifleman and went to France in August 1944. Claiming he was "too scared and too nervous" to be a rifleman, he left his unit, only to return, where he signed a confession of desertion, claiming he would run away again if forced to fight. Tossed in a stockade, he was offered a choice: enter into combat or be court-martialed. Choosing the latter, he was tried for desertion and convicted. The punishment: "to be shot to death with musketry."

1950: Harry Truman vowed to build the hydrogen bomb. The president's decision came five months after the American monopoly on nuclear weapons ended with the Soviet Union's first test of its own atomic bomb. On November 1, 1952, America's first hydrogen bomb—vastly more powerful than the nuclear devices dropped on Japan during World War II— was tested.

1958: The United States entered the space age, with the launch of Explorer 1, the first U.S. satellite successfully launched into orbit. The Soviet Union had beaten America into space with its launch of Sputnik in October 1957.

2002: Secretary of Defense Donald Rumsfeld warned Americans to prepare for potential terror attacks "vastly more deadly" than the terror attacks on New York and Washington four months before (see September 11).

★ QUOTE OF THE DAY

"It is part of my responsibility as commander in chief of the Armed Forces to see to it that our country is able to defend itself against any possible aggressor. Accordingly, I have directed the Atomic Energy Commission to continue its work on all forms of atomic weapons, including the so-called hydrogen or superbomb. Like all other work in the field of atomic weapons, it is being and will be carried forward on a basis consistent with the overall objectives of our program for peace and security."

Harry Truman

Havana, Cuba, funeral procession for *Maine* crewman killed in the explosion. NH 46765 courtesy of Naval History & Heritage Command.

February

February 1

1862: "The Battle Hymn of the Republic" was first published. The lyrics, the work of Julia Ward Howe, was based on chapter 63 of the Old Testament's Book of Isaiah and published in the *Atlantic Monthly* as an anonymous poem. Soon it was widely sung by Union troops as they marched during the Civil War.

1941: As war clouds gathered on the horizon, the U.S. Navy was reorganized into three fleets: the Atlantic, the Pacific and the Asiatic. A significant beefing up of the Atlantic fleet—under the command of Admiral Ernest King—was made a top priority.

1984: President Ronald Reagan ordered a withdrawal of U.S. Marines from Beirut, Lebanon, three months after terrorists destroyed a barracks, killing 241 Americans (see October 23).

 QUOTE OF THE DAY

"Mine eyes have seen the glory of the coming of the Lord;
He is trampling out the vintage where the grapes of wrath are stored;
He hath loosed the fateful lightning of His terrible swift sword:
His truth is marching on."

Julia Ward Howe, "The Battle Hymn of the Republic"

February 2

1848: The Treaty of Guadalupe Hidalgo was signed, ending the Mexican-American War. The war added 525,000 square miles to the United States, including the area that would become the states of Texas, California, Nevada, Utah, New Mexico, and Arizona, as well as parts of Colorado and Wyoming. The United States was now a continental power, with the American flag flying from the Atlantic to the Pacific. The war took the lives of 1,773 men and cost $100 million—the equivalent of about $3.1 billion today.

1948: Harry Truman moved to desegregate the U.S. military. The president told Congress that he had ordered the secretary of defense to take steps "to have the remaining instances of discrimination in the armed services eliminated as rapidly as possible" (see July 26).

1945: B-24 and B-29 bombers began attacking Iwo Jima ahead of a planned invasion. An average 450 tons of bombs would be dropped daily over the next two weeks.

1962: The Air Force lost its first plane in South Vietnam. The C-123, a transport aircraft, crashed while spraying defoliant on a Viet Cong position. The defoliant was part of a broader U.S. campaign—Operation Ranch Hand—to defoliate and therefore expose roads and trails used by the Viet Cong (see January 12).

1974: The F-16 Fighting Falcon made its first official flight. The General Dynamics (now Lockheed Martin) plane is a single-engine, supersonic multirole aircraft. More than 4,500 have been built. Although no longer being bought by the U.S. Air Force, various versions are still manufactured and sold to the air forces of two dozen countries. The F-16 is often referred to as the "Viper" by pilots, because of a perceived resemblance to a viper snake.

★ QUOTE OF THE DAY

"The world has nothing to fear from military ambition in our Government."

James K. Polk

February 3

1917: The United States edged closer to World War I, after President Woodrow Wilson said the United States was severing ties with Germany. Wilson's announcement, made during a speech to Congress, came three days after Germany said it would again practice unlimited submarine warfare in the Atlantic.

1943: The "Four Chaplains" were among those lost when the *Dorchester*, a U.S. troop transport ship, was torpedoed off Greenland. The four U.S.

Army chaplains—George L. Fox, Alexander D. Goode, Clark V. Poling, and John P. Washington—gave their life belts to four other men, and went down with the ship. More than 600 men were lost. But 230 were saved by two other ships using the new "retriever" technique, which involved swimmers clad in wet suits swimming to victims in the water and securing lines to them so they could be hauled onto the rescue ship.

1944: The United States consolidated control of the Kwajalein Atoll in the Marshall Islands, a major advance in the Pacific War, after a battle that began January 31. Most of the 8,700 forces in the Japanese garrison were killed; U.S. losses included 348 killed and almost 1,500 wounded.

1945: More than 1,000 B-17 bombers of the Eighth Air Force covered by almost 600 P-51 Mustangs attacked Berlin, Germany—the heaviest raid on the Nazi capital up to that time. Some 2,266 tons of bombs were dropped.

1961: Operation Looking Glass began. In the event that the headquarters of SAC—the Strategic Air Command—were destroyed, the U.S. Air Force made sure to have a "Doomsday Plane" in the air around the clock that could, if necessary, take direct control of all U.S. bombers and missiles. The Operation Looking Glass mission would continue until 1992.

1988: The Air Force Aerial Achievement Medal was established. It is awarded to military and civilian personnel for sustained meritorious achievement while participating in aerial flight that is considered above and beyond that normally expected of professional airmen.

⭐ QUOTE OF THE DAY

"We do not desire any hostile conflict with the Imperial German Government. We are the sincere friends of the German people and earnestly desire to remain at peace with the Government which speaks for them. We shall not believe that they are hostile to us unless and until we are obliged to believe it."

Woodrow Wilson

February 4

1777: George Washington engaged Nathaniel Sackett as a spymaster, offering him $50 a month (initially out of his own funds). Sackett created an intelligence group that would become known as the Culper Ring. The Culper Ring was responsible for obtaining intelligence on British forces during the Revolutionary War. Sackett, and then replacement Benjamin Tallmadge, developed a network of agents and informers who used invisible ink, dead drops, and code names (Washington was Agent 711)—spycraft that established the playbook for future generations of intelligence agents.

1779: John Paul Jones took command of *Bonhomme Richard*. Originally a merchant ship in the French East India Company (called the *Duc de Duras*), the *Bonhomme Richard* was renamed in honor of Benjamin Franklin by King Louis XVI of France.

1789: The first U.S. president—the commander-in-chief—was elected. It was, of course, 57-year-old George Washington, who had commanded the Continental Army during the Revolutionary War. John Adams became vice-president.

1941: The United Service Organization, better known as the USO, was founded to offer support for U.S. service members and their families. The USO sent many actors, musicians, and other performers to entertain the troops. In 1948, it was disbanded but was reformed the following year and still exists today.

1944: President Franklin D. Roosevelt authorized the Bronze Star Medal, and made the awarding of it retroactive to December 7, 1941—the day Pearl Harbor was attacked.

1945: The last German troops were pushed out of Belgium, as the Allied drive towards Germany accelerated in World War II.

1945: Bombing of Iwo Jima began, ahead of a planned invasion. Over the next two weeks, B-24 and B-29 bombers would drop an average 450 tons of bombs a day on Japanese positions. Heavy bombing would continue throughout the bitter fight for the island which would end with a U.S. victory (see March 26).

1962: The first U.S. helicopter was shot down in Vietnam. It was one of the 15 choppers carrying South Vietnamese Army troops into battle in the Mekong Delta.

★ QUOTE OF THE DAY

"The advantage of obtaining the earliest and best Intelligence of the designs of the enemy, the good character given of you by Colonel Duer added to your capacity for an undertaking of this kind have induced me to entrust the management of this business to your care till further orders on this head."

George Washington, letter to Nathaniel Sackett, February 4, 1777

February 5

1918: An American pilot shot down an enemy aircraft for the first time. Stephen W. Thompson's unit—the 1st Aero Squadron—had not yet begun combat operations, but Thompson, visiting a French unit, was invited to fly as a gunner/bombardier on a French raid over Germany. The squadron was attacked and Thompson shot down a German plane. He was awarded France's Croix de Guerre with Palm.

1958: The United States lost a nuclear weapon off Tybee Island, Georgia. An Air Force B-47 collided with another plane in midair, and, while the crew regained control of the craft, it became necessary to unload the 7,600-pound Mark 15 bomb before landing. Numerous recovery efforts in Wassaw Sound have been unsuccessful.

1960: The South Vietnamese government requested that Washington double U.S. Military Assistance and Advisory Group (MAAG-Vietnam) strength from 327 to 685. The advisory group had been formed on November 1, 1955, to provide military assistance to South Vietnam. In May 1964, MAAG-Vietnam was replaced by the new U.S. Military Assistance Command Vietnam (MACV).

★ QUOTE OF THE DAY

"Leaders have to have a feel for small things…"

Colin Powell, *It Worked for Me: In Life and Leadership*

February 6

1802: The First Barbary War had begun May 14, 1801. On this date, Congress passed an act giving President Thomas Jefferson the authority to instruct the U.S. Navy to seize Tripoli vessels and cargo and to approach privateers to do the same.

1862: The first major Union victory of the Civil War: General Ulysses S. Grant's troops captured Fort Henry on the Tennessee River. His forces would soon seize Fort Donelson on the Cumberland River, giving the Union control of northern Tennessee.

1908: The Army considered its first bids for airplanes. Of 24 proposals, two were approved by the secretary of war.

1966: Lyndon Johnson doubled down in Vietnam. At the Hawaii Conference in Honolulu, Hawaii, with South Vietnam prime minister Nguyễn Cao Kỳ, the president said the United States was "determined to win not only military victory but victory over hunger, disease, and despair."

1968: In heavy fighting, U.S. Marines recaptured Hue's hospital, jail, and provincial headquarters. It would take three more weeks of intense house to house fighting before the Vietnamese city was secured. Nearly a thousand Marines were killed or wounded.

2007: George W. Bush approved a plan to establish a new command center in Africa. The United States Africa Command (USAFRICOM or AFRICOM) become one of the nine Unified Combatant Commands of the U.S. military.

★ QUOTE OF THE DAY

"It shall be lawful for the President of the United States to instruct the commanders of the respective public vessels aforesaid, to subdue, seize and make prize of all vessels, goods and effects, belonging to the Bey of Tripoli, or to his subjects . . ."

An Act for the Protection of the Commerce and Seamen of the United States, against the Tripolitan Cruisers, February 6, 1802

February 7

1815: The Board of Naval Commissioners was established, at the direction of navy secretary Benjamin Crowninshield, to oversee the operation and maintenance of the U.S. Navy.

1942: By executive order, President Roosevelt created the War Shipping Administration, which assumed control over the U.S. Merchant Marine.

1942: The government ordered automakers to convert manufacturing plants for the war effort. The government guaranteed them profits regardless of production costs and also spent $11 billion to build new plants that would be sold to the automobile manufacturers at a discount after the war ended.

1965: The Viet Cong attacked Camp Holloway killing nine Americans and wounding 126. The United States immediately launched a counter attack on the North Vietnamese—Operation Flaming Dart—that endured until February 24. Some members of Congress began to voice concern that the retaliation was a dangerous escalation of the war.

☆ QUOTE OF THE DAY

"I loved my men, and they loved me. I don't consider myself a hero. I just couldn't give them up, just like a mother couldn't give up the child."

Desmond Doss, born February 7, 1919—Army medic and conscientious objector who received a Medal of Honor for saving 75 men during the Battle of Okinawa

February 8

1862: General Ambrose Burnside was victorious in the Battle of Roanoke Island. There were few casualties, but 2,500 Confederate soldiers surrendered. It was one of the first Union victories in the Civil War. Strategically, seizing the North Carolina island gave the North an avenue to threaten Richmond, Virginia.

1957: An agreement with Saudi Arabia gave the United States extended access to a key base at Dhahran. The United States, in return, agreed to continue military support of Saudi Arabia. In addition to its immense oil reserves, Saudi Arabia was seen as a bulwark against possible Soviet expansionism in the Middle East.

1962: MACV, the Military Assistance Command Vietnam, was established as the United States reorganized its military command in South Vietnam. MACV was accompanied by stepped-up American aid and assistance to the South Vietnamese government. Led by General Paul D. Harkins, former U.S. Army Deputy Commander-in-Chief in the Pacific, MACV replaced the U.S. Military Assistance and Advisory Group (MAAG-Vietnam), which was formed on November 1, 1955.

"Ten thousand men to our two thousand on land and nineteen vessels and 54 guns to our eight vessels with nine guns on the water . . ."

Captain William Parker, C.S.S. *Beaufort,* predicting defeat for his Confederates at Roanoke

February 9

1799: The *Constellation*, commanded by Captain Thomas Truxtun, captured the French frigate *L'Insurgente* off Saint Kitts and Nevis Island. The clash occurred during the so-called Quasi-War with France.

1943: Operation Watchtower—the Guadalcanal campaign—ended, a major victory for U.S. and Allied forces. The six-month battle, which began August 7, 1942, and which saw some of the heaviest fighting of the Pacific war, helped secure supply lines and communication routes between the United States, Australia, and New Zealand. A key Japanese airbase that had been under construction was completed by the Allies and renamed Henderson Field—it played a major role in subsequent chapters of the war.

1948: The Marine Corps took delivery of its first helicopters—HO3S-1s (Sikorsky H-5s).

1972: The Boeing E-3 Sentry/Airborne Warning and Control System (AWACS) aircraft made its first flight. In March 1977, it was delivered to the U.S. Air Force. Based on a Boeing 707 platform, the AWACS aircraft features a revolving radar "dome" (the rotodome): 30 feet across, six feet thick, and scanning in six revolutions per minute.

2012: Restrictions on the use of women in combat were removed, when the Pentagon issued new guidelines.

★ QUOTE OF THE DAY

"I hope the President and my country will, for the present, be content with a very fine frigate being added to our infant navy."

Captain Thomas Truxton, February 10, 1799, letter to the Secretary of the Navy

February 10

1807: Worried about British aggression, Thomas Jefferson asked Congress to boost defense spending. Specifically, the president wanted to buy more gun boats to better protect the long U.S. coastline. Jefferson was concerned about growing tension with Great Britain, fueled in part by the British belief that the young United States was rapidly becoming a threat to British maritime supremacy. A battle that summer between an American and British warship off the coast of Virginia was exactly the sort of thing that Jefferson worried about; the United States was also angry that Britain was interfering with American trade with France (which was at war with Britain). Growing tensions between the United States and Britain would lead to the War of 1812—often called America's "second war for independence."

1951: In the Korean War, United Nations forces recaptured the port of Inchon along with the badly damaged Kimpo Airfield.

1954: Dwight Eisenhower warned against U.S. involvement in Vietnam. In 1954, there was heavy fighting between communist forces—led by Ho Chi Minh—and France, which had long enjoyed colonial rule over Vietnam. The French asked Eisenhower for help, but the president refused to send American troops. Yet after the French were defeated—and Vietnam was divided in two by the Geneva Accords—Eisenhower did begin sending military aid to South Vietnam, laying the foundation for direct American involvement in the 1960s.

1962: The first Cold War prisoner swap: U-2 spy plane pilot Francis Gary Powers, imprisoned as an American spy in the Soviet Union since being shot down in 1960 (see May 1), was exchanged for Soviet spy Vilyam Fisher on Glienicke Bridge, Berlin, Germany. Included in the exchange was American graduate student Frederic Power.

1994: The first woman selected for combat pilot training—Lieutenant Jeannie Flynn (now Leavitt)—completed training in an F-15 Eagle.

2015: The Obama administration created the Cyber Threat Intelligence Integration Center, a new federal agency meant to bolster cybersecurity and better coordinate the response of the federal government and private sector.

★ QUOTE OF THE DAY

"I cannot conceive of a greater tragedy for America than to get heavily involved now in an all-out war."

Dwight Eisenhower, in a news conference warning
against U.S. involvement in Vietnam

February 11

1943: Dwight D. Eisenhower was selected to command Allied forces in Europe. The assignment would give the general authority over a planned invasion of Nazi-controlled France, which would occur the next year (see June 6).

1945: The Yalta Agreement. Signed by President Franklin Roosevelt, Prime Minister Winston Churchill and Premier Joseph Stalin, the agreement finalized the post-World War II future of Europe. Germany, soon to surrender, would be divided into four portions, with the United States, Great Britain, France, and the U.S.S.R. each controlling one. The Soviets also agreed to declare war on Japan 90 days after Germany's surrender. The agreement quickly became controversial, as it allowed the Soviet Union to cement its hold on—and spread communism across—Eastern Europe.

1962: Eight U.S. crewmen and one South Vietnamese officer were killed in an SC-47 crash about 70 miles north of Saigon. Their mission had been part of Operation Farm Gate, with the objective of providing advisory support to the South Vietnamese Air Force. In December 1961, President John F. Kennedy expanded Farm Gate's scope to include limited combat missions by U.S. forces.

1991: President George H.W. Bush met with Secretary of Defense Dick Cheney and Joint Chiefs Chairman Colin L. Powell, who had just returned from the Persian Gulf region. Afterward, Bush said he would hold off on a ground war against Iraq for the time being, saying allied air strikes had been "very, very effective."

★ QUOTE OF THE DAY

"Never before have the major Allies been more closely united—not only in their war aims but also in their peace aims."

Franklin D. Roosevelt

February 12

Generals Dwight D. Eisenhower and Omar Bradley at a memorial service for John J. Pershing, July 19, 1948. Library of Congress.

1893: Omar Bradley was born in Randolph County, Missouri. The West Point graduate (in the famous Class of 1915, which included Dwight Eisenhower) and instructor rose to the rank of five-star general during World War II. In 1950 he became the fifth and last man to receive the title of General of the Army (the other four were George C. Marshall, Eisenhower, Henry H. Arnold, and Douglas MacArthur).

1947: The first guided missile—the "Loon"—was launched from the submarine *Cusk* (SS 348). The Loon was America's version of Nazi Germany's V-1—the flying "buzz bomb" used to terrifying effect against London, England. The Loon could carry a 2,200-pound warhead to a range of 150 miles and could be launched from the ground, ships, or aircraft.

1955: The first U.S. military advisors were sent to South Vietnam by the Eisenhower administration, to aid the newly created Government of the Republic of Vietnam.

1973: Operation Homecoming—the release of U.S. POWs from North Vietnam—began. By March 29, all 591 Americans that had been held were freed. Thirteen prisons and prison camps were used to incarcerate the American prisoners, the most infamous of which was Hanoi's Hỏa Lò Prison (derisively nicknamed the "Hanoi Hilton"). One POW, Colonel

This Day in U.S. Military History

Floyd James "Jim" Thompson, had been held for nearly nine years (1964-1973)—the longest time spent as a prisoner of war by any American service person.

★ QUOTE OF THE DAY

"For military command is as much a practice of human relations as it is a science of tactics and a knowledge of logistics. Where there are people, there is pride and ambition, prejudice, and conflict."

Omar Bradley, *A Soldier's Story*

February 13

1923: Charles Elwood "Chuck" Yeager was born in Myra, West Virginia. He is a former U.S. Air Force officer, World War II combat pilot, and a record-setting test pilot. In 1947, he became the first pilot confirmed to have exceeded the speed of sound in level flight (see October 14).

1945: U.S. and British bombers began a devastating attack on Dresden, Germany. Over the next two days, 1,249 planes would drop more than 3,900 tons of bombs on the city. The bombing and resulting firestorm killed up to 135,000 people—one of the deadliest military attacks in history.

1951: United Nations troops held off the Chinese at Chipyong-ni. The four-day Chinese offensive had U.N.—including U.S. and French—troops surrounded while U.S. aircraft dropped supplies at night over a zone outlined by burning gasoline-soaked rags. The surrounded troops held out until relieved by reinforcements.

1965: President Johnson ordered sustained bombing of North Vietnam. The president's decision, which he had been weighing for months, resulted in Operation Rolling Thunder, which would continue until October 31, 1968. During that period an estimated 643,000 tons of bombs were dropped on North Vietnam; nearly 900 U.S. aircraft were lost—and 1,054 U.S. airmen killed, wounded, or captured.

1991: Two U.S. F-117 stealth fighters bombed a civilian air raid shelter in Amiriyah, Baghdad, killing more than 400 people. The United States claimed it had intelligence that it was being used as a command post, but may have confused signals coming from a nearby Iraqi communications center. The Iraqis denied any military aspect to the bunker.

✯ QUOTE OF THE DAY

"To continue to live, a veteran test pilot needs both skill and luck."

Chuck Yeager, *Yeager: An Autobiography* (1985)

February 14

1778: For the second time the American flag (this time the recently adopted Stars and Stripes) was officially recognized by a foreign nation: the *Ranger*, helmed by Lieutenant Thomas Simpson (who had recently been given command by John Paul Jones), was sailing off the coast of Brittany, France, when French admiral Toussaint-Guillaume Picquet de la Motte offered a nine-gun salute. (The first foreign recognition of the American flag came from the Dutch in 1776—see November 16.)

1864: As a dress rehearsal of sorts for his March to the Sea, General William T. Sherman attacked Meridian, Mississippi. Through February 20, Sherman's troops destroyed the city and its infrastructure, including 115 miles of railroad. Sherman reported, "For five days, 10,000 men worked hard and with a will in that work of destruction, with axes, crowbars, sledges, clawbars, and with fire." It is regarded as the first attempt by the Union at warfare that aimed not just to defeat opposing military forces, but the will of the Southern people.

1912: The first U.S. diesel-powered submarine, the *E-1*, was commissioned at Groton, Connecticut. Originally named *Skipjack*, the boat was launched the prior spring by the Fore River Shipyard, Quincy, Massachusetts (see May 27). Lieutenant Chester W. Nimitz—the future World War II giant—was the commander.

1962: President John F. Kennedy authorized U.S. military advisors in Vietnam to return fire if fired upon. Kennedy drew a distinction between these advisors and full-blown combat troops, which he said the United States had not deployed.

2007: Operation Imposing Law, also known as Operation Law and Order, began in Baghdad. The joint operation between U.S. and Iraqi forces was part of President George W. Bush's "surge" plan to clear the Iraqi capital of Shiite militias and Sunni insurgents.

✯ QUOTE OF THE DAY

"Meridian with its depots, store-houses, arsenal, hospitals, offices, hotels, and cantonments no longer exists."

William T. Sherman

February 15

1898: At 9:40 p.m., the U.S. battleship *Maine* blew up in Havana harbor, killing 260 of the 350-member American crew. Spain was accused of blowing up the ship—though there is no definitive evidence of this—sparking what would soon become the Spanish-American War. In 1976, an American investigation instigated by Admiral Hyman Rickover concluded that the *Maine* exploded after an on-board fire ignited ammunition stocks.

1946: Financed by the Army, the first electronic general-purpose computer—was dedicated at the University of Pennsylvania in Philadelphia. In its day, ENIAC's ability to solve "a large class of numerical problems" dazzled scientists and military officials.

1951: President Harry Truman stated that the United Nations had authorized General Douglas MacArthur to recross the 38th parallel into North Korea. MacArthur was, of course, the top U.N. commander in Korea— but would soon be fired by his commander-in-chief (see April 11).

1954: Canada and the United States agreed to construct the Distant Early Warning Line (DEW), a system of radar stations in the Arctic regions of Canada and Alaska. The DEW Line, operational from 1957 to the late 1980s, helped monitor Soviet military activity and alert commanders of a missile or bomber attack.

✯ QUOTE OF THE DAY

"Remember the *Maine!*"

February 16

1804: The daring Decatur raid into Tripoli Harbor: it occurred during the First Barbary War, when President Thomas Jefferson ordered U.S. Navy vessels to the Mediterranean Sea to respond to ongoing raids against American merchant ships by pirates from the Barbary states—Morocco, Algeria, Tunis, and Tripolitania. After disguising themselves as Maltese sailors, Lieutenant Stephen Decatur's force of 74 sailed into Tripoli harbor, approached an American ship that had been seized—the *Philadelphia*—and attacked its pirate crew, capturing or killing all but two. They then set fire to the ship.

1862: Ulysses S. Grant earned the nickname "Unconditional Surrender" Grant after the Battle of Fort Donelson. The battle, waged around a Confederate fort near the Kentucky-Tennessee border, proved to be an important Union victory—the Army of Central Kentucky had almost 14,000 casualties. Grant, already a brigadier general, would be promoted to a major general.

1865: Union forces under General William T. Sherman captured and set ablaze Columbia, South Carolina.

1945: The Bataan Peninsula was re-occupied by American troops. Nearly three years earlier (see April 3), a major Japanese offensive had begun against the strategic peninsula, which guards Manila Bay in the Philippines, resulting in a strategic defeat for American forces—many of whom would perish in the brutal Bataan Death March or during lengthy Japanese captivity.

1945: U.S. planes blasted Tokyo. Task Force 58, part of 5th Fleet, attacked with planes from 12 fleet carriers and four light carriers, which were escorted by eight battleships, 15 cruisers, and 83 destroyers, along with numerous support ships.

1951: The U.S. siege of Wonsan began. The 861-day blockade and bombardment of the North Korean port was one of the largest ever initiated by the Navy.

★ QUOTE OF THE DAY

"The most bold and daring act of the age."

> British admiral Horatio Nelson's reported
> comment on the Decatur raid in Tripoli

February 17

1864: The navy sloop-of-war *Housatonic* was torpedoed and sunk in Charleston Harbor, South Carolina, by the Confederate submarine *H.L. Hunley*. It was the first time a submarine sunk a ship.

1944: Operation Hailstone began. It was a massive United States Navy air and surface attack on Japanese forces in Truk Lagoon, in the Pacific theater. Over two days, U.S. aircraft would conduct 1,250 sorties.

1865: Union forces recaptured Fort Sumter, nearly four years after the fort in Charleston harbor surrendered to Confederate forces (see April 12).

2009: The Obama administration ordered 17,000 additional U.S. troops to Afghanistan. The move in the seven-year-long war was to bolster security. There were already 36,000 American troops there.

★ QUOTE OF THE DAY

"This increase is necessary to stabilize a deteriorating situation in Afghanistan, which has not received the strategic attention, direction, and resources it urgently requires."

Barack Obama on his Afghan troop surge

February 18

1944: Operation Hailstone concluded. More than 260 Japanese planes and almost 50 Japanese vessels—including four destroyers—were destroyed. Truk Island of the Caroline Islands was neutralized.

1968: Lyndon Johnson dug in on Vietnam. Addressing the crew of the aircraft carrier *Constellation*, he vowed that communist forces would not break America's will.

★ QUOTE OF THE DAY

"In Vietnam today, the foes of freedom are making ready to test America's will. Quite obviously, the enemy believes—he thinks—that our will is vulnerable. Quite clearly, the enemy hopes that he can break that will.

And quite certainly, we know that the enemy is going to fail—so we have taken our stand."

Lyndon Johnson

February 19

1862: The *Monitor* made its trial run in New York harbor. Quickly built in just 101 days, the iron-hulled warship she would soon change the face of naval warfare in the epic Battle of Hampton Roads (see March 9).

1917: President Woodrow Wilson ordered American troops back from the Mexican border, ahead of possible deployment in Europe. The troops had been hunting for Pancho Villa, the Mexican revolutionary general.

1941: The Coast Guard Reserve and Auxiliary Act was passed, establishing a military reserve to what had been a civilian reserve.

1945: Operation Detachment—the invasion of Iwo Jima—began. The battle—some of the bloodiest fighting of World War II—would last for five weeks. It is estimated that all but 200 or so of the 21,000 Japanese forces on Iwo Jima were killed—as were nearly 7,000 U.S. Marines. The capture of Iwo Jima gave the United States three airfields from which air raids could be launched on Japan itself—just 660 miles away.

2005: The *Jimmy Carter* entered the navy's fleet as the most heavily armed submarine ever built—and one with vast intelligence gathering capabilities. The $3.2 billion vessel was the last of the Seawolf class of attack subs. Former president and submariner Jimmy Carter was in attendance.

★ QUOTE OF THE DAY

"My background and my interest, my commitment, my dedication and appreciation to the navy is deep and everlasting."

Jimmy Carter, *U.S.S. Jimmy Carter* commissioning

February 20

1864: The Battle of Olustee: the only major Civil War battle fought in Florida was a Union defeat, when Confederate forces under Brigadier General

Joseph Finnegan routed Union troops led by Brigadier General Truman Seymour. The victory kept the Confederates in control of Florida's interior for the remainder of the war.

1942: Navy Lt. Cmdr. Edward O'Hare became the first U.S. flying ace of World War II. Operating from the aircraft carrier *Lexington*, O'Hare, flying a F4F-3 Wildcat, shot down five Japanese G4M1 Betty bombers. (The designation "ace" is given to any pilot who had five or more downed enemy planes to his credit.) For his actions this day, O'Hare received the Medal of Honor. O'Hare would be shot down himself the next year (see November 26). Chicago's O'Hare International Airport is named in his honor.

1945: American B-17 bombers pounded Nuremberg, Germany, for a second time (see January 2). Escorted by 700 fighters, the raid smashed railroad facilities and aircraft. A total of 23 American aircraft were lost.

1951: Operation Killer began in Korea, the second major counteroffensive launched against Chinese and North Korean forces. Led by General Matthew Ridgeway, commander of the Eighth Army, its objective was to annihilate enemy troops south of a line designated as the "Arizona Line." Operation Ripper soon followed (see March 7).

1956: The United States Merchant Marine Academy became a permanent service academy. Based in Kings Point, New York, it is tasked with training officers for the United States Merchant Marine, branches of the military, or the transportation industry.

1962: Marine Lt. Colonel John Glenn, on Friendship 7, became the first American and third person to orbit Earth.

★ QUOTE OF THE DAY

"Korea taught us that all warfare from this time forth must be limited. It could no longer be a question of *whether* to fight a limited war, but of *how* to avoid fighting any other kind."

Matthew Bunker Ridgway, *The Korean War* (1967)

February 21

1944: U.S. forces took control of the Marshall Islands, which had been in Japanese control since 1914. After the war, U.S. nuclear weapons would be tested in the region.

1945: Japanese kamikazes sank U.S. escort aircraft carrier *Bismarck Sea* near Iwo Jima with the loss of 318 crew. This was the last U.S. aircraft carrier to be sunk in war.

1964: Twins Mark and Scott Kelly were born in Orange, New Jersey—twin U.S. Navy captains (Scott Kelly is now retired) and the only twin astronauts (space shuttle pilots).

✭ QUOTE OF THE DAY

"This is a risky business, but it's got a big reward. So, you know, everybody on board *Discovery* and the space station here thinks it's worthwhile."

Mark Kelly, Associated Press interview, July 11, 2006

February 22

1732: America's first president, George Washington, was born on the family plantation at Bridges Creek, Colony of Virginia. His military career began in the British army, fighting in the French and Indian War. As the commander of the Continental Army during the Revolutionary War from 1775 to 1783, Washington led his troops to victory at Yorktown. He also established the importance of intelligence-gathering to the military effort (February 4) and the Purple Heart.

1909: The Great White Fleet returned to Hampton Roads, Virginia, following its 14-month around-the-world cruise. The fleet of 16 battleships (along with escort craft) had been ordered to travel the world by President Theodore Roosevelt, to demonstrate America's power—and its desire for peace. All had their hulls painted a bright white.

1917: Defense spending ramped up, as Congress passed a $250 million arms appropriations bill. The increase in military spending signaled the Wilson administration's determination to be ready for possible war with Germany. The United States would formally enter the war six weeks later (see April 6).

1943: The *Iowa*, the lead ship of the last class of American fast battleships, was commissioned. "The Big Stick," as it was affectionately referred to, would be decommissioned for the final time in 1990.

1974: Lt. j.g. Barbara Ann (Allen) Rainey became the first navy-designated female aviator.

✮ QUOTE OF THE DAY

"The 22nd being the anniversary of the birth of Washington, all of the ships of the squadron fired the usual salute. Many of the Japanese gentlemen came by permission on board the flagship to witness the firing, with which they were much interested."

Commodore Matthew Perry, 1854,
in Tokyo Bay

February 23

1837: Congress called for an inspection of the coast from Chesapeake Bay to the Sabine River "with regard to the location of additional light-houses,

Future president Zachary Taylor commanded U.S. forces at the Battle of Buena Vista, February 22-23, 1847. Library of Congress.

beacons, and buoys." Captain Napoleon L. Coste, commanding the Revenue cutter *Campbell* was dispatched. He reported that the first addition to aids to navigation on this entire coast should be at Egmont Key, Tampa Bay. A lighthouse was authorized immediately and built the next year. The station (not the same tower) still exists as one of the three manned lights on the Gulf of Mexico.

1847: U.S. troops defeated Mexican forces at the Battle of Buena Vista near Saltillo, Mexico. The Americans, led by General—and future president— Zachary Taylor, defeated the army of General—and future president of Mexico—Antonio López de Santa Anna. The battle featured the American use of artillery to repulse a much larger force. This was Taylor's last battle of the Mexican-American War.

1903: The United States leased Guantánamo Bay from Cuba. The base on the southeastern part of that island, was the first, and remains the oldest, American military base. The leasing agreement calls for the United States to pay the Cuban government just $4,085 a year. Since 2002, one portion of the base has been used as a detention camp for combatants captured during the U.S. GWOT—global war on terror.

1904: The United States acquired control of the Panama Canal Zone for $10 million; the ensuing construction of the Panama Canal would provide the United States with a key passage for military and commercial ships between the Atlantic and Pacific oceans.

1942: A Japanese submarine shelled an oil refinery at Ellwood, near Santa Barbara, California—the first enemy bomb to fall on the U.S. mainland during World War II.

1945: U.S. Marines raised the American flag on Iwo Jima. The flag raising on Mount Suribachi, the island's highest peak and most strategic position, was accomplished by six Marines. Michael Strank, Harlon Block, Ira Hayes, Franklin Sousley, Harold Keller, and Harold Schultz. A photo taken by Joe Rosenthal of the Associated Press became one of the most iconic images of the war and served as the basis for the U.S. Marine Corps War Memorial.

★ QUOTE OF THE DAY

"I took the picture, the Marines took Iwo Jima."

Joe Rosenthal

February 24

1885: Chester Nimitz was born at Fredericksburg, Texas. A graduate of the U.S. Naval Academy in 1905, the admiral had overall responsibility for Pacific forces during World War II—which culminated in Japan's surrender in 1945 (see September 2). Nimitz sat at the table on the deck of the battleship *Missouri* in Tokyo Bay as representatives from the vanquished enemy signed the surrender documents.

1917: British intelligence gave the United States a copy of the "Zimmermann Note," a coded Western Union telegram from German foreign office aide Arthur Zimmermann to Germany's ambassador to Mexico sent on January 19, 1917. It said that in the event of war with the United States, Germany would ask Mexico to fight on the German side—and in return would help Mexico recover territory it lost in the Mexican-American War seven decades earlier. The telegram began a spark that led to a U.S. declaration of war against Germany (see April 6).

1944: "Merrill's Marauders" launched operations in northern Burma. Named for Maj. Gen. Frank Merrill, the unit of 2,750 trained in jungle warfare would harass and disrupt the Japanese forces that occupied Burma.

1947: The first flight of the B-45 Tornado bomber. The North American B-45 Tornado (Boeing) was the U.S. Air Force's first operational jet

Fleet Admiral Chester Nimitz looking at a chart of the Japan Sea in his office at Guam, 1945. NH 58060 courtesy of Naval History & Heritage Command.

This Day in U.S. Military History

bomber, and the first multi-jet-engined bomber in the world to be refuelled in midair. It was an important part of the U.S. nuclear deterrent for several years in the 1950s. It was also the first jet bomber of the NATO Alliance, which was formed in 1949.

1968: The Tet Offensive ended with the U.S. and South Vietnamese recapture of Hue. The three-week battle (see January 30) began with a surprise North Vietnamese-Vietcong attack throughout South Vietnam, including the capital of Saigon. Although it resulted in a (costly) American and South Vietnamese victory, Tet increased domestic pressure on President Lyndon Johnson to end the war.

1984: The United States completed its withdrawal from Lebanon, three months after a devastating terror attack on a Marine Corps base (see October 23).

1991: After a six-week air campaign, the U.S. and coalition allies launched a ground attack on Iraq forces, designed to push them out of occupied Kuwait. After 100 hours, President George H.W. Bush declared a ceasefire, and Iraq pledged to honor future coalition and U.N. peace terms. One hundred twenty-five American soldiers were killed in the Persian Gulf War.

★ QUOTE OF THE DAY

"We intend to begin on the first of February unrestricted submarine warfare. We shall endeavor in spite of this to keep the United States of America neutral. In the event of this not succeeding, we make Mexico a proposal of alliance. . ."

Arthur Zimmermann, opening of his infamous
January 19, 1917, telegram

February 25

1836: Samuel Colt patented a mechanism that enabled a gun to be fired multiple times without reloading. During the Mexican-American War, the federal government became a large customer of the revolving-breech pistol. The relationship grew and by the beginning of the Civil War in 1861, the Colt revolver was arguably the world's best known weapon. Colt was also known for developing advanced manufacturing techniques such as interchangeable parts and an organized production line.

The Colt company remains in business and has sold more than 30 million guns.

1933: The first Navy aircraft carrier was launched: the *Ranger* (CV-4). During World War II, *Ranger* was considered too slow for use in the Pacific theater against Japan, but saw action in the Atlantic, against a less robust German navy. *Ranger* saw combat in that theater and provided air support for Operation Torch (see November 8).

1991: A Scud missile fired by Iraq killed 27 U.S. troops. The Army Reserve troops from Pennsylvania were in their barracks in Dhahran, Saudi Arabia, when they were attacked.

⭐ QUOTE OF THE DAY

"Your pistols . . . keep the various warlike tribes of Indians and marauding Mexicans in subjection."

Texas Ranger Samuel Walker, letter to Samuel Colt

February 26

1940: The U.S. Air Defense Command was established at Mitchell Field, near Uniondale, New York. It was tasked with developing air defenses for cities, vital industrial areas, continental bases, and military facilities across the United States.

1944: Sue Sophia Dauser became the first woman in the U.S. Navy to be promoted to captain. She was superintendent of the Navy's Nurse Corps, appointed in 1939.

1945: Eighth Air Force bombers pummeled Berlin, dropping 3,000 tons of bombs on the Nazi capital. Some 500,000 incendiaries—designed to start fires—inflicted significant damage on the city.

1949: A B-50 Superfortress set off on the first nonstop around-the-world flight. Taking off from Carswell Air Force Base in Fort Worth, Texas, the *Lucky Lady II*, piloted by Captain James Gallagher, and featuring a crew of 14 men, traveled 23,452-miles, averaging 249 miles per hour. It was refueled four times in midair by B-29 tanker planes. It landed on March 2 after 94 hours in the air. General Curtis LeMay kept the mission secret, and *Lucky Lady II* switched tail numbers during the flight.

⭐ QUOTE OF THE DAY

"To err is human, to forgive is not SAC policy."

General Curtis LeMay, Commander of Strategic
Air Command (1948-57)

February 27

1776: The first decisive victory of the Revolutionary War occurred at Moore's Creek Bridge near Wilmington, North Carolina, when a colonial force smashed a detachment of Scottish fighters. The colony of North Carolina would soon vote to declare its independence from the British.

1864: Union prisoners arrived at Andersonville. The Confederate prison in southern Georgia (also known as Camp Sumter) quickly became known as a place of suffering, brutality, and death. Of the estimated 45,000 Union prisoners held there during the Civil War, nearly 13,000 died, largely from scurvy, diarrhea, and dysentery. The Confederate commander of the camp, Captain Henry Wirz, was tried and executed after the war for war crimes.

1942: The Battle of the Java Sea began, when 14 Allied ships (American, Dutch, British, and Australian) took on 28 Japanese ships that were invading the Dutch East Indies colony of Java. Over a three-day battle, the Japanese beat Allied forces, sinking at least 11 ships, killing more than 3,370, and taking nearly 1,500 prisoners.

⭐ QUOTE OF THE DAY

"For a man to find, on waking, that his comrade by his side was dead, was an occurrence too common to be noted. I have seen death in almost all the forms of the hospital and battlefield, but the daily scenes in Camp exceeded in the extremity of misery all my previous experience."

Private Prescott Tracy, Andersonville POW, August 16, 1864,
describing the prison camp to the United States Sanitary Commission

February 28

1843: The first steam ship with screw propeller, *Princeton*, launched September 5, 1843, was taken out for a demonstration cruise on the Potomac River with President John Tyler on board and key cabinet and military officials. In a tragic turn, a gun—the "Peacemaker"—exploded and killed Secretary of State Abel P. Upshur, Secretary of the Navy Thomas Gilmer, and six other passengers. Tyler was unharmed, as were former first lady Dolley Madison and future first lady Julia Gardiner.

1847: In the Battle of Sacramento River, near Chihuahua, Mexico, Colonel Alexander Doniphan's force of less than 1,000 defeated Mexican troops numbering more than 4,000, allowing the Missouri volunteers to take Chihuahua and control Mexico's northwest.

1893: The first U.S. Navy battleship was launched: *Indiana*. Designed for coastal defense, and not action on the open ocean, *Indiana* served in the Spanish-American War (1898), supporting the Battle of Santiago de Cuba. It was decommissioned in January 1919.

1991: George H.W. Bush declared victory over Iraq in the Persian Gulf war. In announcing an end to Operation Desert Storm, Bush said his principal strategic goal—pushing Iraq out of Kuwait, which it had invaded the prior August—had been achieved. The United States did not occupy Iraq itself in 1991. Secretary of Defense Dick Cheney told the president it wasn't worth the casualties or "getting bogged down."

1994: U.S. fighter planes shot down four Serbian warplanes which were violating Bosnia's no-fly zone. It was the first military action in the 45-year history of the North Atlantic Treaty Organization (NATO).

★ QUOTE OF THE DAY

"Nations with allies thrive, and those without wither."

General James Mattis, former Secretary of Defense (2017-19),
on NATO, in *Call Sign Chaos* (2019)

February 29

1840: John Philip Holland, the "father of the modern submarine," was born in Ireland. After he immigrated to the United States in 1873, he began working on a submersible ship, and in 1881 launched the *Fenian Ram*, a 31-foot-long submersible powered by a 15-horsepower internal combustion engine. It submerged 64 feet beneath New York Harbor. In 1895, his J.P. Holland Torpedo Boat Company received its first contract from the U.S. Navy.

1864: President Abraham Lincoln signed a bill reviving the rank of lieutenant general and then sent a letter to the Senate nominating Ulysses S. Grant to that rank. Previously, only George Washington and Winfield Scott attained the rank of lieutenant general.

1944: Operation Brewer began: the U.S. campaign to take the Admiralty Islands north of New Guinea.

★ QUOTE OF THE DAY

The president is authorized "to appoint, by and with the advice and consent of the senate, a lieutenant-general, to be selected among those officers in the military service of the United States, not below the grade of major general, most distinguished for courage, skill, and ability...."

H.R. 26, December 14, 1863, signed by
Abraham Lincoln, February 29, 1864

March

March 1

1912: The first parachute jump from an airplane was made, when Captain Albert Berry jumped from an airplane over Jefferson Barracks Army Base, Missouri, at an altitude of 1,500 feet. His parachute—36 feet in diameter—was contained in a metal canister attached to the underside of the plane, and when Berry fell, his weight pulled the parachute from the canister.

1917: Woodrow Wilson told the American people of the Zimmermann Telegram, the final straw in his decision to ask Congress to declare war against Germany (see April 2).

1942: The United States sank its first German submarine of World War II, when Navy Ensign William Tepuni, piloting a Lockheed Hudson, PBO, attacked *U-656* off the coast of Newfoundland.

2002: Operation Anaconda began. It was the first large-scale battle in the U.S. war in Afghanistan since the Battle of Tora Bora (see December 6). It involved U.S. military, CIA paramilitary, Afghan military, and North Atlantic Treaty Organization (NATO) and non-NATO forces. At the end of the operation (see March 18), coalition forces had pushed most of al Qaeda and Taliban forces, who fought fiercely, from the Shah-i-Kot Valley. American casualties were estimated at eight killed and 72 wounded.

2003: The alleged mastermind of the September 11, 2001, terror attacks was captured by U.S. and Pakistani forces. Khalid Shaikh Mohammed is today held at the U.S. detention facility at Guantanamo Bay Naval Base.

★ QUOTE OF THE DAY

"Never again!"

Albert Berry, on whether he'd parachute again. His resolve held until March 10, 1912, when he jumped again.

March 2

Stephen Decatur. Library of Congress.

1799: Coast Guard cutter ships were authorized to fire on uncooperative vessels in American territorial waters. They were also authorized to search ships as needed and "perform such other duties for the collection and security of the Revenue" as directed by the Secretary of the Treasury.

1815: The United States declared war on Algiers, in what became known as the second Barbary War. Several North African states (also called the Barbary States), sent pirates into the waters of the southern Mediterranean to collect "tributes" from passing merchant ships and to seize passengers and crew for ransom. Preoccupied by the War of 1812, the United States had been unable to act on the situation until this day's declaration. A much enlarged U.S. Navy was dispatched. Commodore Stephen Decatur later secured a treaty to end the practices of tribute and ransom.

1864: Abraham Lincoln's February 29 nomination of Major General Ulysses S. Grant to lieutenant general of the Army of the United States was confirmed by the Senate on this day. Lincoln had great confidence in

Grant, who had led Union forces to a series of sweeping victories, including those at Fort Donelson (see February 16), Shiloh (see April 6), and Vicksburg (see May 18). Grant would become the first soldier to attain that rank since George Washington.

1865: In the Battle of Waynesboro, Union forces brought their Shenandoah Valley campaign to a successful conclusion. General George Armstrong Custer's Third Cavalry Division smashed Confederate troops led by General Jubal Early.

1943: A U.S. and Australian offensive began in the Battle of the Bismarck Sea, in the western Pacific. Using land-based aircraft, they destroyed eight Japanese troop transports and four Japanese destroyers. More than 3,000 Japanese troops and sailors drowned, and of 150 Japanese fighter planes that attempted to engage the Allied planes, 102 were shot down.

1949: *Lucky Lady II*, a B-50 Superfortress, completed the first around-the-world nonstop flight (begun February 26), arriving at Carswell Air Force Base, Fort Worth, Texas, to the cheers of a gathered military and media crowd. *Lucky Lady II* had refueled four times aloft, using the drogue system—over the Azores, Saudi Arabia, the Philippines, and the Pacific.

1951: The USS *K-1* (SSK-1) was launched. Later named *Barracuda*, this submarine was the fruit of the navy's Project Kayo, a post-World War II research initiative to develop submarines to attack and destroy enemy submarines. Such subs originally had the hull classification SSK, for "hunter-killer submarine."

1965: Operation Rolling Thunder began. It was the beginning of a sustained, three-and-a-half-year bombing campaign of North Vietnam—and is regarded as the biggest air campaign ever waged during the half-century Cold War. Before President Lyndon Johnson, under political pressure, stopped it on the event of the 1968 presidential election, 643,000 tons of bombs were dropped. Approximately 900 American aircraft were lost—and 1,054 U.S. airmen killed, wounded, or captured.

★ QUOTE OF THE DAY

"We've kicked the Vietnam syndrome once and for all."

President George H.W. Bush, following the allied victory in the first Gulf War.

March 3

1776: The first American amphibious landing operation took place in the Raid on Nassau when Continental sailors and Marines landed on New Providence Island in the Bahamas, where they seized British ordnance and gunpowder.

1873: The Army Signal Corps established a storm signal network to assist ships at sea. Communication stations with telegraph lines were constructed, allowing stations to communicate with each other. It was the precursor to the National Weather Service.

1915: The U.S. Navy Reserve was created by an act of Congress.

1915: The post of Chief of Naval Operations (CNO) was created by Congress. Admiral William S. Benson was appointed as the first CNO.

1945: U.S. forces captured Manila, the Philippine capital, as Japanese resistance crumbled after a month-long battle. Most of the 20,000 Japanese defenders were killed.

★ QUOTE OF THE DAY

"[Some Signal Corps weather watchers] were so confident of their ability to successfully counterfeit the laws of nature that they wrote up their observations several hours before or after the schedule time."

Signal Corps records officer William A. Glassford,
complaining of a few bad apples among the observers

March 4

1776: British troops were forced to end their siege of Boston, Massachusetts, after Continental Army forces fortified Dorchester Heights with cannons.

1814: American troops defeated British forces at the Battle of Longwoods near present-day Wardsville, Ontario. The victory resulted in British troops abandoning parts of upper Canada.

1944: The United States bombed Berlin for the first time. Fourteen bomber wings from the Eighth Air Force attacked, but only one plane reached the

German capital (the rest dropped their loads elsewhere). Although few planes were lost to German defenses, the raid was considered "none too successful" (as recorded in the official history of U.S. Army Air Force). Subsequent attacks grew more effective.

2002: Takur Ghar—the heaviest battle to date of Operation Anaconda (see March 1)—occurred. U.S. forces made three helicopter landings on the Afghan mountain top, only to be greeted by heavy al Qaeda fire each time. Takur Ghar was eventually seized, but seven U.S. service members were killed and many were wounded. The fight also became known as Battle of Roberts Ridge, in honor of its first casualty, Navy SEAL Neil C. Roberts. Roberts fell from his Chinook helicopter and appeared to single-handedly fight al Qaeda attackers for more than an hour before being killed. Tech. Sgt. John Chapman, who died in the battle after also fighting his adversaries single-handedly, received the Medal of Honor posthumously. The other Medal of Honor recipient from the Battle of Roberts Ridge was Navy SEAL Britt Slabinski, who attempted to rescue Roberts.

☆ QUOTE OF THE DAY

"In this simple grave, in this quiet cemetery, in our small town in Central Pennsylvania, lies a national hero."

Memorial service for Neil C. Roberts, 2006, Prospect Hill Cemetery, York, Pennsylvania

March 5

1770: Prelude to the Revolutionary War: a scuffle between British troops and a clutch of colonists in front of Boston, Massachusetts' Custom House burst into violence as the British fired into the crowd killing five. Initially called "The Bloody Massacre Perpetrated in King Street" after the title of an engraving by Paul Revere, it later became known as the Boston Massacre and helped grow support for a war for independence.

1906: Army troops overwhelmed native Moro fighters in the First Battle of Bud Dajo in the Philippines. After the U.S. occupied parts of the Philippines following the Spanish-American War, Philippine rebels, who had been fighting the Spanish, began fighting the Americans.

1918: The Tank Service was established. Armor would become a permanent branch of the U.S. Army in 1950.

1942: The United States Naval Construction Battalions, better known as the Seabees, was established. Formed in World War II, the Seabees (taken from the initials "C.B.") built bases for advancing U.S. forces. The Seabees remain an integral part of the U.S. military today.

⭐ QUOTE OF THE DAY

"The difficult we do now; the impossible takes a little longer."

Seabee sign at Bougainville Navy Yard, 1944

March 6

1836: In Texas, where settlers were battling Mexico for independence, the Alamo fell after a 13-day siege. Mexican general Santa Anna had attacked with around 3,000 men, overwhelming the 187 defenders of the Catholic mission-turned fortress. The affairs of Texas and Mexico came to a consequential crisis when the United States annexed Texas in 1845, helping spark the Mexican-American War.

2007: The U.S. and its NATO allies launched Operation Achilles, the largest land-based offensive in Afghanistan since the United States first attacked in 2001 (see October 7). One major goal of the operation was to flush out Taliban fighters, who had been avoiding direct confrontation with NATO troops by using guerrilla tactics.

⭐ QUOTE OF THE DAY

"I am besieged, by a thousand or more of the Mexicans under Santa Anna. I have sustained a continual Bombardment and cannonade for 24 hours and have not lost a man. The enemy has demanded a surrender at discretion, otherwise, the garrison are to be put to the sword, if the fort is taken. I have answered the demand with a cannon shot, and our flag still waves proudly from the walls. . . ."

William Barrett Travis, Texan commander at the Alamo, sent this impassioned letter "To the People of Texas and All Americans in the World" on February 24 calling for reinforcements

This Day in U.S. Military History　　　　　　　　　　　　　　**67**

March 7

1862: Union forces defeated Confederates at the Battle of Pea Ridge. The battle, in the northern part of Arkansas, began March 7 and concluded March 8. It was part of a larger campaign for control of Missouri. Union troops, led by General Samuel Curtis, suffered 1,384 men killed, wounded, or captured out of 10,000 engaged. The comparable Confederate figure was estimated at 2,000.

1951: Operation Ripper began, with the objective of inflicting maximum damage on Chinese and North Korean forces around Seoul and nearby towns. Led by General Matthew Ridgway, commander of the Eighth Army, it was the immediate follow-up to a prior counteroffensive designated Operation Killer (see February 20).

1994: The U.S. Navy issued its first permanent orders assigning women to regular duty on combat ships.

★ QUOTE OF THE DAY

"I'd learned long before in Europe that a man with a grenade in his hand can often blast his way out of a tight spot."

General Matthew Ridgway, commenting about why he wore
a live grenade attached to his uniform in Korea

March 8

1965: 3,500 Marines from the 9th Marine Expeditionary Brigade landed at Da Nang, led by Brigadier General Frederick J. Karch. They were the first U.S. ground combat troops to be committed to the Vietnam War.

1973: The Coast Guard made its first drug seizure, when the cutter *Dauntless* seized a fishing boat that was carrying one ton of marijuana.

1977: The Army reported that from 1949 to 1969 it had conducted 239 open-air, germ warfare experiments in secret. Unknowing test subjects included army personnel and passengers at Washington D.C.'s Greyhound bus terminal and National Airport (now Reagan National Airport).

★ QUOTE OF THE DAY

"Any Marine worth his salt can load, sight, and fire in four seconds."

Sergeant in Da Nang, 1965, responding to complaints
by Marines of Brigadier General Karch's order to carry
personal arms unloaded after lethal accidents

March 9

1847: The Battle of Veracruz began. Led by General Winfield Scott, it was a 20-day siege of the strategically important Mexican port—and began with the first large-scale amphibious assault conducted by U.S. troops. It ended with an American victory later that month (see March 29). U.S. forces then marched to Mexico City.

1862: The most important naval battle of the Civil War occurred when the northern ironclad *Monitor* and Confederate ironclad *Merrimack* clashed off Hampton Roads, Virginia. The Confederate warship was trying to end

Officers on the deck of the *Monitor* surveying damage, July 9, 1862. NH 577 courtesy of Naval History & Heritage Command.

This Day in U.S. Military History

a Union blockade of Virginia ports—and thus much of the Confederacy's access to international trade. The ships battled for three hours, but their duel essentially ended in a draw—thus ensuring that the Union blockade remained in place. The larger significance of the battle was that it received worldwide attention; Great Britain and France soon stopped building wooden-hulled ships, and others followed suit. The Battle of Hampton Roads ushered in a new era of naval warfare.

1863: Ulysses S. Grant was appointed commander-in-chief of Union forces.

1945: In Operation Meeting House, the United States dropped 2,000 tons of firebombs on Tokyo. Nearly 16 square miles in and around the Japanese capital were destroyed, taking the lives of between 80,000 and 130,000 Japanese civilians. The attack was regarded as the worst single firestorm in recorded history and the single deadliest air raid of World War II, some historians claim, greater than Dresden (see February 13), Hamburg (see July 24), or even the atomic bombings of Hiroshima (see August 6) and Nagasaki (see August 9).

1976: The first female cadets were accepted to West Point, the U.S. military academy in upstate New York.

☆ QUOTE OF THE DAY

"Now comes the reign of iron and cased sloops are to take the place of wooden ships."

Union captain John A. Dahlgren

March 10

1848: The Treaty of Guadalupe Hidalgo, signed on February 2, was ratified by the U.S. Senate, bringing the Mexican-American War to an end.

1948: Jets were assigned to operational duty on board an aircraft carrier for the first time. The carrier was the *Boxer.*

1968: In the Battle of Lima Site 85 on the Laotian mountain Phou Pha Thi, North Vietnamese forces overwhelmed the U.S. Air Force facility helmed by airmen of the 1st Combat Evaluation Group and its Laotian and Thai defenders. Thirteen airmen died.

★ QUOTE OF THE DAY

"There shall be firm and universal peace between the United States of America and the Mexican Republic, and between their respective countries, territories, cities, towns, and people, without exception of places or persons."

Article I, Treaty of Guadalupe Hidalgo

March 11

1853: Marines were deployed to Nicaragua to protect American lives and business interests. One of those business interests was a possible canal that could link the Atlantic and Pacific Oceans, which would save merchant vessels time and money.

1862: Abraham Lincoln demoted his top general. Frustrated by what he considered too much cautiousness about taking the battle to the enemy, the president removed General George McClellan as general-in-chief. McClellan would remain commander of the Army of the Potomac, but later would be removed from that post as well after failing again to decisively engage the Robert E. Lee's Confederate Army (see November 5). Lincoln also appointed General Henry Halleck as commander of U.S. forces in the western United States and General John C. Fremont in command of troops in the Appalachia region.

1916: The first "super-dreadnought" was commissioned. The *Nevada* was the lead ship of the two Nevada-class battleships; her sister ship was *Oklahoma*. It featured triple-gun turrets, was powered by oil instead of coal and had geared steam turbines for greater range. It was also coated in armor.

The *Nevada* saw action in World War I, and when Pearl Harbor was attacked on December 7, 1941, managed to steam away from battleship row despite being hit by one torpedo and at least six bombs. It was repaired and later supported the Allied invasion of Nazi-controlled France on D-Day and the 1945 invasions of Iwo Jima (see February 19) and Okinawa (see April 1).

1942: General Douglas MacArthur left Corregidor under orders from President Franklin D. Roosevelt, as Japanese forces closed in. Left behind on the Bataan Peninsula were some 90,000 American and Filipino troops who would soon be overrun by Japanese invaders. The infamous Bataan Death March followed (see April 9). As for MacArthur, he vowed to return—a promise he kept (see October 20).

1958: A B-47 bomber accidentally dropped a nuclear weapon over Mars Bluff, South Carolina. A conventional explosive detonated, leaving a crater 75 feet wide and 35 feet deep.

1967: Operation Junction City involved more than 25,000 U.S. troops and 575 aircraft sorties. It was an effort to force North Vietnamese and Viet Cong forces away from populated areas and into the open, where superior American firepower could be used against them. The operation included a massive airmobile assault, involving 240 troop-carrying helicopters. The United States claimed to have inflicted more than 2,700 casualties on the enemy by March 17.

2012: An Army staff sergeant murdered sixteen civilians and wounded six others in Panjwayi, Kandahar, Afghanistan. Nine victims were children; 11 of the dead were from the same family. Robert Bales was court martialed and sentenced to life in prison without parole.

★ QUOTE OF THE DAY

"I shall return."

General Douglas MacArthur, March 20, 1942

March 12

1942: With the U.S. now in a two-front war, President Roosevelt named Admiral Ernest J. King to serve as the Chief of Naval Operations. King kept a prior title as well: Commander-in-Chief, United States Fleet, to which he had been appointed on December 30, 1941.

1965: The U.S. Navy's Operation Market Time began. It was an effort to interrupt communist supply lines along river and coastal routes. The strategy led to the Navy's request for Coast Guard vessels and crews to participate in patrols during the Vietnam War.

1975: The seventh and final draft lottery was held. Had the draft still been in effect, men born in 1956 would have been called to report for induction the following year.

2003: The Air Force first tested its Massive Ordnance Air Blast (MOAB), a 9,450 kg munition—the biggest conventional bomb in its arsenal.

★ QUOTE OF THE DAY

"Don't tell them anything. When it's over, tell them who won."

> Ernest J. King, when asked about forming a
> U.S. Navy public relations strategy

March 13

1852: For the first time "Uncle Sam" was depicted in print, appearing in a cartoon by artist Frank Bellew in the *New York Lantern* periodical. The origins of Uncle Sam are lost in history, but he's mentioned in a 1775 verse of "Yankee Doodle Dandy." His most famous incarnation is as an army recruiter in a 1917 poster by J.M. Flagg.

1895: A contract for the first submarine was awarded to the John P. Holland Torpedo Boat Co. After some initial difficulties, the first ship was produced, and christened *Holland*. The ship wasn't certified for the open ocean but became a useful prototype for the development of more advanced subs. The *Holland* had a top speed of about 7 knots on the surface (about 8 m.p.h.) and about 5.5 knots (about 6.3 m.p.h) submerged. The crew consisted of one officer and five enlisted men.

★ QUOTE OF THE DAY

"Old Uncle Sam come there to change
Some pancakes and some onions,
For 'lasses cakes, to carry home
To give his wife and young ones."

> "Yankee Doodle Dandy" lyrics, 1775

March 14

1812: The first war bonds were issued. With the possibility of war with Great Britain growing, President James Madison asked Congress to help raise revenue to pay for the nation's defense. Lawmakers responded with the first bond, and authorized six more during the war itself.

1862: Union forces conquered New Bern, a strategic port and rail hub in North Carolina. The North pitted 13 infantry regiments and 14 gunboats against the Confederacy's fewer numbers. Brigadier General Ambrose Burnside was the victorious Union commander.

2003: The B-1B bomber was used in combat for the first time. The long-range bomber struck targets in Iraq's southern no-fly zone.

★ QUOTE OF THE DAY

"To cherish peace and friendly intercourse with all nations having correspondent dispositions; to maintain sincere neutrality toward belligerent nations; to prefer in all cases amicable discussion and reasonable accommodation of differences to a decision of them by an appeal to arms . . ."

James Madison, citing goals in his first inaugural
address of March 4, 1809

March 15

1916: U.S. troops began a pursuit of Pancho Villa and his forces in Mexico. Led by General John J. Pershing, the troops sought to capture Villa, who was accused, along with his men, of killing 18 people on U.S. soil in Columbus, New Mexico, on March 9. Pershing's men failed to bring Villa to account. Villa was assassinated seven years later.

1919: The American Legion was founded in Paris, France, by 1,000 WWI veterans of the American Expeditionary Forces. Their objectives were to discuss veterans transitioning to civilian life and the overall rights of American veterans. Among the founding members were Wild Bill Donovan and Alvin C. York.

1947: Ensign John W. Lee became the first African-American officer commissioned in the regular Navy. He was assigned to *Kearsage*.

2003: The United States revealed that a long-range B-1B bomber was used for the first time against Iraqi targets in the no-fly zone in southern Iraq.

★ QUOTE OF THE DAY

"These are the times which distinguish the real friend of his country from the town-meeting brawler and the sunshine patriot. While these are covering their conduct with the thinnest disguises and multiplying excuses to keep them at home, the former steps forth and proclaims his readiness to march."

Andrew Jackson, born this day in 1767, speaking on
the loss of Detroit on August 16, 1812

March 16

1802: The United States Military Academy was founded at West Point, New York.

1955: Dwight Eisenhower upheld the use of nuclear weapons. At a news conference, the president was asked whether the United States would use "tactical small atomic weapons" if necessary in wartime. Eisenhower, the former five-star Army general, said yes. "In any combat where these

West Point graduation events, June 6, 1914, showing the 7th Regiment N.G.N.Y.
Library of Congress.

This Day in U.S. Military History

things can be used on strictly military targets and for strictly military purposes, I see no reason why they shouldn't be used just exactly as you would use a bullet or anything else. I believe the great question about these things comes when you begin to get into those areas where you cannot make sure that you are operating merely against military targets. But with that one qualification, I would say, yes, of course they would be used."

1968: In Vietnam, Army Lt. William Calley led troops on a massacre of innocent Vietnamese civilians. As many as 500 villagers—mostly women, children, infants, and the elderly—had been systematically killed. Calley would be convicted by court-martial for the premeditated murder of 22 of them. He was sentenced to a life of hard labor at Fort Leavenworth, Kansas, but was released after three-and-a-half years.

1973: Ten days before the ninth anniversary of his capture in Vietnam, American P.O.W. Floyd James Thompson was released as part of Operation Homecoming.

★ QUOTE OF THE DAY

"I was able to withstand that long agony because I never lost my determination to live—no matter how painful that became—because I love my country and never lost faith in her."

Floyd James Thompson, at his 1982 retirement ceremony

March 17

1776: The Siege of Boston ended as the British evacuated in 120 ships—a victory for the American Revolutionary forces.

1918: The 5th Marine Regiment became the first Marine unit to move into front-line trenches during World War I.

1960: Dwight Eisenhower approved a CIA plan to form an anti-Cuban Army. Angry at Cuba's embrace of Soviet communism, the president okayed the plan, which called for Cuban exiles to attack Cuba and attempt to overthrow Castro. President John F. Kennedy inherited the plan, which went down in history as the Bay of Pigs (see April 17).

★ QUOTE OF THE DAY

"Every vessel which they [the British] did not carry off, they rendered unfit for use."

Timothy Newell, Select Man of Boston, in his journal

March 18

1969: President Richard Nixon ordered the bombing of Cambodia. The president believed the nation, neighboring Vietnam, was being used as a staging area for attacks on U.S. troops. The administration was able to keep the bombings secret for two months. They continued through April 1970.

2002: General Tommy Franks declared that Operation Anaconda had concluded. It was the first large-scale battle in the U.S. war in Afghanistan since the Battle of Tora Bora (see December 6). It involved U.S. military, CIA paramilitary, Afghan military and North Atlantic Treaty Organization (NATO) and non-NATO forces. At the end of the operation, begun March 2, coalition troops had pushed most of al Qaeda and Taliban forces from the Shah-i-Kot Valley. American casualties were estimated at eight killed and 72 wounded. But key al Qaeda leaders, likely including Osama bin Laden, escaped.

★ QUOTE OF THE DAY

"Early on, the situation changed pretty quickly. But in the main, the bad guys have gotten whipped badly."

U.S. military spokesman, on Operation Anaconda, 2002

March 19

1916: Eight Curtiss "Jenny" planes of the First Aero Squadron took off from Columbus, New Mexico, in the first combat air mission in U.S. history. The First Aero Squadron, formed on March 5, 1913, was on a support mission for the U.S. troops who invaded Mexico to capture Mexican revolutionary Pancho Villa.

1945: Off the coast of Japan, a Japanese kamikaze attack hit the aircraft carrier *Franklin*, killing 724 crew. Badly damaged, the ship was nonetheless able to return to the United States under her own power.

2003: A U.S.-led coalition invaded Iraq. President George W. Bush said the goal of Operation Iraqi Freedom was to "disarm Iraq, to free its people and to defend the world from grave danger." The president reported that Iraq possessed weapons of mass destruction, but none were found. In 2008, Bush announced that U.S. forces would leave Iraq by the end of 2011. During those 105 months of "official" war and various operations since, 4,574 Americans were killed (as of August 25, 2019) and more than 32,000 wounded. Direct spending on the Iraq war has been estimated at $757 billion, a figure that does not include interest on money borrowed to finance it, or long-term health care costs for veterans.

2011: Barack Obama ordered air strikes on Libya, as part of a U.N. Security Council decision to enforce a no-fly zone. The president told Congress that attacks were undertaken with French, British, and other allies, would be limited in scope and duration, and that preventing a humanitarian disaster in Libya was in the best interest of U.S. national security.

★ QUOTE OF THE DAY

"It must be apparent to anyone that a limit to the distance we could go would nullify any effort to capture any of this outlaw band, as they would merely step across the line, put their thumbs to their noses and laugh at us."

> General John J. Pershing, complaining about the limitations
> governing his hunt for Pancho Villa

March 20

1922: The 11,500-ton *Langley* was commissioned into the U.S. Navy as America's first aircraft carrier. The carrier was converted from a collier. Its flight deck was 533 feet long and 64 feet wide with an open-sided hanger deck, inspiring the nickname "the Old Covered Wagon."

1951: The battleship *Missouri* fired 246 tons of 16-inch shells and 2,000 rounds of 5-inch ammunition on Wonsan, North Korea, in the heaviest such attack of the Korean War.

1965: President Johnson ordered the Alabama National Guard to protect civil rights activists on their march from Selma to Montgomery on March 21 to March 24.

★ QUOTE OF THE DAY

"Leadership is the thing that wins battles. I have it, but I'll be damned if I can define it."

General George S. Patton

March 21

1865: The Battle of Bentonville, North Carolina ended, marking the last Confederate attempt to stop Union General William T. Sherman.

1943: Cornelia Fort, a pilot with the Women's Auxiliary Ferry Squadron (WAFS, later WASP), crashed as a result of a midair collision with another ferry pilot at Mulberry Canyon, Texas, becoming the first female pilot to die on active duty. She was also one of the first witnesses to the Japanese attack on Pearl Harbor as she was in the air instructing a student when the attacking planes approached.

★ QUOTE OF THE DAY

"I have yet to have a feeling which approaches in satisfaction that of having signed, sealed and delivered an airplane for the United States Army."

Cornelia Fort, from a posthumously published article in *Woman's Home Companion*

March 22

Tuskegee Airmen, Ramitelli, Italy, March 1945. Photographed by Toni Frissell. Toni Frisell Collection, Library of Congress.

1820: U.S. Navy officer Stephen Decatur, hero of the Barbary Wars, was mortally wounded in a duel with disgraced Navy commodore James Barron at Bladensburg, Maryland. Although once friends, Decatur had sat on the court-martial (concerning the 1807 *Chesapeake–Leopard* Affair) that suspended Barron from the Navy for five years in 1808 and later opposed his reinstatement, leading to the fatal quarrel between the two men.

1941: The 99th Pursuit Squadron, also known as the Tuskegee Airmen— the first all-black unit of the US Army Air Corps—was activated. The Tuskegee Airmen is the popular name of a group of African-American military pilots (fighter and bomber) who fought in World War II. Despite their heroism and service to country, the Tuskegee Airmen were subjected to racial discrimination, both within and outside the army.

★ QUOTE OF THE DAY

"We would go through any ordeal that came our way, be it in garrison existence or combat, to prove our worth,"

Benjamin O. Davis Jr, commander of the Tuskegee Airmen

March 23

1965: The first American two-person space flight began, with the liftoff of Gemini 3. Astronauts Virgil I. Grissom and John W. Young were aboard. Gemini 3 completed 3 orbits of the earth in 4 hours, 53 minutes.

1983: Ronald Reagan introduced his Strategic Defense Initiative—designed to protect the United States from Soviet ballistic missiles. SDI—also known as "Star Wars"—was a shift from the prior, U.S. offensive-oriented strategy of mutual assured destruction with Moscow. Mutual Assured Destruction (MAD) was a Cold War theory that neither the United States or the Soviet Union would attack the other because both knew they would be destroyed in return.

★ QUOTE OF THE DAY

"Give me liberty or give me death!"

Patrick Henry, March 23, 1775, pleading to the Commonwealth of Virginia to form a military force to combat British forces

March 24

1920: The first Coast Guard air station was established at Morehead City, North Carolina. It would close a year later, however, due to a lack of funding.

1945: The 9th Army began to cross the Rhine into Nazi Germany. as British and Canadians forces advanced further north.

1999: The U.S. and NATO allies began a bombing campaign against Serbia. The attacks, President Bill Clinton said, were meant to halt "ethnic cleansing"—genocide—the worst in Europe since World War II—being perpetrated by Serb forces against ethnic Albanians in Kosovo and Albania.

★ QUOTE OF THE DAY

"Aggression unopposed becomes a dangerous disease."

Jimmy Carter

This Day in U.S. Military History

March 25

1745: John Barry, who, with John Paul Jones, is considered the "father of the U.S. Navy," was born in Tacumshane, Ireland. He received his first commission in the Continental Navy on March 14, 1776.

1994: The last U.S. troops withdrew from Somalia, effectively ending the United Nations Operation in that war-torn African country. The operation had begun in 1993 and included the Battle of Mogadishu (see October 3)

★ QUOTE OF THE DAY

"I suggest you get out of here while you can."

Lieutenant David Wolcott, Somalia, to reporters on March 25, 1994

March 26

1945: Iwo Jima was declared secure, after a fierce five-week battle that saw some of the bloodiest fighting in World War II. Some 7,000 Marines were killed, along with, it is estimated, all but 200 of the 21,000 Japanese troops who were deployed on the island. Operation Detachment, as the U.S. operation had been called, gave the United States control of three airfields, which would be used for attacks on the Japanese main islands.

1964: Lyndon Johnson signed a "Predelegation of Authority" document, authorizing the use of nuclear weapons if the president could not be reached during a nuclear attack on the United States.

1964: On this day, the Viet Cong captured U.S. Army captain Floyd James Thomspon after the observation plane he was in was shot down. He was held as a prisoner of war for nine years, attaining release on March 16, 1973. He was the longest-held prisoner of war (known) in American history.

★ QUOTE OF THE DAY

"Among the Americans serving on Iwo island, uncommon valor was a common virtue."

Fleet Admiral Chester Nimitz, describing the U.S. invasion and seizure of Iwo Jima

March 27

1794: In the Naval Act of 1794, Congress authorized the construction of the first ships of the United States Navy: the frigates *Constitution*, *Chesapeake*, *Constellation*, *President*, *United States*, and *Congress*.

1813: U.S. troops captured a key British garrison near the mouth of the Niagara River, during the War of 1812. British forces withdraw from Lake Erie, permitting Captain Oliver Hazard Perry to surreptitiously evacuate five vessels from a nearby shipyard.

1814: Leading a confederacy of American, Cherokees, and friendly Lower Creeks, Major General Andrew Jackson defeated the Red Sticks (Creeks) at the Battle of Horseshoe Bend in central Alabama. About 800 of the 1,000 Red Stick warriors died in what became a slaughter, and the battle brought to a close the Creek War. Injured in the battle was Sam Houston, later governor of Tennessee as well as president of the Republic of Texas.

1945: Operation Starvation began—the aerial mining of Japan's ports and waterways.

★ QUOTE OF THE DAY

"The sun was going down, and it set on the ruin of the Creek nation."

Sam Houston, on the Battle of Horseshoe Bend

March 28

1846: U.S. troops commanded by General Zachary Taylor crossed the Rio Grande into Mexican territory during the Mexican-American War.

1862: Battle of Glorieta Pass: Union forces stopped a Confederate invasion of New Mexico territory when they pushed the rebels back at Glorieta Pass. By June, U.S. troops had full control of the region and would for the rest of the war.

1962: The Air Force announced research into the use of lasers to intercept missiles and satellites.

★ QUOTE OF THE DAY

"I do not think there was ever a more wicked war than that waged by the United States on Mexico. I thought so at the time, when I was a

This Day in U.S. Military History

youngster, only I had not moral courage enough to resign. I had taken an oath to serve eight years, unless sooner discharged, and I considered my supreme duty was to my flag. I had a horror of the Mexican War, and I have always believed that it was on our part most unjust. The wickedness was not in the way our soldiers conducted it, but in the conduct of our government in declaring war."

Ulysses S. Grant, 1879, to journalist John Russell Young

March 29

1847: Some 12,000 U.S. troops led by General Winfield Scott occupied the city of Vera Cruz, a strategic target during the Mexican-American War. American forces would continue their offensive to Mexico City itself.

1865: The final campaign of the Civil War began, when Union troops led by General Ulysses S. Grant moved against Confederate forces around Petersburg, Virginia.

1916: During the Punitive Expedition against Pancho Villa, the 7th Cavalry under Colonel George A. Dodd surprised Villista troops in Guerrero, Mexico, after six o'clock in the morning and routed them—the survivors escaped to the hills. (An injured Villa had already left the area.) It was one of the only victories against Villa that the United States enjoyed.

1945: General George S. Patton's Third Army captured Frankfurt, as World War II in Europe wound down.

1973: The last U.S. combat troops left South Vietnam, as North Vietnam freed the last of 591 Americans it said it held as prisoners of war. The moves came two months after the signing of the Vietnam peace agreement (see January 27). Thirteen prisons and prison camps were used to house the American prisoners, the most famous of which was Hanoi's Hoa Lo prison (nicknamed the "Hanoi Hilton").

☆ QUOTE OF THE DAY

"In order to reach this point [Guerrero] the command marched 17 hours out of 24 covering 55 miles and then kept up the fight for five hours."

George A. Dodd, report to General John J.
Pershing, March 29, 1916

March 30

1942: The Coast Guard was put under the jurisdiction of the Navy, similar to the administration of the Marine Corps.

1942: The Joint Chiefs divided the Pacific into two command zones. Admiral Chester Nimitz was appointed Commander in Chief of the Pacific Ocean zone and General Douglas MacArthur Commander in Chief of the Southwest Pacific.

1951: The heaviest air attack of the Korean War was staged by 38 B-29's on twin bridges over the Yalu River. They dropped some 280 tons of bombs. F-80 and F-86 fighter escorts destroyed three enemy MiG-15s and damaged six.

★ QUOTE OF THE DAY

"The days of the frontal attack are over. Modern infantry weapons are too deadly, and frontal assault is only for mediocre commanders. Good commanders do not turn in heavy losses."

Douglas MacArthur, *Reminiscences* (1964)

March 31

1801: Escorted by Marine Commandant William W. Burrows, President Thomas Jefferson selected a site for the Marine Barracks in the nation's capital. They chose a square in the southeast quadrant of the city, near the Navy Yard and within easy marching distance of the Capitol.

1854: In Tokyo, Commodore Matthew Perry, representing the U.S. government, signed the Treaty of Kanagawa with the Japanese government, opening ports to American trade and permitting the establishment of a U.S. consulate in Japan.

1899: Malolos, capital of the First Philippine Republic, was captured. The Capture of Malolos, alternately known as the Battle of Malolos, occurred during the Philippine-American War. U.S. forces were led by General Douglas MacArthur.

1968: In a speech to the nation, President Lyndon Johnson announced a partial halt of bombing missions over North Vietnam and proposed peace talks. He also said he would not run for re-election.

1992: The last active American battleship—*Missouri* (BB-63)—was decommissioned. "Mighty Mo" (or "Big Mo") saw action in the Pacific throughout World War II and was the site of the surrender of Japan in 1945 (see September 2). Mighty Mo also fought in the Korean War from 1950 to 1953.

★ QUOTE OF THE DAY

"There is no need to delay the talks that could bring an end to this long and this bloody war."

Lyndon Johnson

1917 U.S. Navy recruiting poster. Library of Congress.

April

April 1

1865: Union forces routed Confederate troops at Five Forks, Virginia, sealing the immediate fate of General Robert E. Lee's armies. Lee would surrender to Union general Ulysses S. Grant eight days later, ending the Civil War (see April 9).

1884: Florence Blanchfield was born in Shepherdstown, West Virginia. This dedicated nurse became the first woman to become a fully ranked officer in the U.S. Army. Superintendent of the Army Nurse Corps (1943 to 1947) and recipient of the Distinguished Service Medal, Blanchfield died May 12, 1971, at Washington, DC, and is buried at Arlington National Cemetery.

1893: The rank of Chief Petty Officer was established by the Navy.

1945: The invasion of Okinawa began. It was Easter Sunday, and more than 180,000 Army and Marine Corps troops were involved in the invasion's initial phase. The invasion was part of Operation Iceberg, a larger plan to invade and occupy the Ryukyu Islands, a chain of Japanese islands that stretch southwest from Kyushu to Taiwan. Okinawa produced some of the bloodiest fighting of the Pacific war, and when it was over in late June (see June 22), the United States had suffered more than 49,000 casualties, with an estimated 12,520 killed. Japanese losses were even greater—about 110,000 Japanese soldiers were also killed (or took their lives), while an estimated 40,000 to 150,000 Okinawa citizens were also killed.

1945: The 1st and 9th armies linked up, cutting off the German forces in the Ruhr—trapping some 325,000 Nazi troops. Along with British troops to the North and Soviet troops in the East, Nazi Germany's collapse accelerated; it would surrender May 8.

1952: Air Force Colonel Francis S. Gabreski became the eighth ace of the Korean War. "Gabby" was also an ace during World War II, when—flying single-engine P-47 Thunderbolt fighters—he downed 28 Messerschmitts and Focke-Wulfs and destroyed three more German aircraft on the ground. In Korea, flying an F-86 Sabre jet, he shot down six Soviet-built MiG-15 fighters and shared credit for the downing of another.

1954: The U.S. Air Force Academy was founded in Colorado Springs, Colorado.

⭐ QUOTE OF THE DAY

"Not everyone is cut out for flying fighter aircrafts."

Colonel Jeannie Leavitt, the USAF's first female fighter pilot

April 2

1781: Captain John Barry, at the helm of the *Alliance*, captured the British privateer brigs *Mars* and *Minerva*.

1865: The Civil War entered its final week, with Union forces putting Confederate troops on one final, desperate retreat in Virginia. Union forces, led by General Ulysses S. Grant, pushed Robert E. Lee's Army beyond Petersburg, Virginia. Grant's army had grown to more than 120,000, overwhelming Lee's increasingly ragged and under-equipped army.

1916: Lt. R.C. Saufley set an altitude record for a Navy aircraft, flying 16,072 feet in a Curtiss plane at Pensacola, Florida. He beat his own record that had been set just four days earlier.

1917: Woodrow Wilson asked Congress to declare war on Germany. Four days later, Congress did so and the United States formally entered World War I. Wilson's decision to go to war was prompted by Germany's anti-American aggression, including attacks on neutral shipping in the Atlantic and its efforts to help Mexico regain Texas, New Mexico, and Arizona if it fought against America. Wilson learned of this through the Zimmermann Telegram (see March 1) and the resulting public anger against Germany was such that a declaration of war became inevitable. During "the war to end all wars," 116,516 Americans were killed and 204,002 others were wounded.

1951: The first Navy use of a jet fighter as a bomber occurred when two F9F-2B Panthers were catapulted from *Princeton* for an attack on a railroad bridge near Songjin, North Korea. Each carried four 250- and two 100-pound general-purpose bombs.

2003: U.S. forces crossed Iraq's Tigris River as they neared Baghdad. Marines took Numaniya, a city of 80,000.

★ QUOTE OF THE DAY

"The world must be made safe for democracy."

Woodrow Wilson, addressing both houses
of Congress, April 2, 1917

April 3

1797: For the Navy's fleet, Captain Thomas Truxtun issued the first known American signal book using a numerical system entitled *Instructions, Signals, and Explanations*.

1865: Union troops captured the Confederate capital of Richmond. President Abraham Lincoln would visit the vanquished city the next day.

1942: Chester Nimitz was named Commander-in-Chief, Pacific Ocean Areas, a joint command. The admiral also kept his other title, Commander-in-Chief, Pacific Fleet.

1942: U.S. and Allied forces retreated in Bataan, the peninsula guarding Manila Bay of the Philippine Islands. Japanese forces had already forced General Douglas MacArthur's troops from the Philippine capital, and MacArthur himself fled for Australia on President Franklin D. Roosevelt's orders. U.S. troops, commanded by his replacement, Admiral Edward King, would surrender within days (see April 9).

1951: The Eighth Army crossed the 38th parallel in Korea.

★ QUOTE OF THE DAY

"We took Richmond at 8:15 this morning. I captured many guns. The enemy left in great haste. The city is on fire in two places. Am making every effort to put it out. The people received us with enthusiastic expressions of joy."

General Godfrey Weitzel, telegram to General Ulysses S. Grant

April 4

1776: The first American capture of a British armed vessel occurred when the Continental Navy frigate *Columbus* seized the schooner HMS *Hawk.*

1790: Congress established the Revenue Cutter Service, an armed customs enforcement branch of the government. In 1915 it was merged with the United States Life-Saving Service to form the Coast Guard.

1945: American troops of the 4th Armored Division and 89th Division liberated Ohrdruf, a Nazi concentration camp near Gotha, Germany. U.S. troops forced locals to tour the camp and see the horrors inflicted by the Nazis upon their victims.

1949: Harry Truman signed the North Atlantic Pact; a mutual defense treaty among 12 nations. Known today as the North Atlantic Treaty Organization (NATO) 28 nations are members.

1951: Supreme Headquarters of the Allied Powers in Europe (SHAPE) was established. General Dwight D. Eisenhower was appointed commander.

★ QUOTE OF THE DAY

"The visual evidence and the verbal testimony of starvation, cruelty, and bestiality were so overpowering as to leave me a bit sick. . . . I made the visit deliberately, in order to be in a position to give first-hand evidence of these things if ever, in the future, there develops a tendency to charge these allegations merely to 'propaganda.'"

General Dwight D. Eisenhower, after touring Ohrdruf

April 5

1869: Daniel Bakeman, the last surviving soldier of the U.S. Revolutionary War, died at 109 years of age.

1944: U.S. bombers attacked oil and rail facilities in Romania, deemed critical to the German war effort.

2003: U.S. troops entered Baghdad for the first time, less than three weeks after the U.S.-led invasion of Iraq began.

⭐ **QUOTE OF THE DAY**

"Good generalship is a realization that ... you've got to try and figure out how to accomplish your mission with a minimum loss of human life."

General H. Norman Schwarzkopf,
interview on CNN

April 6

1862: The Battle of Shiloh took place on April 6 and 7, 1865. U.S. troops led by General Ulysses S. Grant were attacked at Pittsburgh Landing, Tennessee, by Confederate forces. After two days of fierce fighting, Confederate troops retreated, giving federal troops greater control of the critical Tennessee Valley.

1909: Navy Cmdr. Robert E. Peary, Matthew A. Henson and four Inuit guides became the first humans to reach the North Pole. "I have this day hoisted the national ensign of the United States of America at this place, which my observations indicate to be the North Polar axis of the earth, and have formally taken possession of the entire region, and adjacent, for and in the name of the President of the United States of America," Peary declared. The claim, disputed for decades by skeptics, was later upheld by the National Geographic Society.

1917: At the request of Woodrow Wilson, Congress voted to declare war on Germany. The House of Representatives vote was 373-50; the Senate vote was 82-6.

1917: President Wilson signed an executive order making the Coast Guard part of the Navy. The Coast Guard at that time consisted of 15 cruising cutters, 200 commissioned officers, and 5000 warrant officers and enlisted men. Coast Guard aviators were assigned to naval air stations stateside and abroad.

1945: Desperate Japanese fighters conducted heavy kamikaze strikes against American ships off Okinawa. The *Bush, Colhoun, Emmons,* and LST 447 were hit and unable to be salvaged.

☆ QUOTE OF THE DAY

"I saw an open field... so covered with dead that it would have been possible to walk across... in any direction, stepping on dead bodies without a foot touching the ground."

Ulysses S. Grant, describing
the Battle of Shiloh.

April 7

1818: In the First Seminole War, General Andrew Jackson captured the Spanish fort of San Marcos, Florida, and from there made attacks against villages of Seminoles and fugitive slaves.

1862: The Battle of Shiloh ended in a Union victory. The fierce two-day battle in southwestern Tennessee produced some of the worst casualties of the Civil War. The North suffered more than 13,000 casualties, including 1,700 killed. The Confederates had 10,000 casualties, with also about 1,700 soldiers killed. Ironically, the battle took place near a church named Shiloh, which is a Hebrew word for place of peace.

1917: With the United States now in World War I, the Navy took control of all wireless radio stations. They were considered essential for the war effort.

1945: U.S. forces sank the Japanese battleship *Yamato* in the East China Sea. It took ten torpedo and five bomb hits to sink it. Almost 2,500 of the 2,700 crew were killed. A cruiser and four destroyers were also sunk. A total of ten planes were lost.

1954: Dwight D. Eisenhower coined one of the most famous Cold War-era phrases, when he warned of the "domino theory." The president's theory speculated that if one country in a region—say Vietnam—fell to communism, that others would eventually follow—as a domino falling in a line of dominoes. The domino theory would influence presidents John F. Kennedy and Lyndon Johnson (particularly Johnson) to increase U.S. military involvement in Vietnam.

1979: The first Trident submarine, the *Ohio*, was launched at Groton, Connecticut. *Ohio* was the lead boat of her class of nuclear-powered fleet ballistic missile submarines.

2017: Two Navy ships, *Ross* and *Porter,* fired Tomahawk missiles at Syrian targets. It was retaliation for the Syrian government's use of nerve agents against its own people.

QUOTE OF THE DAY

"You have a row of dominoes set up and you knock over the first one and what will happen to the last one is the certainty that it will go over very quickly. So you have the beginning of a disintegration that will have the most profound influences."

Dwight D. Eisenhower

April 8

1832: The Black Hawk War: Brigadier General Henry Atkinson led more than 200 troops from the Jefferson Barracks (near St. Louis, Missouri) to confront the Meskwakis, who had been involved in intertribal massacres.

1864: In the Red River campaign, the Battle of Mansfield: U.S. troops attempting to take Shreveport, Louisiana, were engaged by Confederate forces—who came away with the victory.

1865: Confederate general Robert E. Lee asked to meet with Union general Ulysses S. Grant to discuss possible surrender. Lee's request came after his retreat was cut off by Union forces near Appomattox Court House, Virginia.

1925: The first night landing on board a U.S. Navy carrier was made when Lt. John D. Price landed his VF-1 aircraft on *Langley,* off San Diego.

1952: Citing national security, Harry Truman ordered the U.S. Army to take control of the steel industry. Contract talks between steel workers and owners failed, and with the Korean War raging, the president determined that steel production was necessary for the war effort. A federal court ruled that Truman's actions were unconstitutional, a decision upheld by the Supreme Court.

1968: U.S. and South Vietnamese forces began their largest offensive to date. Operation Toan Thang (Complete Victory) was designed to destroy the Viet Cong and North Vietnamese forces operating in the Capital Military District (Saigon).

This Day in U.S. Military History

"After it is all over, as stupid a fellow as I am can see that mistakes were made. I notice, however, that my mistakes are never told me until it is too late, and you, and all my officers, know that I am always ready and anxious to have their suggestions."

Robert E. Lee, to Henry Heth

April 9

1865: The Civil War came to end, when Confederate general Robert E. Lee surrendered to Union general Ulysses S. Grant at the McLean House in Appomattox, Virginia. The Civil War remains by far the bloodiest war in U.S. history: 750,000 Americans were killed.

1942: In the largest such action since the Civil War, General Ernest King surrendered a combined American/Filipino force of around 79,000 men at Mariveles, Bataan, Philippines, to the Japanese Army, setting the stage for the Bataan Death March. The prisoners were forced to walk almost 70 miles to Camp O'Donnell in Capas in brutal heat and humidity without sufficient water or food. Many were tortured and killed along the way. Those who

The McLean House today, site of the Civil War surrender. NPS.

survived the march were transported to POW camps, where starvation and disease took more lives. Casualty data varies considerably, but it is generally believed that 5,000 to 18,000 Filipinos and 500 to 650 Americans perished. After the war, an International Military Tribunal convicted and executed the Japanese commander responsible for these war crimes.

1987: The Special Forces Branch was formally established as a basic branch of the Army. The first operating Special Forces unit had been formed in 1952 (see June 11).

1959: NASA announced the selection of America's first seven astronauts: Scott Carpenter, Gordon Cooper, John Glenn, Gus Grissom, Wally Schirra, Alan Shepard, and Donald Slayton. Grissom, Cooper, and Slayton were Air Force pilots; Shepard, Carpenter, and Schirra were Navy pilots, and Glenn was a Marine Corps pilot.

2003: Baghdad fell as American troops raised the Stars and Stripes over the Iraqi capital. The collapse of the Iraqi regime was symbolized by the toppling of a huge statue of Saddam Hussein.

☆ QUOTE OF THE DAY

"General Lee surrendered the Army of Northern Virginia this afternoon on terms proposed by myself. The accompanying additional correspondence will show the conditions fully."

General Ulysses S. Grant, on the surrender of the Confederate Army

April 10

1941: While rescuing survivors of a torpedoed ship, American destroyer *Niblack* dropped depth charges on German submarine *U-52*. It was the first action of war between the U.S. and German navies—and came months before the two countries formally declared war on each other (see December 11).

1963: *Thresher* (SSN-593), a nuclear-powered submarine, failed to surface 220 miles east of Boston, Massuchusetts. *Thresher* was the lead boat of her class of nuclear-powered attack submarines; the disaster claimed 129 lives.

1972: The United States, Soviet Union, and scores of other nations signed an agreement banning biological warfare. The Biological and Toxins

Weapons Convention banned the development, production, and stockpiling of bacteriological and toxic weapons.

☆ QUOTE OF THE DAY

"[We] see, and ages yet may see, on monuments and gravestones, singly or in masses, to thousands or tens of thousands, the significant word *Unknown*."

Walt Whitman, poet and nurse, lamenting the Civil War dead buried anonymously

April 11

1898: As anger grew over the *Maine* explosion, President William McKinley asked Congress for authority to send American troops to Cuba to aid the Cuban bid for independence.

1900: The U.S. Navy took possession of its first submarine—the *Holland*.

1904: Midway Island was garrisoned for the first time, by 20 Marines.

1945: The Third Army liberated the Buchenwald concentration camp in Germany. Among those saved by the Americans was Elie Wiesel, who would go on to win the Nobel Peace Prize in 1986.

1951: Harry Truman fired General Douglas MacArthur, for what Truman considered insubordinate comments about the Korean War. Example: Since both the Soviet Union and China backed North Korea, Truman worried that an expansion of the war could trigger World War III. MacArthur disagreed and spoke publicly about expanding the Korean conflict. He continued to do so even after being reprimanded.

2003: Brigadier General Vincent Brooks, in a press conference, announced that 200 decks of playing cards featuring the likenesses of the most-wanted members of Saddam Hussein's regime would be distributed to troops in Iraq. Saddam Hussein was the ace of spades. Cards printed from military files sold briskly on reseller websites.

☆ QUOTE OF THE DAY

"With deep regret I have concluded that the General of the Army Douglas MacArthur is unable to give his wholehearted support to the policies of the United States government and of the United Nations in matters pertaining to his official duties. . . . I have decided that I must make a change of command in the Far East."

President Harry Truman, part of his statement regarding MacArthur's dismissal

April 12

1861: The first shots of the Civil War were fired, when Confederate forces shelled Fort Sumter, South Carolina. Union forces held out for 34 hours before surrendering.

1864: The Massacre at Fort Pillow occurred when Confederate forces led by General Nathan Bedford Forrest attacked a Union garrison commanded by Major Lionel F. Booth just north of Memphis, Tennessee, killing more than 200 African-American soldiers—even though most of them had surrendered. The Confederate refusal to treat the surrendering Union forces as traditional prisoners of war infuriated the North and is considered one of the most controversial events of the Civil War.

1911: Lt. Theodore Ellyson became Naval Aviator No. 1 when he completed his training at the Glenn Curtiss Aviation Camp at North Island, San Diego, California.

1951: The largest jet battle in history was fought over Korea, when 115 F-84s and F-86s, escorting 32 B-29 Superfortresses, engaged 80 MiG-15s and destroyed 46 of them.

1966: The first B-52 bombing of North Vietnam took place.

1991: Defense Secretary Dick Cheney announced plans to close 31 major US military bases, including Fort Ord in California and Fort Dix in New Jersey.

★ QUOTE OF THE DAY

"After resistance had ceased the enemy, in gross violation of all honorable warfare, butchered in cold blood the prisoners and wounded."

General Stephen A. Harlbut, April 15, 1864, report to General J.B. McPherson on the atrocities at Fort Pillow

This Day in U.S. Military History

April 13

1777: U.S. forces were ambushed and defeated in the Battle of Bound Brook, New Jersey. The Battle of Bound Brook was a surprise attack conducted by British and Hessian forces against a Continental Army outpost. General George Washington moved quickly to recapture the site.

1861: Fort Sumter, after being subjected to 34 hours of bombardment, surrendered.

1960: Navy's navigation satellite, Transit 1B, was shot into orbit from Cape Canaveral, Florida. The satellite went into service in 1964 and was part of the first geopositional satellite navigation system, providing information to Polaris submarines.

2017: The US Air Force dropped the MOAB (GBU-43/B Massive Ordnance Air Blast) bomb on the Nangarhar Province of Afghanistan, targeting ISIS terrorists. It was the first operational use of the 21,600-pound weapon—the most powerful non-nuclear weapon among U.S. armaments.

★ QUOTE OF THE DAY

"MacArthur was too distanced from us for his going to make much impact. The only sort of thing we noticed was the food getting better after [General Matthew] Ridgway took over."

Lieutenant Jim Sheldon, 17th Infantry, commenting on
the April 11 leadership change in Korea, quoted in
The Korean War (1987), by Max Hastings

April 14

1865: President Abraham Lincoln was shot as he attended a play at Ford's Theatre in Washington, D.C. He died early the next morning. His assassin, actor John Wilkes Booth, killed Lincoln to avenge the surrender—five days before—of the Confederacy. Secretary of War Edwin Stanton, at Lincoln's deathbed, soon organized a massive federal manhunt and a $100,000 reward for the capture of the assassins.

1918: America's first aerial dogfight occurred when two American pilots from the U.S. First Aero Squadron tangled with German aircraft over Toul, France. U.S. fliers Douglas Campbell and Alan Winslow shot down two German two-seaters. Campbell went on to become the first American to qualify as a "flying ace" in World War I.

★ QUOTE OF THE DAY

"Doug went out looking for trouble."

> Eddie Rickenbacker, commenting on fellow pilot
> Douglas Campbell's first dogfight

April 15

1861: Following the Confederate shelling of Fort Sumter, South Carolina, Abraham Lincoln called for 75,000 volunteers to join the Union Army. 92,000 did, and the Civil War—the most devastating war in American history—was on. Lincoln quickly adapted to the role of commander-in-chief, assuming vast powers. Supreme Court rulings declared some of Lincoln's wartime conduct unconstitutional, but the president ignored them, saying his priority was to preserve the Union.

1918: The First Marine Aviation Force was formed at Marine Flying Field in Miami, Florida. Its commander was Capt. Alfred A. Cunningham.

1952: The first B-52 prototype test flight was made. The Boeing B-52 Stratofortress, a long-range, subsonic, jet-powered strategic bomber, remains in service to this day and is expected to serve into the 2040s.

1961: The first nuclear-powered frigate was launched at Quincy, Massachusetts—*Bainbridge.*

1969: North Korea shot down an unarmed reconnaissance plane, killing all 31 Americans on board. The Lockheed EC-121 Warning Star was an American Airborne early warning and control radar surveillance aircraft that was used by the navy and air force. President Richard Nixon did not retaliate and ordered reconnaissance flights to resume three days later.

1986: The United States bombed Libya and the government of Muammar Gaddafi in retaliation for its sponsorship of terrorism against American troops and citizens. More than 100 U.S. Air Force and Navy aircraft were involved in Operation El Dorado Canyon. Gaddafi himself escaped the attack.

This Day in U.S. Military History

1999: U.S. and NATO allies bombed TV transmitters, military installations and bridges throughout Yugoslavia. Military targets in Montenegro were struck as was the city of Subotica, near the Hungarian border.

★ QUOTE OF THE DAY

"Now he belongs to the ages."

Edwin Stanton, on Lincoln's death

April 16

1947: Congress passed the Army-Navy Nurses Act of 1947 giving Army, Navy, and Air Force Nurse Corps members commissioned rank. Also, this act made the Nurse Corps of the Army and the Navy permanent. Florence A. Blanchfield pursued this legislation.

1947: The term "cold war" was coined by Bernard Baruch, for decades an advisor to presidents on economic and foreign policy issues. It would define the relationship between Washington and Moscow for the next four decades.

1972: After a four-year lull, the United States resumed bombing of Hanoi and Haiphong in North Vietnam. It was part of the U.S. response to a North Vietnamese offensive, which had begun on March 30.

★ QUOTE OF THE DAY

"[A]fter several years of cold war, we are intensely aware that a military effort cannot be separated from political objectives."

Omar Bradley, *A Soldier's Story* (1951)

April 17

1961: Operation Zapata—better known as the Bay of Pigs—began. Planning for the attempted ouster of Cuba's Communist leader Fidel Castro began during the Eisenhower administration, but the final go-ahead was given by President John F. Kennedy. The plan was to invade Cuba with

Cubans who had fled to the United States after Castro came to power. It failed: the U.S.-trained Cuban invasion force of around 1,500 (Brigade 2506) was overwhelmed by a much larger pro-communist force (more than 200,000). Out of ammunition and options, Brigade 2506 surrendered on April 20. The White House and Central Intelligence Agency would later blame each other for the debacle.

★ QUOTE OF THE DAY

"It was a very intense thing. We were under heavy artillery fire, and it continued for 48 straight hours."

Alfredo Duran, Brigade 2506 veteran, to CNN, 2001

April 18

1847: In one of the bloodiest battles of the Mexican-American War, U.S. forces under Winfield Scott defeated the Mexicans at the mountain pass of Cerro Gordo, near Xalapa, Veracruz. More than 1,000 Mexicans were killed and another 3,000 were captured. Making fruitful reconnaissance for the United States was young captain Robert E. Lee.

Lieutenant Colonel James H. Doolittle (left) and Captain Marc A. Mitscher, Commanding Officer of USS *Hornet* (CV-8), with a 500-pound bomb and USAAF aircrew members on the *Hornet*'s flight deck, while en route to the launching point for the raid. NH 64472 courtesy of Naval History & Heritage Command.

This Day in U.S. Military History

1942: *The Stars and Stripes* resumed publication. The military newspaper was originally published by four Union soldiers in 1861, using a captured newspaper plant in Missouri. It ceased publication after the Civil War, made a brief—as in one day—return in 1918.

1942: In the daring Doolittle Raid, Tokyo was bombed for the first time. It was revenge for Japan's attack on Pearl Harbor, and gave a big boost to American morale. The raid—involving 16 B-25B Mitchell bombers—was launched without fighter escort from the aircraft carrier *Hornet* deep in the Western Pacific Ocean, each with a crew of five men, and led by Army Air Force Lt. Col. James "Jimmy" Doolittle.

1943: Taking advantage of intercepted intelligence of his movements, U.S. Army Air Force P-38s shot down a plane carrying Imperial Japanese Navy Admiral Isoroku Yamamoto, Commander in Chief of the Japanese Combined Fleet—and mastermind of the attack on Pearl Harbor attack.

1988: The largest naval operation since World War II occurred when the United States launched Operation Praying Mantis against Iranian forces in Persian Gulf. The U.S. operation was in retaliation for the Iranian mining of the gulf during the Iran-Iraq War and the subsequent damage to an American warship. It also marked the U.S. Navy's first exchange of anti-ship missiles by ships.

★ QUOTE OF THE DAY

"[General] Scott in his order assigning positions to the different corps, issued on the 17th says the pass will be in our possession by 10 o clock AM, and strange to say it was just about that time."

Francis Woodbridge, soldier at Cerro Gordo, in
an April 23, 1847, letter to his wife

April 19

1775: The Battles of Lexington and Concord occurred, recognized as the first battles of the Revolutionary War. In "Concord Hymn," Ralph Waldo Emerson described the first shot fired by the Patriots as the "shot heard round the world."

1861: Abraham Lincoln ordered a naval blockade of Confederate ports. It was a tall order for the president. The navy only had 42 ships when the Civil War began, and there were 3,550 miles of Confederate coastline to

A contemporary engraving of the Battle of Lexington. Library of Congress.

patrol. But the blockade eventually helped weaken the South by stopping the import of supplies from Europe.

1960: The Grumman A-6 Intruder made its first flight. The all-weather, carrier-based Intruder became the primary fighter for the Navy and Marine Corps and first saw action in the Vietnam War.

★ QUOTE OF THE DAY

"Stand your ground. Don't fire unless fired upon; but if they mean to have a war, let it begin here."

John Parker's order, at Lexington Green

April 20

1861: As the Civil War broke out, Colonel Robert E. Lee resigned from U.S. Army—writing a note to General Winfield Scott in front of his gathered family. Virginia had voted to secede on April 17. Lee would head its army.

1964: *Henry Clay* launched Polaris A-2 missiles—the first demonstration of a Polaris submarine's ability to launch missiles from the surface as well as from a submerged position.

This Day in U.S. Military History   **105**

1898: William McKinley signed a Congressional resolution demanding Cuban independence and sent it to Spain, who severed diplomatic ties the next day.

★ QUOTE OF THE DAY

"Leadership is the art of accomplishing more than the science of management says is possible."

General Colin Powell

April 21

1898: The Spanish-American War began: the United States made a declaration of war on April 25, but made it retroactive to April 21, when President William McKinley ordered the U.S. Navy to begin a blockade of Cuba and Spain.

1951: Marine carrier-based airplanes made their first aerial contact with enemy planes over Korea. Captain Philip C. Delong shot down two YAK fighters and 1st Lieutenant Harold D. Daigh destroyed one more and damaged another.

★ QUOTE OF THE DAY

"Whenever I have been in a difficult situation, or in the midst of such a confusion of details that the simple and right thing to do seemed hazy, I have often asked myself, 'What would Farragut do?'"

Admiral George Dewey, hero of the Spanish-American War

April 22

1778: During the American Revolution, two boats of volunteers from the sloop-of-war *Ranger*, commanded by John Paul Jones, went ashore at Whitehaven, England. They torched ships in the harbor and spiked defensive guns.

1944: The United States used helicopters in combat for the first time, when the 1st Air Commando Group, led by Lt. Col. Clinton B. Gaty, deployed Sikorsky R-4s during search and rescue operations in the China-Burma-India theater.

"It seems to be a law of nature, inflexible and inexorable, that those who will not risk cannot win."

John Paul Jones

April 23

1898: Spain declared war on the United States. U.S. president William McKinley called for 125,000 volunteers to fight. Among those who answered the call: Theodore Roosevelt, who resigned as secretary of the navy to serve.

1945: America's first automated, radar-guided missile was used in combat for the first time. The Bat missile (ASM-N-2) was deployed against Japanese targets off Borneo. The weapon sunk several Japanese coastal defense ships.

"[Dr. Leonard] Wood and I were speedily commissioned as Colonel and Lieutenant-Colonel of the First United States Volunteer Cavalry. This was the official title of the regiment, but for some reason or other the public promptly christened us the 'Rough Riders.'"

Theodore Roosevelt, from *The Rough Riders* (1899)

April 24

1778: *Ranger,* commanded by John Paul Jones, defeated and captured HMS *Drake* off the coast of Ireland.

1980: Operation Eagle Claw—an attempt to rescue American hostages in Iran—failed, when two helicopters went down in the Iranian desert with engine trouble. Another crashed into a C-130, killing eight Americans and wounding five others.

"A strange series of mishaps, almost completely unpredictable . . ."

Jimmy Carter, *White House Diary* (2010),
on Operation Eagle Claw

April 25

1862: Having broken through its defenses, David Farragut asked the city of New Orleans to surrender. Despite the fact that the Confederate military had departed, it refused.

1864: The North was defeated at the Battle of Marks' Mills near New Edinburg, Arkansas.

1898: The United States declared war against Spain, two days after Spain declared war, but made their declaration retroactive to April 21.

1945: U.S. troops advancing from the west and Soviet troops advancing from the east met at the Elbe River, near Torgau in Germany. Lt. Bill Robertson and his men met Lt. Alexander Sylvashko and his men on the bridge. Soldiers of both allied nations embraced and exchanged toasts. Germany was now cut in two.

2009: The Boeing P-8 Poseidon flew for the first time. The aircraft, based on a 737, is a submarine hunter and would replace the Lockheed P-3 Orion.

☆ QUOTE OF THE DAY

"Treat them nicely."

General Courtney Hodges, instructions to his troops for when they met the Soviets

April 26

1805: The first recorded land battle the United States fought on foreign soil occurred when U.S. forces captured the port city of Derne, Cyrenaica (now Derna, Libya), during the first Barbary War. Led by Lt. William Eaton and First Lt. Presley O'Bannon, the attacking group was made up of a small unit of Marines and around 500 mercenaries. They traveled over 500 miles of desert from Alexandria, Egypt, to reach their target.

1865: The 16th New York Volunteer Cavalry cornered Abraham Lincoln's assassin, John Wilkes Booth, and accomplice David Herold at the Richard Garrett farm in Port Royal, Virginia. Herold was captured, but Booth was shot and killed—by Sergeant Boston Corbett, who was a survivor of the Andersonville prison camp.

1944: U.S. troops seized offices at retailer Montgomery Ward, after it refused to obey a federal order to recognize a union. Government control would end two weeks later.

★ QUOTE OF THE DAY

"I was under the impression at the time that he [Booth] had started to the door to fight his way through, and I thought he would do harm to my men if I did not."

Sergeant Boston Corbett, explaining why he violated orders to take Booth alive

April 27

1805: "...to the shores of Tripoli," joined Marine Corps lore when leathernecks raised the U.S. flag for the first time over a conquered fortress of the Old World at Derna, a stronghold of the Tripolitan pirates. The Battle of Derna was the Marines' first battle on foreign soil.

1813: American troops captured York (present day Toronto) during the War of 1812. York was the capital of the province of Upper Canada (present-day Ontario) at the time. The victory came at a cost of heavy casualties, and Brigadier General Zebulon M. Pike, acclaimed explorer of the West and namesake of Pike's Peak, was killed in an explosion. British troops would retaliate the next year with their attack on Washington, D.C. (see August 24).

1822: Ulysses S. Grant was born at Point Pleasant, Ohio. The West Point graduate saw action in the Mexican War under General Zachary Taylor and was later appointed by President Lincoln to command the Union army during the Civil War. Grant accepted the surrender of General Robert E. Lee's Army of Northern Virginia on April 9, 1865, ending the Civil War. The war hero would serve two terms as U.S. president, from 1869-1877.

★ QUOTE OF THE DAY

"Let us have peace."

Ulysses S. Grant, motto

April 28

1919: The first jump in free fall from an airplane with a backpack parachute occurred when Leslie Irvin jumped from a plane flown at 1,500 feet by James "Floyd" Smith. The parachute, designed by Irvin, Smith, and Major E. L. Hoffman, incorporated elements from other parachute designs, but in a novel way. The parachute, in a soft backpack, included a rip cord, allowing the jumper to manually activate the chute away from the aircraft he or she jumped from.

1965: In Operation Power Pack, President Lyndon Johnson sent 22,000 troops to the Dominican Republic, to prevent what he called a "communist dictatorship" in the Caribbean nation that was roiled by civil war.

1975: Gerald Ford ordered an American evacuation of Saigon, as troops from communist North Vietnam neared the South Vietnamese capital. The U.S. presence in Vietnam was reduced to its embassy—which would soon be evacuated.

1993: Secretary of Defense Les Aspin announced the women would be allowed to serve in combat roles—as fighter pilots, but also on most naval combat ships.

☆ QUOTE OF THE DAY

"This truly makes an assignment based on an officer's pilot abilities, flying skills, maturity, and judgment with no regard to gender."

Captain Eileen Isola, responding to Aspin's announcement

April 29

1862: Union troops seized New Orleans, completing a four-day operation. Its capture was a major blow to the Confederacy, which had planned for a Union attack not from the Gulf of Mexico, but from down the Mississippi River.

1945: U.S. troops from the 42nd and 45th infantry divisions liberated Dachau concentration camp, freeing 33,000 prisoners. Established in 1933, Dachau was the first concentration camp opened in Germany and was just ten miles north of Munich. An estimated 32,000 people lost their lives there.

2011: President Barack Obama authorized Operation Neptune Spear to kill or capture terrorist Osama bin Laden.

⭐ QUOTE OF THE DAY

"Inmates of the camp hugged and embraced the American troops, kissed the ground before them and carried them shoulder high around the place."

Marguerite Higgins, American war correspondent at Dachau

April 30

1798: Congress established the Department of the Navy as a separate cabinet department. Benjamin Stoddert was named as the first Secretary of the Navy.

1863: The Battle of Chancellorsville began. The week-long engagement, one of the most important battles of the Civil War, was fought in Spotsylvania County, Virginia, near the village of Chancellorsville. Even though Union Army Maj. Gen. Joseph Hooker's Army of the Potomac was twice the size of General Robert E. Lee's Army of Northern Virginia, Lee won because of his bold decision to divide his army. But Lee lost many men, including Lt. Gen. Thomas J. "Stonewall" Jackson, leaving some historians to conclude that Lee's victory was largely a Pyrrhic one.

1970: President Richard Nixon announced that U.S. troops were invading Cambodia—a nation being used by North Vietnam as a stage from which to wage war on South Vietnam. Nixon's public announcement came after a year of Cambodian bombing that the administration had attempted to keep quiet. The invasion sparked nationwide protests.

⭐ QUOTE OF THE DAY

"[T]his is the decision I have made. In cooperation with the armed forces of South Vietnam, attacks are being launched this week to clean out major enemy sanctuaries on the Cambodian-Vietnam border. A major responsibility for the ground operation is being assumed by South Vietnamese forces."

Richard Nixon, from his address to the nation
on military action in Cambodia

1898 lithograph depicting Rear Admiral George Dewey on the *Olympia* at the Battle of Manila Bay. Library of Congress.

May

May 1

1896: Mark W. Clark was born at Madison Barracks, Sackets Harbor, New York. A veteran of World War I, Clark became the youngest four-star general in 1945. During World War II, he liberated Rome and accepted the surrender of German troops in Italy on May 2, 1945. In the Korean War, he took over United Nations Command in 1952 and oversaw the armistice.

1898: In Manila Bay, Philippines, in the first battle of the Spanish-American War, U.S. forces destroyed the Spanish Pacific fleet. The Spanish fleet consisted of ten out-of-date warships and was no match for the modern U.S. Asiatic Squadron. The battle is known for the famous comment made by Commodore George Dewey, who told the captain of his flagship, the *Olympia*, "You may fire when ready, Gridley."

1951: In the only use of aerial torpedoes during the Korean War, AD-4 Skyraiders from *Princeton* attacked Hwacheon Dam with Mark 13 torpedoes. Six torpedoes exploded and incapacitated the dam, which North Korean forces had used previously to flood U.N. forces.

1960: An American U-2 spy plane flying at 60,000 feet was shot down over Sverdlovsk, U.S.S.R. This sparked one of the tensest chapters of the Cold War, as the United States claimed that the plane was part of a weather reconnaissance mission—until the Soviets produced pilot Francis Gary Powers and wreckage from the plane. The incident scuttled a planned summit between President Dwight Eisenhower and Soviet leader Nikita Khrushchev. Powers was later traded for a captured Soviet spy.

1961: The Situation Room began operations on or about May 1. President John F. Kennedy requested the "Sit Room" after the bungled Bay of Pigs operation in Cuba (see April 17). Frustrated with the quality and speed of information he received during that crisis, Kennedy ordered that a bowling alley built for Harry Truman in the basement of the West Wing be replaced with a command post that brought in information from the CIA and Defense and State Departments. It would prove invaluable during the Cuban Missile Crisis a year and a half later (see October 16).

2003: President George W. Bush announced that "major combat operations in Iraq have ended." Bush, speaking on the aircraft carrier *Abraham Lincoln* off California, spoke below a banner that read "Mission Accomplished." The announcement was premature, as the war continued for seven and a half more years.

2011: President Barack Obama announced that U.S. forces operating near Abbottabad, Pakistan, had killed Osama bin Laden, leader of the terror group al Qaeda, which had attacked New York City and Washington, D.C., a decade before (see September 11). Code-named Operation Neptune Spear, the raid was one of the most daring in U.S. history—carried out in a Central Intelligence Agency-led operation featuring Navy SEALs of the Naval Special Warfare Development Group (also known as DEVGRU or SEAL Team Six). Participating units also included the Army Special Operations Command's 160th Special Operations Aviation Regiment (Airborne) and CIA operatives. Bin Laden was killed on May 2, but it was still May 1 in the United States.

⭐ QUOTE OF THE DAY

"You may fire when ready, Gridley."

Commodore George Dewey, Battle of Manila Bay

May 2

1863: In the Battle of Chancellorsville, Confederate general Thomas J. "Stonewall" Jackson was wounded by friendly fire while on reconnaissance. He died eight days later.

1942: Admiral Chester J. Nimitz predicted that Japan would attack Midway. He ordered preparations to be stepped up. Japan would attack—and suffer a crippling defeat (see June 4).

1945: German forces in Italy—230,000 men—surrendered to General Mark Clark's 15th Army Group in the Po Valley.

1999: NATO aircraft hit a key power plant in Belgrade, blacking out much of Serbia. The bomb sprayed graphite over the power plant, shorting its circuits.

★ QUOTE OF THE DAY

"He has lost his left arm; but I have lost my right arm."

Robert E. Lee, on Stonewall Jackson's injury at Chancellorsville

May 3

1861: President Abraham Lincoln urgently called for Civil War volunteers. In Proclamation 83, the commander-in-chief asked for 42,034 army volunteers to serve for three years, and another 18,000 seamen to serve for "not less than one or more than three years."

1898: U.S. forces raised the American flag over Cavite, Philippines, at the conclusion of the Battle of Manila Bay during the Spanish-American War.

1952: A ski-modified U.S. Air Force C-47 became the first American aircraft to land on the North Pole. It was piloted by Lieutenant Colonel William P. Benedict and Lieutenant Colonel Joseph O. Fletcher.

★ QUOTE OF THE DAY

"I earnestly invoke the cooperation of all good citizens in the measures hereby adopted for the effectual suppression of unlawful violence, for the impartial enforcement of Constitutional laws, and for the speediest possible restoration of peace and order, and with those of happiness and prosperity throughout our country."

Abraham Lincoln, closing of Proclamation 83

May 4

1864: The biggest Union campaign of the Civil War—the Overland Campaign (also known as the Wilderness Campaign)—began when the Army of the Potomac crossed the Rapidan River in Virginia. It was part of an overall plan by Union commander Ulysses S. Grant to destroy the two major remaining Confederate armies: Joseph Johnston's Army of Tennessee, which was guarding Atlanta, and Robert E. Lee's Army of Virginia. Grant sent General William T. Sherman to take on Johnston, and then rode along with the Army of the Potomac, which was still under the command of George Meade, to confront Lee. It was the first time that Union armies launched a coordinated offensive along multiple fronts and is regarded as a strategic success for the Union, despite severe casualties over seven weeks of fighting.

1904: The U.S. took control of the Panama Canal and construction began immediately. The Isthmian Canal Commission was in charge of the immense project, reporting to Secretary of War William Taft. The 51-mile passageway linking the Pacific and Atlantic Oceans would be completed in 1914.

1942: One of the most important naval battles in history began—the Battle of the Coral Sea. The four-day fight between U.S. and Japanese forces was the first air-naval battle in which warplanes operating off aircraft carriers fought each other as well as the first in which neither side's ships sighted nor fired directly upon the other. One American carrier, the *Lexington*— nicknamed "the Blue Ghost"—was badly damaged (216 crewmen died) and had to be sunk by its crew. Both sides claimed victory: Japan because it destroyed an American carrier and the United States because Japan lost so many planes and experienced pilots that it had to abandon plans for additional offensives in the South Pacific,

1942: The Coast Guard Auxiliary was ordered to form an anti-submarine patrol force. The move was a response to the growing German submarine threat to America's East Coast.

★ QUOTE OF THE DAY

"Dewey! Dewey! Dewey!
Is the hero of the day!
And the *Maine* has been remembered
In the good old fashioned way."

Popular song that sprang up as American learned
of Dewey's victory in Manila

May 5

1862: President Lincoln visited the Civil War front, traveling on the steamer *Miami* to Hampton Roads, where he personally directed the stalled Peninsular Campaign. Accompanying the commander-in-chief were Secretary of War Edwin Stanton and Secretary of the Treasury Salmon P. Chase. Lincoln directed gunboat operations in the James River and the bombardment of Sewell's Point by a blockading naval squadron.

1945: The War Department said that 400,000 U.S. troops would remain in defeated Germany. It also said that two million troops would be discharged from the military. The war against Japan, meantime, continued, with six million service members assigned to the Pacific theater.

1950: The Uniform Code of Military Justice was approved by Congress.

1961: Navy Commander Alan Shepard became the first American to travel in space. His journey aboard his tiny Freedom 7 space capsule, which lasted 15 minutes, was a suborbital flight. The first American to travel in actual orbit would be John Glenn the following year (see February 20). In 1971, Shepard would become the fifth American to walk on the moon, during the Apollo 14 mission.

★ QUOTE OF THE DAY

"Everything is A-O.K.!"

Alan Shepard, on Freedom 7

May 6

1875: William D. Leahy was born in Hampton, Iowa. During World War II, he was the senior-most military officer on active duty; as fleet admiral, Leahy was the first U.S. naval officer ever to hold a five-star rank in the U.S. armed forces.

1916: A first on board the *New Hampshire*: ship-to-shore radio telephone communication. The dreadnought was off the Virginia Capes.

1941: The first flight of the Republic P-47 Thunderbolt took place. The P-47 was one of the main United States Army Air Forces (USAAF) fighters of World War II.

1942: U.S. forces surrendered on Corregidor Island—the last Allied stronghold in the Philippines (see April 9). The senior American officer, General Jonathan Wainwright, who remained a POW until 1945 and was the highest ranking American POW of the war, was present on the *Missouri* for the formal Japanese surrender ceremony in 1945 (see September 2).

1945: 36th Infantry Division troops took Hermann Goering into custody near Radstadt, Austria. Goering had been commander of the German Luftwaffe during World War II and at one point was Adolf Hitler's designated successor. Sentenced to death in the Nuremberg trials, he committed suicide before he could be hanged.

1970: The United States opened three new fronts in Cambodia, as efforts to rout North Vietnamese staging areas were stepped up.

★ QUOTE OF THE DAY

"[H]is example of courage, fortitude and unshakable patriotism, all exhibited in the face of the most discouraging conditions, will long be an inspiration to Americans and free men everywhere."

Dwight D. Eisenhower, on the death of Jonathan
Wainwright in 1953

May 7

1945: Nazi Germany surrendered at Reims, Germany, ending World War II in Europe. At first, Nazi Field Marshal Alfred Jodl tried to limit the surrender to German forces fighting in western Europe. But General Dwight D. Eisenhower, the Supreme Allied Commander, demanded complete surrender of all German forces, those fighting Soviet forces in the East as well as in the West. Jodl signed an unconditional surrender. Russia refused to accept this surrender, so on May 8, a second unconditional surrender was signed at Berlin. End of hostilities were set for May 9, at 12:01 a.m., local time.

☆ QUOTE OF THE DAY

"The mission of this Allied force was fulfilled at 0241 local time, May 7, 1945."

General Dwight D. Eisenhower

May 8

1846: In the Battle of Palo Alto, General Zachary Taylor defeated a superior Mexican force near Brownsville, Texas. The battle came before the United States formally declared war on Mexico.

1911: The Navy ordered its first airplane, the Curtiss A-1. The date is regarded as the birthday of naval aviation.

1945: President Harry Truman, on his 61st birthday, announced the surrender of Nazi Germany. V-E (Victory in Europe) Day meant the end of World War II in Europe, but the war against Japan would continue for four months.

1972: President Richard Nixon said the United States would mine North Vietnamese ports to stem the flow of weapons to that communist nation. Nixon noted that the North Vietnamese had spurned American offers to end the war peacefully, and had actually stepped up its attacks in South Vietnam.

☆ QUOTE OF THE DAY

"There is only one way to stop the killing. That is to keep the weapons of war out of the hands of the international outlaws of North Vietnam."

Richard Nixon, 1972

May 9

1916: President Woodrow Wilson mobilized the national guards of Arizona, New Mexico, and Texas to patrol the Mexican border. The

General John J. Pershing. Library of Congress.

move came as Brigadier General John J. Pershing led Army troops into northern Mexico to try to capture or kill the revolutionary leader Pancho Villa and his followers. Villa and his men had raided the town of Columbus, New Mexico, on March 9, killing 18 soldiers and civilians.

1926: Navy Lt. Cmdr. Richard E. Byrd and Chief Aviation Pilot Floyd Bennett, flying in a Fokker plane christened *Josephine Ford*, reported flying over the North Pole. For their achievements—as aviators, polar explorers, and organizers of polar logistics—they received the Medal of Honor. Some critics have disputed their claim.

1942: The first German prisoners taken in combat by U.S. forces in World War II were captured when their U-boat was sunk by U.S. Coast Guard cutter *Icarus* off the coast of North Carolina. Thirty-three Nazis from *U-352* were rescued from the sunken submarine.

★ QUOTE OF THE DAY

"One must be so soaked in military lore that he does the military thing automatically."

General George S. Patton

May 10

1775: The Green Mountain Boys, led by Ethan Allen and Benedict Arnold, captured Fort Ticonderoga from the British. Later that summer, the fort was used as a staging area for the invasion of Quebec.

1797: The first U.S. frigate was launched in Philadelphia, Pennsylvania—the *United States*. The "Old Wagon" fought in the "Quasi-War," the War of 1812, the Second Barbary War, and, briefly, as a seized Confederate ship in the Civil War. The ship was broken up in 1865. A famous *United States* sailor was *Moby-Dick* author Herman Melville.

1815: President James Madison ordered the Navy into battle against Mediterranean pirates. During the War of 1812, the North African Barbary States of Tripoli, Tunis, and Algeria often attacked American ships that did not pay tribute (bribes) for right of safe passage. In June, a fierce U.S. attack led by Captain Stephen Decatur put an end to the practice. It was the second war against the Barbary States, the first was waged by Thomas Jefferson between 1801 and 1805.

1863: Confederate general Thomas J. "Stonewall" Jackson died. His reported last words were, "Let us cross over the river, and rest under the shade of the trees."

1865: Union forces captured Jefferson Davis, president of the fallen Confederate government. Davis and his wife were nabbed by a detachment of Union general James H. Wilson's cavalry near Irwinville, Georgia. Imprisoned for two years, Davis was indicted for treason, but was never tried.

1917: With the United States now in World War I, General John J. Pershing was appointed commander of the American Expeditionary Forces (AEF), which was being formed to fight on the Western Front.

1960: The first submerged circumnavigation of the world was completed by *Triton* (SSRN-586). It took 84 days and 46,000 miles, following many of the routes taken by Magellan.

1969: As part of Operation Apache Snow, battalions of the 101st Airborne, the 9th Marine Regiment, and battalions of the ARVN 1st Infantry Division were sent to Dong Ap Bia mountain (Hill 937) in the A Shau Valley, South Vietnam, to take out an encampment of the North Vietnamese—the beginning of the ferocious Battle of Hamburger Hill that lasted 11 days.

1972: The A-10 Thunderbolt II (a.k.a. "Warthog") made its first flight. The Fairchild Republic aircraft, a twin-engine, straight wing jet aircraft was designed solely for close air support, including attacking tanks, armored vehicles, and other ground targets with limited air defenses.

⭐ QUOTE OF THE DAY

"I make you a present of a Major, a Captain, and two Lieutenants of the regular Establishment of George the Third."

Ethan Allen, letter to Connecticut governor Jonathan Trumbull accompanying British prisoners from Fort Ticonderoga

May 11

1864: At the Battle of Yellow Tavern, in Virginia, flamboyant Confederate cavalry commander J.E.B. Stuart was mortally wounded, dying the next day.

1898: In the Raid of Cienfuegos, U.S. sailors and Marines under enemy fire severed two undersea cables (out of three) near Cienfuegos, Cuba, cutting off Spanish communication on the island and in the region.

1942: The Air Medal was authorized by President Franklin D. Roosevelt. It was designated for "any person who, while serving in any capacity in the Army, Navy, Marine Corps, or Coast Guard of the United States subsequent to September 8, 1939, distinguishes, or has distinguished, himself by meritorious achievement while participating in an aerial flight."

1945: A Japanese kamikaze attack on the carrier *Bunker Hill* killed 496 Americans. The attack near Okinawa also knocked the ship out of the war.

1961: John F. Kennedy upped U.S. involvement in Vietnam, sending 400 Special Forces and 100 military advisors to South Vietnam. He also ordered a secret warfare program to begin—to be conducted by U.S.-trained South Vietnamese forces.

☆ QUOTE OF THE DAY

"Over 97 percent of the snakes in the A Shau are deadly poisonous; the other three will eat you."

Army warning, Battle of Hamburger Hill, 1969

May 12

1938: Aircraft carrier *Enterprise* (CV-6) was commissioned. During World War II the "Big E" was involved in the Doolittle Raid, the Battle of Midway, the Guadalcanal Campaign, the Battle of the Santa Cruz Islands, the Battle of the Philippine Sea, the Battle of Leyte Gulf, and the Okinawa Campaign (April 1).

1949: Soviet leader Joseph Stalin lifted his blockade of West Berlin one minute after midnight. Eleven months earlier, the Soviets began a blockade in an effort to force U.S. and British troops out of the divided city. There were fears that West Berlin's two million people could starve. President Harry Truman averred: "We stay in Berlin. Period." And thus the Berlin Airlift began on June 26, 1948—a symbol of American (and British) determination to stand up to communism. Truman ordered round-the-clock flights to drop food and clothing and necessities to West Berliners. The Berlin crisis also led to the creation of NATO—the North Atlantic Treaty Organization—that has helped maintain European security for seven decades.

1975: Gerald Ford was informed that a U.S. merchant ship, the *Mayaguez*, had been seized by the Cambodian Khmer Rouge. Ford ordered an attack to free the 39-member crew; but by the time the attack began, the crew had already been released.

1952: General Mark W. Clark succeeded General Matthew Ridgway as commander of U.N. forces in Korea as Ridgway replaced the retiring General Dwight Eisenhower as supreme commander of Allied Powers in Europe.

1958: NORAD—the North American Aerospace Defense Command—was formed by the United States and Canada.

This Day in U.S. Military History

★ QUOTE OF THE DAY

"Heroes come when they are needed; great men step forward when courage seems in short supply."

President Ronald Reagan, presenting General Matthew Ridgway
the Presidential Medal of Freedom, May 12, 1986

May 13

1846: At the request of President James Polk (on May 11), Congress declared war against Mexico. The Mexican-American War would end in 1848 with the United States gaining 525,000 square miles of land, including what is now Texas, California, Nevada, Utah, New Mexico, Arizona, and parts of Colorado and Wyoming.

1863: Union forces, led by generals William T. Sherman and James B. McPherson, arrived at Jackson, Mississippi, as part of the Vicksburg Campaign.

★ QUOTE OF THE DAY

"In further vindication of our rights and defense of our territory, I invoke the prompt action of Congress to recognize the existence of the war, and to place at the disposition of the Executive the means of prosecuting the war with vigor, and thus hastening the restoration of peace."

President James K. Polk

May 14

1812: The Ordnance Department was established by act of Congress.

1863: The Battle of Jackson, Mississippi: Union troops under William Sherman and James McPherson took the city in battle against General Joseph E. Johnston, a key strategic goal in the Vicksburg Campaign.

1864: Union and Confederate troops fought at Resaca, Georgia. It was one of the first engagements in a summer-long campaign by Union general William T. Sherman to capture the Confederate city of Atlanta.

1942: Congress passed a law making women eligible for noncombat duties in the Women's Auxiliary Army Corps (WAAC), Women Accepted for Voluntary Emergency Service (WAVES), Women's Auxiliary Ferrying Squadron (WAFS) and Coast Guard or Semper Paratus Always Ready Service (SPARS), the Women's Reserve of the Marine Corps.

1975: President Gerald Ford ordered an attack on Koh Tang Island, Kampuchea, to free the crew of the merchant vessel *Mayaguez*. It was the first use of U.S. troops on foreign soil under the War Powers Act. Thirty-eight Marines were killed in the operation, with 50 wounded and three missing and later executed by the Khmer Rouge. The action occurred after all 39 members of the crew of the cargo ship had already been released. The names of the Americans killed in the battle with the Khmer Rouge are the final names inscribed on the Vietnam Veterans Memorial in Washington, D.C.

★ QUOTE OF THE DAY

"For all the girls in the WAFS, I think the most concrete moment of happiness came at our first review. Suddenly and for the first time we felt a part of something larger."

Cornelia Fort, first female pilot to die in the line of duty
(see March 21), 1943

May 15

1800: The frigate *Essex* became the first U.S. Navy warship to cross the Equator. Commanded by Captain Edward Preble, the *Essex* was on a mission to escort American merchant ships in southeast Asia.

1939: A contract was awarded to the Curtiss-Wright Company for the XSB2C-1 dive bomber. The "Hell-Diver" bomber would play an integral role in World War II before being retired from the U.S. Navy in 1947.

1942: The Women's Auxiliary Army Corps (WAACs) was created and women were granted official military status. It stemmed from legislation introduced in Congress on May 14, 1941, by Representative Edith Nourse Rogers of Massachusetts, the first congresswoman from New England.

★ QUOTE OF THE DAY

"[The WAAC Act] gives women a chance to volunteer to serve their country in a patriotic way."

Representative Edith Nourse Rogers

May 16

1863: The Battle of Champion Hill. After a standoff of nearly a year around the strategic Mississippi River city of Vicksburg, Mississippi, Union forces under Ulysses S. Grant defeated Southern forces under General John Pemberton. Pemberton's forces withdrew into Vicksburg, which would soon be under Union siege (see May 19 and 25).

1965: *Henry W. Tucker* (DD-875) provided the first U.S. naval gunfire in Vietnam when it pounded the Viet Cong on the coast near Saigon.

★ QUOTE OF THE DAY

"As the officers and soldiers of the United States have been subjected to repeated insults from women (calling themselves ladies) of New Orleans . . . when any female shall . . . show contempt for the United States, she shall be regarded as a woman of the town plying her avocation."

General Benjamin Butler, military governor of New Orleans,
the infamous "Woman Order"—General Order
Number 28, May 16, 1862

May 17

1973: Captain Robin Lindsay Catherine Quigley became the first woman to hold a major Navy command when she became head of U.S. Navy Service School at San Diego, California.

1987: During the Iran-Iraq War, U.S. patrol frigate *Stark* (FFG-31) was struck by two Exocet missiles fired by an Iraqi fighter jet in the Persian Gulf. Thirty-seven U.S. sailors were killed and 21 wounded.

'The crew of the *Stark* did not believe they were in any danger. . . . The surprise was incredible."

> Rear Admiral Harold J. Bernsen, press conference on the *Stark* attack

May 18

1861: In the first Union offensive of the Civil War, Union troops engaged Confederate batteries at Sewall's Point, Virginia.

1917: At Woodrow Wilson's urging, Congress passed the Selective Service Act—allowing men to be drafted into the military. After the United States entered World War I in April 1917, the president asked for military volunteers. Only 97,000 signed up. He then asked for the draft. At peak strength, the U.S. had 4.3 million men under arms. The draft was canceled after the war's end in November 1918. It was America's first draft since the Civil War.

1944: Capture of Monte Cassino. After four months and five Allied attempts to take the key German position at the Benedictine abbey at Monte Cassino in Italy, the site—although reduced to rubble—was finally taken. Allied casualties, at 55,000, were heavy.

"We must economize on youth in the next war if we are to survive even victory."

> William "Wild Bill" Donovan, on World War I

May 19

1863: The assault and siege on Vicksburg began. Led by Major General Ulysses S. Grant's Army of the Tennessee, U.S. forces attacked the Mississippi city, but were stymied by Lt. Gen. John Pemberton's defending troops. Grant tried again on May 22, to no avail. The siege endured until July 4, when Pemberton surrendered. Grant's Vicksburg campaign led to

Union control of the entire Mississippi River and the splitting in two of the Confederacy.

1943: D-Day set: President Franklin D. Roosevelt and British Prime Minister Winston Churchill set May 1, 1944, as the day for an Allied invasion of Nazi-controlled France. Delays would push the invasion back five weeks (see June 6).

★ QUOTE OF THE DAY

"I now determined upon a regular siege—to 'out-camp the enemy,' as it were, and to incur no more losses."

Ulysses S. Grant, remembering Vicksburg in his memoirs

May 20

1815: Aboard his flagship *Guerriere*, Commodore Stephen Decatur led a squadron of nine ships into the Mediterranean Sea in order to combat ongoing piracy.

1956: The United States dropped a thermonuclear bomb from a B-52 on the Bikini Atoll—four miles off-target. It was May 21, local time.

1969: After ten assaults, exhausted U.S. and South Vietnamese forces finally took Hill 937, Dong Ap Bia. Combined U.S/SouthVietnamese casualties were 103 killed (72 Americans) and more than 400 injured. The North Vietnamese saw more than 650 killed. "Hamburger Hill" was the nickname of American servicemen for Hill 937 due to the bloody hand-to-hand combat.

★ QUOTE OF THE DAY

"As soon as the war ended, we located the one spot on Earth that hadn't been touched by the war and blew it to hell."

Bob Hope, comedian, on the nuclear bomb tests at Bikini Atoll

May 21

1917: *Ericsson* (DD-56) became the first U.S. warship to fire a torpedo at a German U-boat.

1944: A terrible accident at Pearl Harbor killed 163 and injured 396. It occurred in an ordnance explosion during preparations for the invasion of Saipan. Six tank landing ships, three tank landing craft, and 17 track landing vehicles were destroyed.

★ QUOTE OF THE DAY

"We decimated a large North Vietnamese unit and people are acting as if it were a catastrophe."

General Melvin Zais, 101st Airborne, responding to American political, media, and public questioning of the value of the Battle of Hamburger Hill

May 22

1863: Congress established the Bureau of United States Colored Troops, which was tasked with providing uniforms and training to soldiers of African descent as well as deploying them. By the end of the Civil War the United States Colored Troops (USCT) had more than 200,000 soldiers of African descent, but also included Native Americans, Hawaiians, Latinos, and Anglos.

1968: Carrying a crew of 99, the nuclear submarine *Scorpion* (SSN-589) was lost with her crew off the Azores observing Soviet naval maneuvers in the area. In October 1968, naval search ships located the submarine's remains on the sea floor more than 9,800 feet below the surface. It appeared that the hull imploded after passing crush depth, but the reason for the sinking remained a mystery.

★ QUOTE OF THE DAY

"The certain cause of the loss of the *Scorpion* cannot be ascertained from evidence now available."

Naval Court of Inquiry report, January 31, 1969

May 23

William H. Carney. Library of Congress.

1865: At President Andrew Johnson's direction, a formal review of U.S. troops took place in Washington, D.C., over two days. The Grand Review of the Armies occurred on Pennsylvania Avenue and, on the first day, stretched for seven miles, kicked off by the Army of the Potomac. The viewing stand, bedecked in patriotic bunting, was placed before the White House and included Johnson, his cabinet, and key military commanders.

1900: Former slave William H. Carney of the 54th Massachusetts Volunteer Infantry, received the Medal of Honor for his heroic actions while wounded at the assault on Fort Wagner at Charleston, South Carolina, on July 18, 1863. His actions made him the first African-American soldier to be given the Medal of Honor, although he was the last of his Civil War comrades to receive it.

1988: The V-22 Osprey, the world's first production tilt-rotor aircraft, made its debut at the Flight Research Center at Bell Helicopter Textron's Arlington, Texas, facility. The Osprey flies like a helicopter and an airplane.

"It works, it's ahead of schedule, and will be a sound investment for taxpayers' money."

William L. Ball III, Secretary of the Navy, at the Osprey unveiling

May 24

1844: The first telegraph line in the United States—between Washington, D.C., and Baltimore—was completed. The telegraph would soon be used by President James Polk to manage the Mexican-American War, and it gave Abraham Lincoln a technological edge during the Civil War.

1861: The first Union combat fatality of the Civil War occurred, in Alexandria, Virginia, when 24-year-old Elmer Ellsworth of the 11th New York Regiment tried to remove a Confederate flag from a hotel roof. He was shot by the hotel keeper, James Jackson, who was then shot by a Union soldier.

Infantry unit with fixed bayonets, followed by ambulances in the Grand Review at Washington, D.C., May 1865. Photography by Matthew B. Brady. Civil war photographs, 1861-1865, Library of Congress, Prints and Photographs Division.

This Day in U.S. Military History   **131**

1865: The Grand Review of the Armies continued for a second day at Washington, D.C. General Sherman's army paraded this day. More than 150,000 troops took part during the review. The Union armies would be disbanded in June.

1917: In World War I, the first American naval convoy left Hampton Roads, Virginia, to cross the North Atlantic.

★ QUOTE OF THE DAY

"The city is full of soldiers, running around loose. Officers everywhere, of all grades. All have the weather-beaten look of practical service."

> Walt Whitman, poet and Civil War nurse, observing preparations
> for the Grand Review, May 1865

May 25

1945: The date for the invasion of Japan—Operation Olympic—was set. The target date was November 1.

1973: Skylab 2, the first U.S. manned orbiting space station, launched with an all-Navy crew: Commander Charles (Pete) Conrad, Jr., Pilot Paul J. Weitz, and Science Pilot Joseph P. Kerwin. The trio broke endurance records and conducted medical experiments while making solar and Earth observations. They returned after making 404 orbits of Earth.

★ QUOTE OF THE DAY

"But I like to think we were a very compatible crew [on Skylab 2], and part of that, I think, is due to our military background. Pete was the boss. I mean, he was the commander, he was the boss. The good thing about Pete, though, is that he would listen to you, and if you had a better idea, he would adapt it."

> Paul J. Weitz, NASA Johnson Space Center
> Oral History Project, March 26, 2000

May 26

1865: Confederate general Edmund Kirby Smith negotiated the surrender of his Army of the Trans-Mississippi at Galveston, Texas, which was formalized June 2. This was the last major field unit—43,000 soldiers—of the Confederacy to surrender.

1948: The Civil Air Patrol became an official auxiliary of the U.S. Air Force. The Civil Air Patrol (CAP) was created in December 1941 as a volunteer aviation organization that performs three congressionally assigned missions: emergency services, which includes search and rescue (by air and ground) and disaster relief operations; aerospace education for youth and the general public; and cadet programs for teenage youth.

★ QUOTE OF THE DAY

"Supporting America's communities with emergency response, diverse aviation and ground services, youth development, and promotion of air, space and cyber power."

Civil Air Patrol, mission statement

May 27

1813: During the War of 1812, American troops captured Fort George, Canada, which served as the headquarters for the Centre Division of the British Army.

1958: The Air Force received its first F-105 Thunderchief—the "Thud." The supersonic tactical fighter-bomber was a replacement for the F-84F.

1958: The F-4 Phantom II made its first flight. The McDonnell Douglas F-4 Phantom II was a tandem two-seat, twin-engine, all-weather, long-range supersonic jet interceptor aircraft/fighter-bomber.

★ QUOTE OF THE DAY

"There's a four-motor job up there about to make a run. Go get 'em McCluskey!"

This Day in U.S. Military History   **133**

Order given during the attack on the Marshall and Gilbert islands to Lt. Cdr. Clarence McCluskey, who received a Distinguished Flying Cross on May 27, 1942, for taking out a Japanese bomber (see February 1)

May 28

1863: The 54th Massachusetts Infantry—the most famous African-American regiment of the Civil War—left Boston for engagement in the South.

1918: Battle of Cantigny: America's 28th Infantry, with French forces, captured Cantigny, France from the Germans—the first major American victory of World War I.

1980: The U.S. Naval Academy celebrated its first female graduates; of which there were 55.

1984: At a ceremony at Arlington National Cemetery, the only unknown American soldier from the Vietnam War was buried after being awarded the Congressional Medal of Honor by President Ronald Reagan, who was honorary next of kin. In his eulogy, Reagan urged Congress and the nation to find those missing in action, because "an end to America's involvement in Vietnam cannot come before we have achieved the fullest possible accounting of those missing in action." Later, in 1998, this serviceman was identified through DNA testing: he was Air Force First Lieutenant Michael J. Blassie. His remains were sent to his hometown of St. Louis, Missouri, for reburial.

★ QUOTE OF THE DAY

"[T]he war in Southeast Asia still haunts a small but brave group of Americans: the families of those still missing in the Vietnam conflict. They live day and night with uncertainty, with an emptiness, with a void we cannot fathom. Today, some sit among you; their feelings are a mixture of pride and fear. They are proud of their sons or husbands, fathers or brothers, who bravely and nobly answered the call of their country, but some of them fear that this ceremony writes a final chapter, leaving those they love forgotten."

President Ronald Reagan, May 28, 1984, at
Arlington National Cemetery

May 29

1781: In a battle with the British ships *Atalanta* and *Trepassey* off Newfoundland, John Barry, U.S. commander on *Alliance*, was injured by shrapnel and taken below to have his wounds dressed while the *Alliance* was dangerously battered. When his second in command asked permission to strike colors, Barry angrily ordered to be carried on deck to resume the fight—which the Americans won.

1940: The Vought F4U Corsair made its first flight. The plane was heavily used in World War II and the Korean War. From 1940 until 1953, 12,571 Corsairs were manufactured.

★ QUOTE OF THE DAY

"No Sir, the thunder! If this ship cannot be fought without me, I will be brought on deck; to your duty, Sir."

John Barry

May 30

1868: The Grand Army of the Republic held a memorial day to honor those who died "in defense of their country during the late rebellion." There are many competing tales of the first Memorial Day—or "Decoration Day"— as it was sometimes known as. May 30 was the agreed-upon observance date for 100 years, until 1968's Uniform Monday Holiday Act was enacted that year on June 28 (Public Law 90-363) which made Memorial Day a movable observance on the last Monday of May.

1942: Cologne, Germany, was bombed by 1,000 allied aircraft—the first use of saturation bombing in World War II.

1943: U.S. troops retook Kiska and Attu islands from occupying Japanese troops. The battle to retake these Aleutian Islands began on May 11. The 7th Infantry faced dug-in Japanese, who made a desperate *banzai* final counterattack. This was the only land battle of World War II fought on U.S. soil.

★ QUOTE OF THE DAY

"We must observe this Memorial Day with the solemn determination that arises from our memories of the December morning at Pearl

This Day in U.S. Military History

Harbor; of the day when the valiant handful of Marines and bluejackets were overcome at Wake; and of still another moment when a few thousand weary defenders relinquished the rocky heights of Bataan.

These are stirring memories for all Americans. We, particularly, shall not forget them. Together they and the ideals for which we are fighting make a compelling force that will carry us forward to the inevitable, ultimate victory."

> Fleet Admiral Chester W. Nimitz at Memorial Day services at Pearl Harbor, May 30, 1942

May 31

1862: Battle of the Seven Pines began, part of the Peninsula Campaign. Confederate general Joseph E. Johnston's forces attacked McClellan's Army of the Potomac. There was no clear victor when the battle ended on June 1, but there were heavy casualties, and Johnston himself was injured, which necessitated Robert E. Lee's appointment as commander.

1900: As China's Boxer Rebellion spread to Beijing, U.S. Marines under Captain John T. Myers arrived in that city as part of a multination force formed to protect foreign legations.

1919: The first transatlantic flight was completed, when a Curtiss flying boat landed at Plymouth, England. The first nonstop flight, of course, would be conducted in 1927 by Charles Lindbergh.

★ QUOTE OF THE DAY

"Victory has no charms for me when purchased at such cost."

> General George McClellan, on the Battle of Seven Pines

General U.S. Grant at Cold Harbor, 1864. Photo by Edgar Guy Fawx. Civil War photographs, 1861-1865, Library of Congress, Prints and Photographs Division.

June

June 1

1812: President James Madison made the case for war against Britain during a speech to Congress. Madison listed several grievances: impressment of American sailors (who were forced to serve in the Royal Navy), renewing and encouraging warfare among Native American peoples in the Northwest, and conducting illegal blockades. Madison said these acts constituted war and that for the United States to ignore them would undermine American sovereignty. On June 4, the House of Representatives voted 79-49 for war, followed by a 19-13 Senate vote on June 17.

1862: The Battle of Seven Pines (also known as the Battle of Fair Oaks) on the outskirts of Richmond, Virginia, ended in a stalemate. The Army of the Potomac had more than 5,000 casualties while the Army of Northern Virginia had more than 6,000 casualties.

1944: USN Blimp Squadron Fourteen (ZP-14), Airships (K-23) and (K-130), completed the first transatlantic crossing by non-rigid, lighter-than-air aircraft. The journey took 50 hours after leaving Naval Air Station, South Weymouth, Massachusetts, and arriving at Naval Air Station Port Lyautey in Morocco (75 miles north of Casablanca). The blimps' task was to patrol German U-boats in the Straits of Gibraltar.

⭐ QUOTE OF THE DAY

"Whether the United States shall continue passive under these … accumulating wrongs, or, opposing force to force in defense of their national rights, shall commit a just cause into the hands of the Almighty Disposer of Events, … is a solemn question which the Constitution wisely confides to the legislative department of the Government. In recommending it to their early deliberations I am happy in the assurance that the decision will be worthy the enlightened and patriotic councils of a virtuous, a free, and a powerful nation."

James Madison

June 2

1865: Two months after the official end of the Civil War, the final remaining Confederate troops formally surrendered. The Army of the Trans-Mississippi, led by General Edmund Kirby Smith, comprised 43,000 soldiers.

1944: Operation Frantic, U.S. shuttle-bombing missions that used Soviet bases to attack Eastern European targets, kicked off with its first mission: "Frantic Joe." Led by Lt. Gen. Ira C. Eaker, Commander-in-Chief of the Mediterranean Allied Air Forces, 130 B-17 bombers and 69 P-51s bombed a railway yard in Hungary, a success. The operation continued through September, hampered by Soviet recalcitrance and lack of protection for U.S. forces.

★ QUOTE OF THE DAY

"There are no reluctant leaders. A real leader must really want the job."

Ira C. Eaker

June 3

1781: Jack Jouett's Ride. Farmer Jack Jouett rode 45 miles on horseback during the night to warn Virginia governor Thomas Jefferson and the Virginia legislature that Tarleton's Raiders, led by Lt. Col. Banastre Tarleton, were coming. Jouett rode from a tavern in Louisa County to Charlottesville, Virginia, in about 6 1/2 hours, arriving at Monticello, Jefferson's home, at dawn on June 4. His warning gave the Americans time to escape.

1864: In the Battle of Cold Harbor, begun May 31, General Ulysses S. Grant launched an all-out attack on the Confederate Army of Northern Virginia near Mechanicsville, Virginia, with disastrous results. Historians estimate that 7,000 Union troops were lost within one-half hour of battle on the first attack. After a second unsuccessful attack, Grant's orders for a third assault were all but ignored. Battlefield tradition held that the first commander who sought a truce in order to tend to the wounded was the loser. Grant refused to admit defeat by seeking such a truce, and the wounded were left on the ground for three days following the battle. As a consequence, all but two of the thousands of wounded men died from their wounds, hunger, thirst, or exposure.

1916: The National Defense Act was enacted, authorizing a standing Army of 175,000 and a National Guard of 450,000. It also included an idea promoted by Douglas MacArthur: the use overseas of the National Guard. Congress would soon pass a defense authorization bill of $128 million—the largest military budget to date. The context for the act was Mexican revolutionary Pancho Villa's raid on Columbus, New Mexico.

1959: The first class graduated from the Air Force Academy in Colorado Springs, Colorado.

★ QUOTE OF THE DAY

"The men bent down as they pushed forward, as if trying, as they were, to breast a tempest, and the files of men went down like rows of blocks or bricks pushed over by striking against one another."

Union officer describing the slaughter of Union general John Martindale's division of the 18th Corps

June 4

1934: *Ranger* (CV-4), the first Navy ship designed from the keel up as an aircraft carrier, was commissioned at Norfolk, Virginia.

1942: The Battle of Midway began. The United States scored a decisive victory in the four-day battle that ended Japanese naval superiority in the Pacific and turned the tide of the Pacific War. U.S. warplanes sank four Japanese aircraft carriers—all of which had been part of the six-carrier force that attacked Pearl Harbor six months earlier. The United States lost one carrier. Military historian John Keegan called it "the most stunning and decisive blow in the history of naval warfare."

1944: Rome was liberated by U.S. forces. The 9th Army, commanded by General Mark W. Clark, entered the southern suburbs of the Italian capital—the first of the three Axis capitals to fall during World War II.

1944: The first Navy capture of an enemy vessel since the early 19th century occurred when a hunter-killer group comprised of five destroyer escorts and *Guadalcanal* (CVE-60) captured German submarine *U-505*.

✯ QUOTE OF THE DAY

"The general seeking to break an enemy defense line and destroy his forces must decide just when and how to strike and precisely to what extent he dare weaken one sector of his front in order to mass overpowering strength at the main point of attack. He, too, must take a chance, although, in the stilted phraseology of military communiqués, he calls it a 'calculated risk.'"

General Mark Clark, *Calculated Risk* (1950)

June 5

1794: The first officers of the U.S. Navy under the new U.S. Constitution were appointed: John Barry, Samuel Nicholson, Silas Talbot, Joshua Barney, Richard Dale, and Thomas Truxtun. They were also asked to supervise the construction of new ships.

1917: With the United States now in World War I, the first of three national registration days for the draft was held on this date—for all men between the ages of 21 and 30. The Selective Service Act of 1917 had been enacted shortly before, on May 18.

✯ QUOTE OF THE DAY

"When we know as much about people as hog specialists know about hogs, we'll be better off."

Major General Lewis Hershey, Selective Service Director, 1956

June 6

1862: Memphis surrendered to Union forces after the First Battle of Memphis. Union gunboats of the Mississippi River Squadron destroyed the Confederate River Defense Fleet, helping to open up the Mississippi River region to Union forces.

1944: Operation Overlord—the Allied invasion of Nazi-occupied France began. Commanded by General Dwight D. Eisenhower, the U.S.-led invasion—the biggest amphibious assault in history—opened the long-awaited western front against Adolf Hitler's so-called "Fortress Europe."

Within eleven months, allied forces converging on Germany from both west and east brought about the Nazi surrender (see May 8).

1957: The first carrier-to-carrier transcontinental flight occurred when two F8U Crusaders and two A3D Skywarriors flew nonstop from *Bon Homme Richard* (CVA-31) off the coast of California to *Saratoga* (CVA-60) off the east coast of Florida.

1969: Four Marines in a bunker at An Hoa combat base were killed by North Korean explosives. One of them was Dan Bullock, who had hidden his true age and enlisted at the age of 14. Bullock was 15 years old on the day of his death, the youngest ever to die in the Vietnam War.

★ QUOTE OF THE DAY

"If we are about to be captured, I'll shoot you first. After all, I am your commanding officer."

William "Wild Bill" Donovan, on Utah Beach to a
subordinate, June 7, 1944

June 7

1942: The Battle of Midway ended after four days. In addition to losing four aircraft carriers, the Japanese suffered more than 3,000 casualties.

1944: The construction of artificial harbors and sheltered anchorages, also known as Mulberries, began off the Normandy coast—hastening the delivery of supplies to Allied forces who were now pouring into France, a day after D-Day.

2006: A key al Qaeda leader—Abu Musab al-Zarqawi—was killed in Hibhib, Iraq, by an American airstrike.

★ QUOTE OF THE DAY

"The annals of war at sea present no more intense, heart-shaking shock than this battle, in which the qualities of the United States Navy and Air Force and the American race shone forth in splendour. The bravery and self-devotion of the American airmen and sailors and the nerve and skill of their leaders was the foundation of all."

Winston Churchill, describing the U.S. victory at Midway

June 8

1830: The sloop of war *Vincennes* became the first U.S. warship to circle the globe when it returned to New York City. With Commander William B. Finch at the helm, the ship had departed New York on September 3, 1826, and had visited islands in the South Seas.

1967: Attack on the *Liberty*. The unescorted intelligence ship, sailing in international waters off the Egyptian coast, was attacked without warning by Israeli forces. Out of a crew of 294 Americans, 34 were killed and 171 wounded. Israel apologized and made reparations, claiming mistaken identity—but surviving crew members charged that it was a deliberate attack.

★ QUOTE OF THE DAY

"I was not on a voyage of discovery; my instructions were distinct and specific . . ."

William B. Finch, report on his 1830 voyage

June 9

Brigadier General Laura Yeager. U.S. Department of Defense.

1959: *George Washington* (SSBN-598), the first U.S. Navy nuclear-powered fleet ballistic missile submarine, was christened at Groton, Connecticut.

2019: The first woman to assume command of a U.S. Army infantry division was announced. Major General Laura Yeager, a former UH-60 Black Hawk pilot in Iraq, leads the 40th Infantry Division based in Los Alamitos, California.

☆ QUOTE OF THE DAY

"To me this is just my next assignment, but I understand it's a milestone."

Major General Laura Yeager, quoted in *Stars and Stripes*

June 10

1801: Thomas Jefferson ordered U.S. forces into war against the Barbary Coast states of North Africa (what are today Morocco, Libya, Tunisia, and Algeria). Jefferson sought an end to the years-long practice of paying ransom or tribute to the Barbary Pirates who had captured merchant ships and their crews.

1854: The U.S. Naval Academy held its first formal graduation. Previously, classes at the Annapolis, Maryland, school had graduated without a ceremony. Graduates—there were six—included Rear Admiral Thomas O. Selfridge and Rear Admiral Joseph N. Miller.

1871: The Battle of Ganghwa began—the first U.S. military action to occur in Korea.

1898: In the Battle of Guantánamo Bay that began June 6, the First Marine Battalion landed on the eastern side of Guantánamo Bay, Cuba. "GITMO," as it is often called today, would soon become the first official—and permanent—U.S. base on foreign soil.

1999: President Bill Clinton ordered an end to Operation Allied Force (or Operation Noble Anvil), the U.S.-led NATO bombing campaign against Serbia, after Serb forces agreed to withdraw from Kosovo. American troops joined a 50,000 man peacekeeping force to enforce the agreement. The bombing campaign had begun on March 24, a response to Serbian aggression in Kosovo and Albania, and reports of ethnic cleansing.

★ QUOTE OF THE DAY

"The sight of the flag upon the midnight sky has thrilled our hearts."

Marine Lt. Col. Robert Huntington, on flying the American flag at
Guantánamo

June 11

1775: The Battle of Machias began—the first naval battle of the Revolutionary War—at Machias, Maine (then Massachusetts).

1871: The Battle of Ganghwa concluded. The Asiatic Squadron of the U.S. Navy, led by Rear Admiral John Rodgers, had traveled to Korea on a peaceful trade mission, but violence erupted when a Korea fort fired on an American ship. As a consequence, almost 1,500 Marines and sailors successfully attacked and destroyed six Korean forts.

★ QUOTE OF THE DAY

"You say to your [Prussian] soldier 'Do this and he doeth it'; but I am obliged to say [to an American soldier]: 'This is the reason why you ought to do that: and then he does it.'"

Baron Friedrich Wilhelm von Steuben, 1778, Prussian officer who
trained American troops

June 12

1775: The Battle of Machias, the first naval battle of the American War of Independence, concluded with an American victory. The British ship *Margaretta*, under Captain James Moore, had skirmished with Colonial locals over provisions for the British in Boston, and was ultimately defeated by the crews of *Unity* and *Falmouth Packet*. Moore died of musket injuries.

1915: The "Class the Stars Fell On": On this day, the U.S. Military Academy's class of 1915 graduated. This class of 164 gained fame due to the fact that 36 percent of the graduates became generals. West Point graduates of this year included later five-star generals Dwight D. Eisenhower and Omar Bradley and four-star generals James Van Fleet and Joseph T. McNarney. Graduating first in that class was William Covell, who attained the rank of major general.

1948: Women could now be admitted into both the regular and reserve forces of the Army, Navy, Marine Corps, and Air Force, after President Harry Truman signed the Women's Armed Services Integration Act. The law capped their numbers at 2 percent of the total force each branch.

1961: The American flag was ordered flown at the Marine Corps War Memorial in Arlington, Virginia, "at all times during the day and night," thanks to a proclamation signed by President John F. Kennedy.

★ QUOTE OF THE DAY

"The master tactician of our forces."

Dwight D. Eisenhower, on Omar Bradley in World War II

June 13

Winfield Scott in an 1847 Currier & Ives lithograph. Library of Congress.

This Day in U.S. Military History

1777: Aboard the cargo ship *Victoire*, 19-year-old French noble Marie-Joseph-Paul-Yves-Roch-Gilbert du Motier, Marquis de Lafayette, arrived in Charleston, South Carolina, to aid the colonial forces in their fight against England.

1786: Winfield Scott was born at Dinwiddie County, Virginia. Known as "Old Fuss and Feathers" for his insistence on proper military etiquette, and the "Grand Old Man of the Army" for his 52 years in uniform, he served as a general from 1814 to 1861. He took part in every U.S. military campaign during this period, including the War of 1812, the Mexican-American War, and the early portion of the Civil War (he developed the Anaconda Plan). General Scott was also involved in various battles with Native Americans. Scott was also the Whig Party's nominee in the 1852 presidential election, but lost to Democrat Franklin Pierce.

1929: The first radio broadcast from an aircraft was made by Coast Guard Radio Technician A. G. Descoteaux. In a Loening amphibian, he reported the takeoff of a French aircraft on a trans-Atlantic flight at Old Orchard Beach, Maine. The account was relayed by ground equipment to an extensive national hookup and was received by U.S. and foreign listeners.

★ QUOTE OF THE DAY

"[In] war all depends on the moment."

Marquis de Lafayette

June 14

1775: The U.S. Army was created by the Second Continental Congress. It began with six companies of expert riflemen in Pennsylvania, two in Maryland, and two in Virginia.

1863: In the Siege of Port Hudson, begun May 22, Union general Nathaniel Banks launched a final, unsuccessful infantry assault on the fort (35 miles north of Baton Rouge, Louisiana) that led to almost 1,800 casualties.

★ QUOTE OF THE DAY

"Could somebody get me a Coke?"

General Dwight D. Eisenhower, at a celebratory luncheon, June 1945

June 15

1775: George Washington became commander in chief of the Continental Army. The Second Continental Congress chose him because of his extensive military experience, impressive appearance, and leadership qualities. He had been nominated by John Adams and Samuel Adams.

1863: President Abraham Lincoln asked for 100,000 troops to protect Washington, D.C., from General Robert E. Lee's advancing Army of Northern Virginia, which had advanced to the Potomac River. Lincoln could see enemy campfires from the White House. But Lee didn't attack the capital—his troops moved into Pennsylvania for a showdown at Gettysburg, regarded as a key turning point in the Civil War (see July 1).

1944: The Battle of Saipan began. Saipan, in the Mariana Islands, was a key node of defense for Japan. A fleet of 800 ships from Guadalcanal and Hawaii carried the 2nd and 4th Marine Divisions, consisting of 162,000 men. By the end of the first day, 20,000 had established a six-mile-long beachhead. The eventual seizure of Saipan left the Japanese mainland within range of the American B-29 bombers.

★ QUOTE OF THE DAY

"[I] feel just a little bit like a man looking for a needle in a hay stack with an armed guard standing over the stack forbidding you to look in the hay."

> General John J. Pershing, letter to General H.H. Crowder on the hunt for Pancho Villa, June 15, 1916, from "Somewhere in Mexico"

June 16

1775: The post of Army Adjutant General was established. Its slogan: "Defend and Serve." In 1950, it was redesignated the Adjutant General's Corps.

1775: The Army's Quartermaster Corps, originally designated the Quartermaster Department, was established. While numerous additions, deletions, and changes of function have occurred, its basic supply and service support functions have continued in existence.

★ QUOTE OF THE DAY

"You do it slow, but you do it right."

General O.P. Smith, 1st Marine Division commander, in Korea

June 17

1775: The Battle of Bunker Hill, an early clash between colonial and British troops during the Revolutionary War, began. Colonial forces discovered that British troops were planning to fortify the hills around Boston in order to gain control of its harbor. In a series of battles, the British won but suffered many casualties, showing that the more inexperienced colonial militia could stand up to the well-trained redcoats. Colonial commander was William Prescott.

★ QUOTE OF THE DAY

"Don't fire until you see the whites of their eyes!"

Famous, perhaps apocryphal, order given to Colonial troops

June 18

1778: British troops—15,000 men—evacuated Philadelphia, after almost nine months of occupation.

1812: James Madison signed a Congressional declaration of war against Great Britain—and the War of 1812 was on. Sandwiched between the Revolutionary and Civil Wars, the War of 1812 is often overlooked, but had enormous consequences for the United States. Often called America's "second war of independence," the war would see the White House and Capitol destroyed by British troops before the United States prevailed.

1945: General Dwight D. Eisenhower arrived at Washington, D.C., to be celebrated with a parade and then luncheon. General George C. Marshall organized the Allied victory in Europe celebrations.

1981: The Lockheed F-117 Nighthawk made its first flight at "Area 51" in Nevada. The Air Force denied the stealth fighter existed until 1988 (see November 10).

2013: In Afghanistan, NATO transferred security of all 403 Afghan districts to local forces.

☆ QUOTE OF THE DAY

"If the subjects of one sovereign may be taken by force from the vessels of another, on the high seas, the right of taking them when found implies the right of searching for them; a vexation of commerce, especially in time of peace, which has not yet been attempted . . ."

James Madison, January 5, 1804, in a letter as U.S. secretary of state to James Monroe, about the British practice of impressment—one of the causes of the War of 1812

June 19

1778: After a severe winter, George Washington's army marched out of Valley Forge, Pennsylvania. The Continental Army had encamped there beginning December 19, 1777. Of the 12,000 men stationed at Valley Forge, almost 2,000 died from typhus, influenza, cholera, and malnutrition. Washington stayed with his men, inspiring loyalty to him and their cause. In the spring of 1778, Prussian military adviser Friedrich von Steuben kept the soldiers busy with drills and training in modern military strategy. By June 1778, the army was stronger and better disciplined. Just ten days later the Americans won a key victory against the British under Lord Cornwallis at the Battle of Monmouth in New Jersey.

1864: Confederate raider C.S.S. *Alabama* met its demise in the Battle of Cherbourg, off Cherbourg, France. *Alabama,* which had burned or sunk 65 Union vessels (most of them merchant ships) since its August 24, 1862 christening, had arrived in France for repairs. Union warship *Kearsarge,* commanded by Capt. J.A. Winslow, sank the *Alabama* just outside French territorial waters.

1944: The "Great Marianas Turkey Shoot": the Battle of the Philippine Sea began. In the two-day battle, around 900 U.S. fighters shot down more than 600 Japanese aircraft—an uneven victory that gave the engagement its nickname. The naval battle eliminated the Imperial Japanese Navy's ability to conduct large-scale carrier operations, as Japan lost three carriers and eight other ships.

1952: The first Special Forces unit in the Army was formed, when the 10th Special Forces Group was activated. The Special Forces Branch was established as a basic branch of the Army effective April 9, 1987, by General Order Number 35, June 19, 1987.

★ QUOTE OF THE DAY

"War is at best barbarism…its glory is all moonshine. It is only those who have neither fired a shot nor heard the shrieks and groans of the wounded who cry aloud for blood, more vengeance, more desolation. War is hell."

General William T. Sherman, in a June 19, 1879, speech to
the Michigan Military Academy

June 20

1924: Audie Murphy, the most decorated soldier in U.S. history, was born in Kingston, Texas, to sharecroppers. As soon as he turned 18 years of age, in 1942, he enlisted in the Army. His bravery in battle garnered 37 medals, including the Congressional Medal of Honor and several Purple Hearts. It is estimated that he killed 240 Germans. On January 26, 1945, in his most famous act of heroism, Murphy held off a German infantry company with a machine gun at Holtzwihr, France. He later became an actor and songwriter.

1934: "Any attack by (Japan) would be made without previous declaration of war or intentional warning" was the conclusion of an analysis of Japanese radio traffic in a report given to the Chief of Naval Operations. The analysis came seven and a half years before Japan's sneak attack on Pearl Harbor.

1964: General William Westmoreland was given command of U.S. Military Assistance Command Vietnam (MACV). His initial task was to provide military advice and assistance to the government of South Vietnam. But as U.S. ground troops were introduced, Westmoreland assumed the added responsibility of commanding them in combat. He would serve in that role until July 1968.

★ QUOTE OF THE DAY

"Just hold the phone and I'll let you talk to one of the bastards."

Audie Murphy, on a field telephone at Holtzwihr, France, responding to the question of how close the Germans were

June 21

1860: The Signal Corps was authorized as a separate branch of the Army by an act of Congress.

1864: Union forces, led by Ulysses S. Grant, tightened their control of Petersburg, Virginia. The goal was to sever Confederate supply lines and seize a key railroad which ran south from the city.

1898: In the Spanish-American War, the protected cruiser *Charleston*, who had fired an unanswered challenge on Fort Santa Cruz on June 20, accepted the surrender of Spanish forces on Guam the next day. The Spaniards, who had no gunpowder, had been unaware of the state of war.

1944: "Frantic II," the second mission of Operation Frantic, revealed the inadequacies of the U.S./Soviet cooperation. The German Luftwaffe discovered the mission and in the early hours of June 22, attacked the American B-17s at Poltava, Ukraine, destroying or damaging 69 and also destroying fuel needed for the missions. Russian military authorities wouldn't authorize U.S. counterattacks.

★ QUOTE OF THE DAY

"Having received the surrender of the Island of Guam, I took formal possession at 2.45 p.m., hoisting the American flag on Fort Santa Cruz and saluting it with 21 guns from the *Charleston*.

From a personal examination of Fort Santa Cruz, I decided that it was entirely useless as a defensive work, with no guns and in a partly ruinous condition, and that it was not necessary to expend any mines in blowing it up."

Captain Henry Glass, commander of the *Charleston,*
to Secretary of the Navy John D. Long, *"At Sea,"* June 24, 1898

June 22

1807: The *Chesapeake–Leopard* Affair: in a surprise attack, British warship *Leopard* fired upon and captured American frigate *Chesapeake*—claiming to be looking for Royal Navy deserters. The U.S. was outraged at the surrender—*Chesapeake* commander James Barron was convicted in an 1808 court martial of being unprepared—and the incident was one of the causes of the War of 1812. Barron later killed Stephen Decatur in a duel, angry at Decatur's part in the court martial.

1944: President Franklin D. Roosevelt signed the GI Bill. The bill gave returning WWII service members low-interest home and business loans and college tuition. Giving veterans tuition assistance (plus living expenses, books, supplies, and equipment) transformed America. Before the war, only 10 to 15 percent of young Americans went to college; by 1947, veterans made up half of the nation's college enrollment, and by 1950 nearly 500,000 Americans had earned diplomas, compared with 160,000 in 1939.

1945: The invasion of Okinawa ended. This final, major battle of the Pacific War came at a grievous price: the United States had suffered more than 49,000 casualties, with an estimated 12,520 killed. Japanese losses were even greater—about 110,000 Japanese soldiers were also killed (or took their lives), while an estimated 40,000 to 150,000 Okinawa citizens were also killed.

1963: Launches of the nuclear-powered submarines *Tecumseh* (SSBN-628), *Daniel Boone* (SSBN-629), *Flasher* (SSN-613), and *John Calhoun* (SSBN-630).

2011: President Barack Obama announced the first U.S. troop withdrawals from Afghanistan and pledged a pullout by the end of 2014. After peaking at about 100,000 troops from 2010 to 2011, troop levels declined to 16,000 by December 2014. He later said in 2016 that conditions were too fragile to leave and that 8,400 troops would remain through the end of his second term on January 20, 2017.

★ QUOTE OF THE DAY

"[This bill] gives emphatic notice to the men and women in our armed forces that the American people do not intend to let them down."

Franklin D. Roosevelt, on the G.I. Bill

June 23

1812: The first shots of the War of 1812 were fired. Commodore John Rodgers led a squadron on board *President* off New York City that fired on H.M.S. *Belvidera*—whose captain was unaware that war had been declared. The *Belvidera* eluded capture.

1939: The Coast Guard Auxiliary was created.

2010: President Barack Obama relieved his top commander in Afghanistan—General Stanley McChrystal—when his comments critical of Obama administration members came to light in an article about to be published in *Rolling Stone* magazine. McChrystal had been in command when al Qaeda terrorist Abu Musab al-Zarqawi was killed in 2006.

2014: Congress designated the month of June "National Post-Traumatic Stress Disorder Awareness Month." In 2010, it had previously designated June 27 PTSD Awareness Day (S. Res. 455). Post-traumatic stress disorder (PTSD) is a mental health problem that can occur after someone goes through a traumatic event like war, assault, an accident, or a disaster.

★ QUOTE OF THE DAY

"Since October 2001, more than 310,000 of the approximately 1,000,000 veterans of Operation Enduring Freedom, Operation Iraqi Freedom, and Operation New Dawn who have received health care from the Department of Veterans Affairs have been diagnosed with PTSD."

From S.Res.481: A resolution designating the month of June 2014 as "National Post-Traumatic Stress Disorder Awareness Month," 113th Congress

June 24

1948: The Cold War in full swing: The Soviet Union blocked access to West Berlin, Germany. Western allies responded with Operation Vittles (the Berlin Airlift) on June 26.

1950: President Harry Truman was informed by Secretary of State Dean Acheson that North Korea had invaded South Korea (it was June 25 in Korea itself). Five days later, the president ordered U.S. forces to respond. America, he said, would contain communism.

★ QUOTE OF THE DAY

"I'm writing in a hurry: I see death coming up the hill."

U.S. soldier during the Battle of Hamburger Hill

June 25

General George Armstrong Custer, 1865. Civil War photographs, 1861-1865, Library of Congress, Prints and Photographs Division.

This Day in U.S. Military History

1845: President James Polk ordered General Zachary Taylor to move his troops to the Mexican border in Texas to discourage a Mexican invasion. Taylor's troops would soon invade Mexico itself, during the Mexican-American war.

1876: The Battle of Little Bighorn. Army Lieutenant Colonel George Armstrong Custer, leading a force of 210 men, attacked an encampment of 2,000 Sioux Indians led by chiefs Sitting Bull and Crazy Horse near Little Bighorn River, Montana. Custer and all men in his immediate command were killed in the two-hour battle.

1886: Henry H. "Hap" Arnold was born in Gladwyne, Pennsylvania. He went on to become a five-star general during World War II. In 1944 he became one of just five men to receive the title of General of the Army. He also became a five-star Air Force general, the only person in American history to hold five-star rank in two branches of the U.S. military.

1942: With at least 400 senior officers to consider, General George C. Marshall chose Major General Dwight D. Eisenhower to lead U.S. forces in Europe—despite the fact that Eisenhower had never been in combat in his 27-year career.

2019: David Bellavia became the only living Iraq War veteran to receive the Medal of Honor. Bellavia, an Army staff sergeant in 2004, was fighting in Operation Phantom Fury, commonly known as the Second Battle of Fallujah, which included scores of close-quarters gun battles in house-to-house fighting. A review previously awarded Army Staff Sgt. Travis Atkins a posthumous Medal of Honor for his service in Iraq.

★ QUOTE OF THE DAY

"There are only so many Knute Rockne pep talks you can give when you're stacked eight to a man in a Bradley."

Staff Sergeant David Bellavia, Medal of Honor recipient, on the eve of the Second Battle of Fallujah, in *Eyewitness to War, Volume II*

June 26

1948: Operation Vittles—better known as the Berlin Airlift—began. It was ordered by President Harry Truman to deliver supplies to West Berlin after access to the city was blocked by the Soviets. The Berlin Airlift was seen as an early test of Cold War wills between the United States and Soviet Union.

1962: The Sound Surveillance System (SOSUS) was a program instigated by the Cold War in 1949-50 where sophisticated underwater microphone posts were positioned to detect Soviet submarines. On this day, SOSUS succeeded for the first time in picking up the sounds of a Soviet diesel submarine. The U.S. Naval Facility at Cape Hatteras, North Carolina, was doing the monitoring.

1993: President Bill Clinton ordered an attack on Baghdad. The president ordered the navy to hit Iraqi intelligence headquarters in the Iraqi capital—after learning that Iraq had plotted to kill former President George H.W. Bush during his April 1993 visit to Kuwait.

★ QUOTE OF THE DAY

"There aren't enough [Chinese] in the world to stop a Marine regiment going where it wants to go!"

Colonel Lewis B. "Chesty" Puller, in Korea—born June 26, 1898, Puller is the most decorated Marine

June 27

1861: The first naval officer was killed in the Civil War. While commanding a gunboat flotilla, flagship *Thomas Freeborn* commander James Harmon Ward was mortally wounded by a musket ball off Mathias Point, Virginia.

1917: The first troops of the American Expeditionary Forces (AEF) arrived in Saint-Nazaire, France, after a two-week voyage from New York City.

1950: Harry Truman ordered the Air Force and Navy to help defend South Korea after the June 25 North Korean invasion. U.S. ground forces would soon get into the Korean fight as well (see June 30). By the time a truce was signed in 1953, 36,516 Americans would be killed. The Korean War— "the forgotten war"—officially has not ended, and a state of war still exists today.

1969: *Life* magazine featured the 242 Americans who had died in Vietnam the week of May 28 to June 3, 1969, raising antiwar sentiment with the general public.

"This is plainly a serious matter—a large-scale attack."

Dean Rusk, Assistant Secretary of State,
on the North Korean invasion

June 28

1862: The siege of Vicksburg began in earnest, when Union admiral David Farragut took his ships past the Mississippi River stronghold on this date. The siege of the Confederate city continued for over a year (see July 4).

1918: The Chemical Warfare Service was established, combining activities that until then had been dispersed among five separate agencies of government. It was made a permanent branch of the Regular Army by the National Defense Act of 1920. In 1945, it was redesignated the Chemical Corps.

1919: The Versailles Peace Treaty was signed, formally ending World War I.

1941: In Executive Order 8807, President Franklin D. Roosevelt established the Office of Scientific Research and Development. The department's remit was to serve as a central organizing unit for all current and future scientific research conducted for military purposes. Its secret S-1 Section evolved into the Manhattan Project, which built the first atomic bomb.

★ QUOTE OF THE DAY

"[To] initiate and support scientific research on the mechanisms and devices of warfare with the objective of creating, developing, and improving instrumentalities, methods, and materials required for national defense."

Office of Scientific Research and Development, purpose

June 29

1945: President Harry S. Truman approved a plan to invade Japan: November 1 (Operation Olympic) and March 1, 1946 (Operation Coronet). Britain would deploy long range bombers in support of the invasions. The successful test of the atomic bomb (see July 16) and predictions that an invasion of Japan would cause up to one million American casualties—and infinitely more Japanese casualties—would convince Truman to use atomic weapons instead.

1966: U.S. aircraft bombed the two biggest cities in North Vietnam—Hanoi and Haiphong—for the first time, destroying oil depots located near both.

★ QUOTE OF THE DAY

"Strategic air attack is wasted if it is dissipated piecemeal in sporadic attacks between which enemy has an opportunity to readjust defenses or recuperate."

General Henry H. "Hap" Arnold

June 30

1812: President James Madison issued an urgent declaration for new military officers. In 1812, the U.S. Army and Navy was an all-volunteer force (as it is today) and was considered weaker in both numbers and weaponry than Britain and deficient in military officers capable of leadership. Madison urged Congress to increase emergency commissions of military officers, adjutants, quartermasters, inspectors, paymasters, and engineers.

1815: Unaware that the Treaty of Ghent had been signed six months before, the U.S. sloop-of-war *Peacock* under Lewis Warrington on this day captured British brig *Nautilus* in the Indian Ocean, making it the last action of the War of 1812.

1950: Three days after the United Nations Security Council voted to provide military assistance to South Korea, President Harry S. Truman authorized air operations and a naval blockade on this day, as well as ordering ground troops to Korea. The 3rd Bombardment Group flew the first air mission north of the 38th Parallel against Heijo Airfield, Pyongyang.

★ QUOTE OF THE DAY

"We gallop toward the enemy, and trot away, always."

General J.E.B. Stuart, Confederate cavalry commander

Three Confederate prisoners at Gettysburg. Civil War photographs, 1861-1865, Library of Congress, Prints and Photographs Division.

Teddy Roosevelt and the Rough Riders on San Juan Hill. Library of Congress.

July

July 1

1850: The Naval School at Annapolis, Maryland, was renamed the U.S. Naval Academy. Commander Cornelius K. Stribling was named its first Superintendent.

1863: One of the pivotal battles of the Civil War—Gettysburg—began. The Battle of Gettysburg lasted three days and produced the greatest number of casualties of the entire Civil War: 46,286 dead, wounded, or missing. The Union victory halted Confederate general Robert E. Lee's invasion of the North; for the remainder of the war he would largely be on the defensive.

1898: One of the most famous battles of the Spanish-American War was a victory for the United States. The Battle of San Juan Hill took place near Santiago de Cuba—the site was actually two hills: San Juan and Kettle. Nearly 8,500 U.S. infantry and cavalry charged a startlingly inferior number of Spanish. Theodore Roosevelt's "Rough Riders" (the 1st Volunteer Cavalry) gained fame for their charge—supported by hand-cranked Gatling guns. The Buffalo Soldiers (10th Cavalry, 24th and 25th infantry regiments) also fought in the battle. Roosevelt received the Medal of Honor posthumously in 2001 for his leadership.

1911: Aviation pioneer and designer Glenn Curtiss sold the U.S. Navy its first aircraft, an A-1 Triad—also the first amphibious airplane. Curtiss trained pilots for the Navy. For his contributions, Curtiss is often called the "father of naval aviation."

1942: Marine Attack Squadron 214 (VMF-214) was commissioned at Ewa, Oahu, Hawaii. In August 1943, the squadron regrouped under Major Gregory "Pappy" Boyington—and gained fame as the "Black Sheep."

1962: The Army created an Intelligence and Security Branch. Five years later to the day it was redesignated as Military Intelligence.

1971: Samuel Lee Gravely Jr. became the first African-American rear admiral. Previously, he had been the first African-American to command a warship (1962, the destroyer *Falgout*).

★ QUOTE OF THE DAY

"After the battle of San Juan my men had really become veterans; they and I understood each other perfectly, and trusted each other implicitly; they knew I would share every hardship and danger with them, would do everything in my power to see that they were fed, and so far as might be, sheltered and spared; and in return I knew that they would endure every kind of hardship and fatigue without a murmur and face every danger with entire fearlessness."

Theodore Roosevelt, *The Rough Riders* (1899)

July 2

1863: The Battle of Gettysburg continued, with Robert E. Lee's forces attacking the left and right flanks of George Meade's Army of the Potomac.

1926: The Distinguished Flying Cross was established by Congress. Richard E. Byrd was the first naval aviator to receive the Distinguished Flying Cross for his flight to the North Pole (see May 9).

1945: In the first successful use of rockets against shore positions, *Barb* (SS-220) bombarded Japanese installations on Kaihyo Island, Japan.

★ QUOTE OF THE DAY

"Come on, you Wolverines!"

George Armstrong Custer, rallying cry to the Michigan Brigade at Gettysburg

July 3

1815: Second Barbary War: Commodore Stephen Decatur secured a treaty to end piracy against American merchant vessels. Signed aboard Decatur's flagship, *Guerriere*, the pact with His Highness Omar Agha in the Bay of Algiers came after Decatur sailed to the Mediterranean with a squadron of nine ships.

1863: Pickett's Charge: the Battle of Gettysburg ended in a Union victory. On the third day, Major General George Pickett of the Confederacy led a disastrous infantry charge at the core of Union forces on Cemetery Ridge. When the smoke cleared, Southern forces had suffered a 50 percent casualty rate.

1894: Grover Cleveland ordered federal troops to Chicago, Illinois, to put down a strike by employees of the Pullman Car Company. Eugene Debs, president of the American Railway Union, organized the strike on May 11 after George Pullman lowered worker wages during the depression of 1893. General Nelson Miles commanded 12,000 U.S. Army troops to get the railways (and mail) moving. Violence later broke out on July 7, resulting in 30 striker deaths.

1898: U.S. warships destroyed the Spanish fleet (the *Flota de Ultramar*) off Santiago, Cuba. Commanded by Admiral William Sampson, the battle was a major victory for the United States in the brief Spanish-American war.

1988: An Iranian civilian airliner was mistakenly shot down in the Persian Gulf, after the *Vincennes* fired two surface-to-air missiles. Iran Air flight 655 was destroyed and all 290 people on board perished. *Vincennes* crew reportedly misread radio signals of the plane, mistaking it for a hostile aircraft. A Pentagon review blamed human failure for the disaster.

⭐ QUOTE OF THE DAY

"Don't cheer, boys. The poor devils are dying."

Captain J. W. Philip, commander of *Texas,* at the Battle of Santiago

July 4

1776: The Declaration of Independence was approved by the Continental Congress—the official birthday of the United States of America.

1801: Thomas Jefferson held the first presidential review of the U.S. Marine Band at the White House. He gave the band its nickname: "The President's Own."

1863: Confederate troops surrendered Vicksburg, Mississippi, following a long bombardment and siege by Union naval and land forces. The Union now had control of the Mississippi River and had cut the Confederacy in two.

1917: The American Expeditionary Forces arrived at Paris, France. General John J. Pershing went to the Marquis de Lafayette's grave at Picpus Cemetery. An aide, Lt. Col. Charles E. Stanton, make an address to the assembled crowd as they placed an American flag on Lafayette's grave. Traditionally, every July 4, a new flag is placed on the grave in acknowledgement of the French noble's support of the new nation.

★ QUOTE OF THE DAY

"Lafayette, nous ici!" ("Lafayette, we are here!")

Lt. Col. Charles E. Stanton, July 4, 1917, at the grave of
the Marquis de Lafayette

July 5

1801: David Glasgow Farragut was born at Campbell's Station, Tennessee, near Knoxville. Known for the rousing command, "Damn the torpedoes, full speed ahead!," during the Battle of Mobile Bay in 1864 (see August 5), he was appointed vice admiral by President Abraham Lincoln in 1864 and was the first-ever commissioned admiral in the Navy. Remarkably, his

David Farragut. Library of Congress.

This Day in U.S. Military History

naval career began at the age of seven, when he was commissioned a midshipman. At age 12, he saw action in the War of 1812, and was wounded at age 13. In 60 years of service, he also fought in the Mexican-American War. He died August 14, 1870, at Portsmouth, New Hampshire. His Tennessee hometown renamed itself Farragut in his honor.

1859: The Midway Atoll, near the Hawaiian Islands in the Pacific Ocean, was sighted by Captain N.C. Middlebrooks, who claimed them for the United States by virtue of the Guano Islands Act of 1856. First named "Middlebrook Islands" after their discoverer, they would soon become one of the first offshore islands annexed by the U.S. government (see August 28).

☆ QUOTE OF THE DAY

"[I must] stick with the flag."

David Farragut, after Virginia's secession

July 6

John Paul Jones.

1747: John Paul Jones was born John Paul on the Arbigland Estate, where his father was a gardener, near Dumfries, Scotland. He added "Jones" to his name after committing manslaughter in the West Indies and fleeing to Virginia. The "dandy skipper" joined the Continental Navy in 1775, and his exploits in the American Revolution made him famous. He is best known for his cry, "I have not yet begun to fight!" during the battle between the Continental frigate *Bonhomme Richard* and HMS *Serapis* in 1779 (see September 23). He died at age 45 in France. In 1905, in a search initiated by Theodore Roosevelt, his remains were found in Paris, and shipped to the United States, where they were reinterred in 1913 at the Naval Academy Chapel in Annapolis.

1953: The Second Battle of Pork Chop Hill began. Previously, on April 18, 1953, the Chinese had withdrawn from the hill near Yeoncheon, Korea. On July 11, the U.S. forces withdrew.

1990: The A-4 Skyhawk was retired. One of the oldest and most versatile attack aircraft in Marine Corps history, the A-4 served the USMC for over 30 years.

★ QUOTE OF THE DAY

"I wish to have no connection with any ship that does not sail fast; for I intend to go in harm's way."

John Paul Jones

July 7

1798: John Adams named 65-year-old George Washington commander in chief (again) of the U.S. Army. A possible war with France loomed, and, ever the patriot, Washington—who had retired a year earlier after two terms as president—accepted.

1846: The Pacific Squadron under Commodore John D. Sloat arrived and occupied Monterey, California, claiming the city for the United States.

1941: The 1st Marine Aircraft Wing was activated at Quantico, Virginia. Within a year, it would participate in the U.S. offensive at Guadalcanal. The 1st MAW would earn five Presidential Unit Citations for gallantry in campaigns spanning World War II, Korea, and Vietnam.

1948: Chief Yeoman Wilma J. Marchal, Yeoman Second Class Edna E. Young, Hospital Corpsman First Class Ruth Flora, Aviation Storekeeper First Class Kay L. Langen, Storekeeper Second Class Frances T. Devaney, and Teleman Doris R. Robertson became the first six enlisted women in the U.S. Navy.

★ QUOTE OF THE DAY

"Feeling how incumbent it is upon every person, of every description, to contribute at all times to his Countrys [sic] welfare, and especially in a moment like the present, when everything we hold dear & Sacred is so seriously threatened, I have finally determined to accept the Commission of Commander in Chief of the Armies of the United States, with the reserve only, that I shall not be called into the field until the Army is in a Situation to require my presence, or it becomes indispensible (sic) by the urgency of circumstances."

George Washington, in a letter to John Adams accepting
Adams' commission

July 8

1853: On his flagship *Susquehanna*, Commodore Matthew Perry entered Edo Bay, Japan, accompanied by four ships. He was on a mission from President Millard Fillmore to open trade with Japan—by force if necessary. Perry refused to go to the only port open to foreigners and fired some volleys to underline his intent. By July 14, Japanese officials agreed to accept a letter from President Fillmore. Perry left after the letter's delivery, vowing to return in February 1854 to receive its reply. Through Perry's action, America became the first Western nation to establish relations with Japan in two centuries.

1950: President Harry Truman named General Douglas MacArthur commander for U.N. forces in Korea under direction of a U.N. resolution (Security Council Resolution 84, July 7).

1959: The first Americans were killed in action in Vietnam. Major Dale R. Buis and Master Sergeant Charles Ovnand were killed by Viet Cong guerrillas, who rushed into their compound in Bien Hoa. Buis and Ovnand were with their troops in a mess hall watching a movie when they were attacked.

☆ QUOTE OF THE DAY

"I regretted that I had not time, and what was still more valuable any coal to spare, to remain longer and to explore further these interesting islands. They will deserve more complete examination, and I hope that the government of the United States will ere long send suitable vessels for such purpose."

Commodore Matthew Perry, journal entry on leaving Japan

July 9

1846: U.S. forces raised the American flag over Yerba Buena—today known as San Francisco—during the Mexican-American War. The troops were led by Cmdr. John B. Montgomery and his detachment of Marines and sailors from the sloop-of-war *Portsmouth.*

1850: Zachary Taylor, "Old Rough and Ready," twelfth U.S. president and hero of the Mexican-American War who served 40 years in the military, died at Washington, D.C.

1943: Operation Husky—the Allied invasion of Sicily, Italy, began under the command of General Dwight D. Eisenhower. Some 1,200 transports and 2,000 landing craft helped land elements of eight divisions, while airborne landings by the 82nd Airborne Division and British units helped disrupt Axis defenses. The operation was engaged through August 17.

Troops soon went ashore, including airborne units, in the first large-scale airborne operation attempted by the allies in World War II.

1968: The battle of Khe Sanh ended in Vietnam. The North Vietnamese claim of victory was dismissed by the United States, which said American forces had withdrawn, because their base was no longer needed. Some historians think the Battle of Khe Sanh may have distracted American and South Vietnamese attention from the buildup of Viet Cong troops in the South ahead of the Tet Offensive (see January 30).

⭐ QUOTE OF THE DAY

"The first page in the liberation of the European Continent."

Allied commander Dwight Eisenhower on the Invasion of Sicily

July 10

1863: The First Battle of Fort Wagner, Morris Island, Charleston, South Carolina, began. U.S. forces were repulsed. See July 18.

1950: Tank warfare entered the Korean War on this day in clashes between the United States and North Korea near Chonui. Near Pyongtaek, the Air Force achieved its greatest single-day destruction of enemy tanks and trucks during the conflict.

1951: The United Nations and North Koreans began truce talks, but the Korean War continued for two more years.

⭐ QUOTE OF THE DAY

"If resistance is broken and the line pierced the tank must and will assume the role of pursuit cavalry and 'ride the enemy to death.'"

George Patton, *Light Tanks* (1917)

July 11

1798: President John Adams signed the act "Establishing and Organizing a Marine Corps" that re-established the Marine Corps. The Continental Congress had disbanded the service in April 1783 at the end of the American Revolution. The Marine Corps, however, recognizes its "official" birthday to be the date that the Second Continental Congress first authorized the establishment of the "Corps of Marines" on November 10, 1775.

1861: Union forces scored a victory in the struggle for western Virginia, at the Battle of Rich Mountain. Their commander was General George McClellan.

1869: Tall Bull, a prominent leader of the Cheyenne Dog Soldier warrior society, was killed during the Battle of Summit Springs in Colorado. Tall Bull was the most distinguished of several Cheyenne warriors who became fierce foes of the U.S. government in the bloody Plains Indian Wars.

1953: Major John F. Bolt became the first jet ace in Marine Corps history. In Korea, he flew an F-86 Super Sabre on temporary duty with the USAF's 51st Fighter Interceptor Wing. Serving in the South Pacific during World War II, Bolt also had six confirmed kills and one probable kill.

⭐ QUOTE OF THE DAY

"The President today, as Commander-in-Chief of the Armed Forces, appointed William J. Donovan Coordinator of Information."

White House announcement, July 11, 1941

July 12

1862: President Abraham Lincoln signed a bill creating the Medal of Honor. It is the highest military decoration awarded by the U.S. government, given to those who have distinguished themselves in actual combat at risk of life beyond the call of duty. The Medal of Honor had a predecessor, the Badge of Military Merit, which had been created by President George Washington in 1792 (see August 7).

1916: The AB-3 flying boat, piloted by Lt. Godfrey de Chevalier, was catapulted from *North Carolina* (ACR 12) while underway in Pensacola Bay, Fla. The launch completed calibration of the first catapult designed for shipboard use.

1990: The first woman to command an operational aviation squadron was named today: Cmdr. Rosemary B. Mariner. It was the Tactical Electronic Warfare Squadron 34 (VAW-34), which she led during Operation Desert Storm. Mariner achieved other several firsts in her career: first woman to qualify as a naval aviator in 1974 and one of the first women to fly light attack aircraft. By the time she retired as captain in 1997, she had flown 15 different types of aircraft.

★ QUOTE OF THE DAY

"In modern warfare, the emphasis is not on physical strength, but on brain power operating sophisticated weapons systems. A machine gun is a great equalizer."

Rosemary B. Mariner, 1982

July 13

1861: The first general to die in the Civil War was Robert S. Garnett of the Confederacy on this day during the Battle of Corrick's Ford in western Virginia. The Union, with 20,000 troops under General George B. McClellan, were victorious and western Virginia remained in federal control until the end of the war.

1921: Brig Gen William "Billy" Mitchell's Martin MB-2 and Handley Page bombers sank several ships off the Virginia Capes. The tests were part of Project B, begun in May, which aimed to study how ship design could counter an air attack.

1950: The first strategic bombing strike on North Korea was conducted, when dozens of B-29s blasted oil refineries and marshaling yards at the port of Wonsan.

★ QUOTE OF THE DAY

"How much I miss the good coffee I use to get at home. I would cheerfully pay one dollar for as much like it as I could drink. . . . We got some ground coffee from the Yanks in the Seven Days fight. . ."

Texas Confederate soldier, July 1862, quoted in *Journey to Pleasant Hill: The Civil War Letters of Captain Elijah P. Petty, Walker's Texas Division, CSA* (1982), edited by Norman D. Brown

July 14

1813: Lt. John M. Gamble, the first U.S. Marine to command a U.S. Navy ship, made a valuable capture during the War of 1812. On the *Greenwich*, he captured the formidable British whaling ship *Seringapatam,* a victory made sweeter by the fact that the larger *Seringapatam* had more crew and more guns.

1952: The keel was laid down to the U.S. Navy's first supercarrier—*Forrestal* (CVA 59)—at Newport News, Virginia. The carrier was named for James Forrestal (1896-1949), the first secretary of defense (1947-49).

2001: A prototype Minuteman ICBM interceptor hit and destroyed an unarmed Minuteman II ICBM over the central Pacific. The interceptor was traveling some 15,000 mph at more than 140 miles in altitude.

★ QUOTE OF THE DAY

"To you, my dear sir, much credit, and even applause, were given for the capture of an enemy's ship so notorious as was the *Seringapatam.*"

Part of a eulogy for John M. Gamble

July 15

1942: The first ship specifically designed to lay mines—*Terror* (CM-5)—was commissioned. *Terror* gave valuable support for Operation Torch in North Africa at Casablanca. The minelayer was also involved at Iwo Jima and Okinawa. A kamikaze attack on May 1, 1945, took 41 lives and injured 123.

★ QUOTE OF THE DAY

"Duties were routine, like calling 155mm artillery when Charley hit a South Vietnamese outpost, and he always did. But the American TOC [tactical operations center] officer didn't call the fire directly, a Vietnamese had to radio the final artillery request and coordinates. After all, we were *advisers.*"

Thomas R. Hargrove, recalling the summer of 1969 in Vietnam in his memoir *A Dragon Lives Forever* (1994)

July 16

1862: David G. Farragut was named the first rear admiral, a rank that Congress established on this day.

1945: Trinity: in the southern New Mexican desert, at 5:30 a.m., the United States detonated the first nuclear bomb, the culmination of the massive Manhattan Project. "The Gadget" sat atop a 100-foot tower for the detonation, the timing of which was meant to occur as the Potsdam Conference was beginning. The energy released was the equivalent of 21 kilotons of TNT. Ground zero was equidistant between Albuquerque and El Paso, Texas. President Harry S. Truman would soon order bombs dropped on the Japanese cities of Hiroshima, Japan (see August 6) and Nagasaki (see August 9), hastening the surrender of Japan and the end of World War II.

1957: Project Bullet: the first supersonic transcontinental flight was made by Marine pilot Major John Glenn. Flying an F8U Crusader, he flew 2,445 miles from Los Alamitos, California, to Floyd Bennett Field, New York City, in three hours, 23 minutes. Operation Bullet earned Glenn a Distinguished Flying Cross (his fifth to that time).

1971: Jeanne Holm became the first female Air Force general. For ten years—1965 to 1975—she was the highest ranking woman in the Air Force, and is credited with helping to increase opportunities for women across the U.S. military.

★ QUOTE OF THE DAY

"Now I am become Death, the destroyer of worlds…"

J. Robert Oppenheimer, responsible for the research and design of an atomic bomb, quoting Hindu scripture after the bomb's first test

July 17

1862: Military pensions were established for wounded service members, when Congress passed a law saying that "every officer, seaman, or marine, disabled in the line of duty, shall be intitled [sic] to receive for life, or during his disability, a pension from the United States." Gradations were set according to the nature and degree of disability and monthly pay.

1898: The United States began occupation of Cuba, which achieved independence in 1902.

1945: The Potsdam Conference began in the Berlin suburb of Potsdam in Germany, attended by President Harry Truman, Prime Minister Winston Churchill, Premier Joseph Stalin of the U.S.S.R. Discussions included postwar management of Germany and the final stage of the war against Japan. It was also decided that U.S. and Soviet troops would occupy the southern and northern halves of Korea.

1989: The first test flight of the B-2 stealth bomber occurred near Palmdale, California. Designed to fly undetected by enemy radar, the B-2 was said to be capable of delivering a 25-ton payload.

★ QUOTE OF THE DAY

"At noon to-day, after a salute of 21 guns, & amidst the hurrahs of our troops, 'Old Glory' was raised over Santiago de Cuba, & the Spaniards stacked their arms."

Private Roger Fitch, Rough Rider, in his journal, July 17, 1898

July 18

1863: The Second Battle of Fort Wagner: three Union brigades, including the 54th Massachusetts Infantry Regiment of African-American soldiers commanded by Robert Gould Shaw, again attempted to take the fort and gain control of Charleston Harbor. Confederate defenders commanded by General William Taliaferro again repulsed the charge with more than 1,500 Union casualties. Shaw died and Frederick Douglass's son, Lewis, was injured.

1945: At the Potsdam Conference, Harry Truman was notified about and in turn informed Joseph Stalin of the Trinity atomic bomb test.

★ QUOTE OF THE DAY

"Boys, the old flag never touched the ground."

William Carney of the 54th, who received the Medal of Honor for heroic actions at the Second Battle of Fort Wagner, including protecting the colors

July 19

1911: Orville Wright delivered the first Wright airplane, a Wright B, to the Navy at Annapolis. It was soon converted to a seaplane by adding twin floats.

1941: The first class of "Tuskegee Airmen" began training under Benjamin O. Davis, Jr. Tuskegee, Alabama, was the focal point for the training of African-American military fighter and bomber pilots during World War II. The Tuskegee Institute had gotten a contract from the military and provided primary flight training while the army built a separate, segregated base. Despite their heroism and service to country, the Tuskegee Airmen were subjected to racial discrimination, both within and outside the army.

1943: As the Potsdam Conference continued, the United States bombed Rome, Italy, with approximately 800 tons of bombs dropped by 521 B-17s and B-24s. Bombing the city was controversial, and despite targeting the rail yards, an estimated 3,000 civilians died.

1958: The Atlas B, a prototype of the Atlas intercontinental ballistic missile (ICBM), made its first flight.

✯ QUOTE OF THE DAY

"If you're at the top, you don't have to plead the way you do you're at the bottom. You can exert hell of a lot more pressure from the top . . ."

General Daniel "Chappie" James, Sr, first African-American four-star general, flight instructor at Tuskegee

July 20

1942: Adm. William D. Leahy became Chief of Staff to the Commander in Chief of the Army and the Navy. Today such a position would be akin to the Chairman of the Joint Chiefs of Staff. Leahy had served as U.S. ambassador to (Vichy) France.

1960: The first launch of a Polaris missile took place when the submarine *George Washington* fired two missiles while submerged off Florida. President Dwight Eisenhower received this message from the submarine's command: "POLARIS - FROM OUT OF THE DEEP TO TARGET. PERFECT."

1969: The United States landed on the moon and two astronauts—former Navy pilot Neil Armstrong and Army pilot Edwin "Buzz" Aldrin—walked on the lunar surface. Command module pilot Michael Collins, meanwhile, would establish a record of 59 hours 27 minutes 55 seconds in lunar orbit.

★ QUOTE OF THE DAY

"That's one small step for [a] man, one giant leap for mankind."

Neil Armstrong

July 21

1861: Union forces were routed in the First Battle of Bull Run. The battle, near Manassas, Virginia, pit Union general Irvin McDowell against Confederate generals P.G.T. Beauregard, Joseph E. Johnston, and Thomas J. "Stonewall" Jackson. The defeat left Washington, D.C., threatened—and uncertainty as to how to halt Confederate forces.

1921: In the culmination of Project B, a series of tests in the summer of 1921 to demonstrate the capabilities of air power, the First Provisional Air Brigade dropped six 2,000-pound bombs on the captured German battleship *Ostfriesland*, sinking it in 20 minutes. General Billy Mitchell had predicted the outcome in an effort to establish a separate air force, and was triumphant at this expression of power.

1944: U.S. forces landed on Guam. The invasion force consisted of the Third Marine Division and the 1st Provisional Marine Brigade, along with the Army's 77th Infantry Division. The island was declared secure on August 9.

1946: The first jet takeoff and landing on an aircraft carrier occurred when Navy Lt. Commander James Davidson flew a McDonnell XFH-1 Phantom off the *Franklin D. Roosevelt.*

★ QUOTE OF THE DAY

"[There are] no conditions in which seacraft can operate efficiently in which aircraft cannot operate efficiently."

General Billy Mitchell, after the sinking of the *Ostfriesland*

This Day in U.S. Military History

July 22

1802: During the First Barbary War, the *Constellation* defeated nine enemy gunboats off Tripoli, sinking two. The ship was commanded by Capt. Alexander Murray.

1864: The Battle of Atlanta: William T. Sherman's Union forces defeated the South's forces of John Hood near Atlanta, Georgia, with heavy casualties: 3,600 for the North and 5,500 for the South—of those 5,500, 1,000 were killed. Union general James B. McPherson was killed.

1943: Allied forces took Palermo, less than two weeks after their invasion of Sicily. Less than a month later the entire island was under Allied control.

☆ QUOTE OF THE DAY

"And when you see General Patton . . . you get the same feeling as when you saw Babe Ruth striding up to the plate. Here's a big guy who's going to kick hell out of something."

Navy lieutenant, watching George S. Patton in Normandy, July 1944, quoted in *Collier*'s magazine

July 23

1846: Commodore Robert Stockton took over the Pacific Squadron from Commodore Sloat at Monterey, California, and continued the successful California Campaign of the Mexican-American War.

1862: General Henry W. Halleck became general-in-chief of all Union forces. The West Point graduate was tasked with better coordinating the overall Union war effort, which President Abraham Lincoln felt was in disarray. In 1864, Lincoln appointed Halleck chief of staff for the army, ostensibly a promotion, while appointing General Ulysses S. Grant general-in-chief—this reorganization was seen as acknowledging Halleck's inability to coordinate the armies. Despite his shortcomings as a strategic planner, Halleck's organizational skills contributed significantly to the Union victory.

1885: "Unconditional Surrender" Grant, 18th president of the United States and hero of the Civil War, died at Wilton, New York.

1956: The Bell X-2 rocket set a new aircraft speed record, when it flew 1,895 mph. The pilot of the "Starbuster" was Air Force Lt. Colonel Frank K. Everest.

★ QUOTE OF THE DAY

"The Union is his monument."

Newspaper editorial on the death of Ulysses S. Grant

July 24

1943: Allied bombers began Operation Gomorrah, a series of devastating air raids on Hamburg, Germany, getting partial revenge for German attacks on British cities. The Royal Air Force and U.S. Army Air Force used a new tactic—dropping strips of aluminum foil—that confused German radar and thus helped minimize loss of aircraft. American planes bombed by day; British planes bombed at night.

1944: U.S. forces landed on Tinian, one of the Marianas Islands. After heavy fighting, the island was captured by July 29, with periodic skirmishes after. Of 8,000 Japanese troops, more than 5,000 were killed or committed suicide.

1967: Race riots broke out in Detroit, Michigan. The next day, President Lyndon Johnson ordered 4,700 federal troops from the 82nd and 101st airborne divisions to Detroit to work with the Michigan National Guard. By the time the riots ended on July 18, an estimated 43 people were killed and at least 500 were injured. The scale of the rioting was probably surpassed only by the 1863 draft riots that erupted in New York City during the Civil War and by the 1992 "Rodney King riots" in Los Angeles.

★ QUOTE OF THE DAY

"If the RAF continues night bombing and we bomb by day, we shall bomb them round the clock and the devil shall get no rest."

Ira C. Eaker, to Winston Churchill, 1942

July 25

1812: Battle of Niagara Falls: British forces repulsed an American attack in a bloody confrontation on Canadian soil. The United States suffered 1,500 casualties—Winfield Scott was injured.

1866: Ulysses S. Grant was named General of the Army, the first officer to hold the rank.

1898: The U.S. gunboat *Gloucester* arrived at Guánica, Puerto Rico, and secured it, with forces disembarking. By the 28th, the city of Ponce surrendered. By mid-August, the island was in American control.

1980: President Jimmy Carter signed Presidential Directive 59 advocating "limited" nuclear war. The order said that if nuclear deterrence with its enemies failed, the United States "must be capable of fighting successfully so that the adversary would not achieve his war aims and would suffer costs that are unacceptable." The plan called for pre-planned nuclear strike options and capabilities for rapid development of target plans against such key target categories as "military and control targets."

✯ QUOTE OF THE DAY

"[By the end of July 1898], there were less than 50 percent who were fit for any kind of work. All the clothes were in rags; even the officers had neither socks nor underwear."

Theodore Roosevelt, on the fatigue and sickness (malaria) wracking the U.S. troops in Cuba, *The Rough Riders* (1899)

July 26

1947: President Harry Truman signed the National Security Act, a major overhaul of the U.S. national security establishment. It created the National Security Council, Central Intelligence Agency, the Department of Defense (which had been the War Department) and National Security Resources Board.

1945: The *Indianapolis*, in a secret mission, delivered enriched uranium and the components necessary to assemble the atomic bomb to Tinian

Indianapolis at the Mare Island Navy Yard, California, on July 12, 1945. 19-N-86915 courtesy of Naval History & Heritage Command.

Island. The cruiser had left San Francisco with the components on July 16.

1948: President Harry Truman desegregated the military. His Executive Order No. 9981 directed "equality of treatment and opportunity" in the armed forces. There was considerable opposition within the military to the president's order. Army chief of staff Omar Bradley, for example, declared that "the Army is not out to make any social reform."

★ QUOTE OF THE DAY

"It is hereby declared to be the policy of the President that there shall be equality of treatment and opportunity for all persons in the armed services without regard to race, color, religion or national origin. This policy shall be put into effect as rapidly as possible, having due regard to the time required to effectuate any necessary changes without impairing efficiency or morale."

Article 1, Executive Order No. 9981

July 27

1775: The Army Medical Department and the Medical Corps were established, when the Continental Congress established the army hospital headed by a Director General and Chief Physician.

1909: Orville Wright, with Lt Frank P. Lahm riding as a passenger, flew the Army's first airplane for 1 hour 12 minutes 40 seconds to set a two-man endurance record. The flight test fulfilled a requirement for a government contract—an hour-long flight with a passenger.

1953: An armistice was signed at Panmunjom, Korea, ending three years of fighting in the Korean War. General Mark W. Clark signed for the United Nations Command. A peace treaty was not signed, however—just an agreement to stop fighting, thus a state of war still exists. The agreement created a Korean Demilitarized Zone near the 38th parallel. Sandwiched between World War II and Vietnam, the Korean War—"the forgotten war"—killed an estimated 36,516 Americans and wounded another 103,284—in less than three years of fighting.

★ QUOTE OF THE DAY

"Korea's mountainous terrain literally soaks up infantry. We never had enough men, whereas the enemy not only had sufficient manpower to block our offensives, but could make and hold small gains of his own."

General Mark W. Clark, *From the Danube to the Yalu* (1954)

July 28

1866: "Buffalo Soldiers"—all-black army units—were formed by an act of the 39th Congress on this date and signed by President Andrew Johnson. The 9th and 10th cavalry regiments and 24th and 25th infantry regiments comprised the Buffalo Soldiers. The meaning of the nickname "Buffalo Soldier" is disputed, but—whether it comes from the buffalo robes the soldiers wore on winter campaigns or from comparisons to the American bison, which, when wounded or cornered, fought ferociously, displaying uncommon stamina and courage—was accepted with pride by all-black units.

1932: President Herbert Hoover ordered the Army to evict protesting Army veterans from Washington, D.C. Around 20,000 World War I veterans, demanding promised benefits and bonus money, had set up camps in Anacostia Flats while trying to pressure Congress and the president to pay up. General Douglas MacArthur, Major Dwight Eisenhower, and Major George S. Patton, among others carried out Hoover's orders to force them out of the nation's capital. They did so—with tanks, cavalry, fixed bayonets, and tear gas.

1965: Lyndon Johnson ordered 50,000 more U.S. troops to Vietnam, bringing the number to 125,000. But the U.S. buildup was just beginning. It would double, and then double again, peaking at 538,000 in 1968.

1973: Skylab 3 was launched, the second mission to the first U.S. manned space station. The commander of the mission was Navy Capt. Alan L. Bean, the pilot was Marine Major Jack R. Lousma, and Science Pilot was former Navy electronics officer Owen K. Garriott. The mission lasted 59 days, 11 hours and included 858 Earth orbits.

★ QUOTE OF THE DAY

"I went to a jet squadron, and I really loved flying airplanes, and rather than getting out in four years like I was planning to do, I decided I'd make a career out of this."

Jack R. Lousma, Johnson Space Center Oral History
Project, March 7, 2001

July 29

1775: Military chaplains were established by a resolution of the Continental Congress. The Office of the Chief of Chaplains was created by the National Defense Act of 1920.

1846: During the Mexican-American War, U.S. forces took control of San Diego and raised the American flag.

1967: In a devastating series of events on the *Forrestal* (CV-59) carrier in the Gulf of Tonkin, a rocket misfired, catalyzing a fuel fire conflagration. Nine 1,000-pound bombs exploded. Killed were 134 sailors and injured more than 161. In addition, 21 aircraft were destroyed. It was the Navy's worst disaster in a combat zone since World War II.

"I've got 45 years of service in the military, nine in the Navy and 36 in the Army, and I will never forget what happened July 29, 1967."

Emmet O'Hare, retired Army colonel, at the *Forrestal* 50th anniversary memorial service, July 29, 2017

July 30

1863: Abraham Lincoln issued his "eye-for-an-eye" order. Angry that black Union soldiers, when taken prisoner by Confederates, were being treated differently from white POWs, Lincoln ordered that similar treatment be applied to Confederate POWs—including execution.

1942: Franklin D. Roosevelt signed an act establishing WAVES (Women Accepted for Volunteer Emergency Service). More than 80,000 officers and enlisted women served in the WAVES during World War II.

1945: *Indianapolis* was sunk by a Japanese submarine. An estimated 800 of the ship's 1,196 sailors and Marines survived the sinking, but after four to

WAVES recruiting poster, 1942. Library of Congress.

This Day in U.S. Military History

five days floating in the Pacific, exposure to the sun, dehydration, drowning, and shark attacks killed hundreds more. Only 316 men survived. The ship had just delivered the first atomic bomb to a base on the island of Tinian.

⭐ QUOTE OF THE DAY

"You've got to fight to live. But all you've got to do to expire is just give up. Let your head drop in the water. And I saw that so, so many times."

Indianapolis survivor Edgar Harrell, 2019

July 31

1912: The first airplane from a catapult, designed and built by Navy Captain W. Irving Chambers made a successful takeoff from its platform in Annapolis, Maryland, but immediately dove into the water.

1942: Transportation operations were originally within the purview of the Quartermaster General, but on this date, the Transportation Corps was established.

1957: The DEW Line, a distant early warning radar defense installation extending across the Canadian Arctic, became fully operational.

1991: George H.W. Bush and Soviet leader Mikhail Gorbachev agreed to cut nuclear arsenals. The Strategic Arms Reduction Treaty (START I) was the first treaty to provide for deep reductions of both U.S. and Soviet/Russian strategic nuclear weapons. The breakup of the Soviet Union, which occurred later that year, complicated matters, given that it created several new nuclear powers: Russia, Belarus, Ukraine, and Kazakhstan.

⭐ QUOTE OF THE DAY

"Innovation is the bridge between doctrine and war."

Captain William A. Andrews, USAF pilot and decorated veteran of Operation Desert Storm

Wright Flyer in a test flight at Fort Myer, 1909. Probably Orville Wright piloting. Library of Congress.

August

August 1

1864: Union general Philip Sheridan was appointed commander of the newly created Army of the Shenandoah by Ulysses S. Grant. His task was to drive out Confederate general Jubal Early. Sheridan took command on August 7. Over the next few months, Sheridan's force of some 40,000 men would skillfully push Confederate troops out of the Shenandoah Valley and destroy every possible source of their supplies.

1943: Operation Tidal Wave: 177 Army Air Force B-24 Liberators attacked oil refineries around Ploesti, Romania, in order to disrupt or stop fuel supply to the Axis. It was the first large-scale, minimum-altitude attack against a strongly defended target, and the longest major bombing mission from base to target undertaken to date. The mission failed in its objective and the raid was costly: 53 aircraft and 660 crewmen lost—the second-worst loss ever suffered by the USAAF in a single mission.

1944: After a week of heavy fighting, Tinian Island was declared secure. Over the next two months Navy construction teams (SeaBees) built six runways, turning Tinian into the biggest air base in the world. It became a staging area for bombing raids on Japan, including, in 1945, the atomic bombings of Hiroshima and Nagasaki.

1955: The Lockheed U-2, a high-altitude reconnaissance plane, made its first test flight.

★ QUOTE OF THE DAY

"[E]at out Virginia clear and clean as far as they [Early's men] go, so that crows flying over it for the balance of the season will have to carry their provender with them."

Ulysses S. Grant, order to Philip Sheridan

August 2

1909: The Wright Flyer was accepted by the Army as its first aircraft, after tests at Fort Myer, Virginia. Purchased by the Signal Corps for $30,000, the Flyer was renamed Signal Corps Airplane No. 1.

1943: Japanese destroyer *Amagiri* collided with and crushed US torpedo boat *PT-109* among the Solomon Islands. In command of *PT-109* was 26-year-old Lieutenant John F. Kennedy. Assumed dead by the Navy, the 11 survivors swam to the nearest island—3.5 miles away. Kennedy towed an injured crewmate by biting into the strap of a life jacket for the four hours. The men of *PT-109* survived for six days before Solomon Island scouts found them.

1945: Survivors of the *Indianapolis* sinking were spotted by a U.S. air patrol and later rescued. Of the 1,195 on board when the ship was torpedoed, about 800 made it into the water in the 12 minutes before the vessel sank. Shark attacks began with sunrise of the first day and continued until only 316 men were still alive when rescued, almost five days later.

1958: The Atlas-B, a prototype of the Atlas intercontinental ballistic missile (ICBM), made its second test flight and flew 2,500 miles down the Atlantic Missile Range after launching from Cape Canaveral, Florida.

1964: Gulf of Tonkin Incident. The Navy destroyer *Maddox* was allegedly provoked by three North Vietnamese torpedo boats, spurring the Johnson administration to seek the Gulf of Tonkin Resolution against North Vietnam (see August 7).

★ QUOTE OF THE DAY

"I know too much about war to glory in it, but wars are made by politicians who neglect to prepare for it."

William "Wild Bill" Donovan

August 3

1904: The first successful controlled dirigible flight in the U.S. was made over Oakland, California, by Thomas S. Baldwin. The airship, *California Arrow*, was equipped with a Curtiss motorcycle motor. Baldwin would later demo powered dirigibles for the Army, who purchased Signal Corps Dirigible No. 1 in 1908 from him. Baldwin later served in World War I maintaining the U.S. airships.

1950: Eight Corsairs of VMF-214, the famed "Black Sheep" squadron of World War II, executed the first Marine aviation mission in the Korean War. Launching from Sicily, the Corsairs hit enemy installations near Inchon.

1958: The world's first nuclear-powered submarine, *Nautilus* (SSN-571), made the first submerged transit of the North Pole.

★ QUOTE OF THE DAY

"For the world, our country, and the Navy—the North Pole."

Commander William R. Anderson, on the *Nautilus*

August 4

1790: At the instigation of Secretary of the Treasury Alexander Hamilton, Congress created the Revenue-Marine to enforce tariff laws and combat smuggling. Renamed the U.S. Revenue Cutter Service in 1894, it became today's Coast Guard after merging with the U.S. Life-Saving Service. The Coast Guard is the oldest seagoing service in the United States and now operates within the Department of Homeland Security.

★ QUOTE OF THE DAY

"As you are speedily to enter upon the Duties of your Station, it becomes proper briefly to point them out to you. Accordingly I send you a copy of the Act under which you have been appointed & in which are contained your powers, & the objects to which you are to attend & I shall add such observations as appear to me requisite to guide you in fulfilling the intent of that Act.

It may be observed generally that it will be, in a particular manner, the province of the Revenue Cutters to guard the Revenue Laws from all infractions or ⟨br⟩eaches either upon the Coasts or within the Bays, or ⟨up⟩on the Rivers & other Waters of the United States, pre⟨vi⟩ous to the anchoring of Vessels within the *harbours* ⟨for⟩ which they are respectively destined."

Alexander Hamilton, letter to the captains of the Revenue
Cutters, June 4, 1791

August 5

1864: Battle of Mobile Bay. A Union fleet under Admiral David Farragut attempted to run past three Confederate forts into Mobile Bay, Alabama. After coming under fire, the fleet headed into a maze of underwater mines, known at that time as torpedoes. The ironclad *Tecumseh* was sunk by a torpedo, after which Farragut is said to have exclaimed, "Damn the torpedoes—full steam ahead!" The Union fleet was successful and Mobile Bay was secured.

1943: The Women Airforce Service Pilots (WASP) was created for noncombat services (training, ferrying aircraft, target towing, test piloting, and more) that would free up men for combat missions. WASP was awarded a Congressional Gold Medal July 1, 2009, with the acknowledgement that "they flew more than 60,000,000 miles for their country in every type of aircraft and on every type of assignment flown by the male Army Air Forces pilots, except combat."

1964: Today marks the official beginning of the Vietnam War for the United States.

Battle of Mobile Bay. Library of Congress.

This Day in U.S. Military History

1964: Operation Pierce Arrow: the United States bombed North Vietnam. Aircraft launched from *Ticonderoga* and *Constellation* hit North Vietnamese PT boat bases and coastal installations, as well as oil storage facilities.

1964: Navy Lieutenant Everett Alvarez Jr. became the first American pilot to be downed in Vietnam and the first to be taken prisoner in North Vietnam (second prisoner in the war), when his A-4 Skyhawk was hit, forcing him to bail out. Alvarez was held as a POW until February 12, 1973. Alvarez's captivity would be second only to that of Army Captain Floyd "Jim" Thompson, who had been captured in South Vietnam four months earlier (see March 26).

1990: George H.W. Bush vowed to remove Iraqi forces from Kuwait, after Iraq, on orders from its leader Saddam Hussein, invaded its oil-rich neighbor on August 2. In doing so, Iraq gained control of 20 percent of the world's oil reserves and, for the first time, a substantial coastline on the Persian Gulf.

✶ QUOTE OF THE DAY

"For years and years we've dreamed of this day, and we kept faith—faith in God, In our President and our country. . . .God bless you, Mr. and Mrs. America, you did not forget us."

Everett Alvarez, Jr., Travis Air Force Base, February 16, 1973

August 6

1945: On President Harry Truman's orders, an atomic bomb was dropped on the Japanese city of Hiroshima. Paul Tibbets, in command, flew B-29 *Enola Gay* from North Field, Tinian Island, and in six hours reached Hiroshima. At 8:15 a.m., the bomb was dropped.

The president ordered the attack after being told an invasion of Japan could cost up to one million American casualties. Truman knew that U.S. and Allied casualties in two recent battles—Iwo Jima and Okinawa—were horrendous: approximately 77,469 killed and wounded. A second atomic bomb would be dropped three days later on another city, Nagasaki (see August 9). Between the initial blast, burns, and exposure to radiation, the atomic bombings of Hiroshima and Nagasaki killed 210,000 people by the end of 1945 and 340,000 within five years—mostly civilians. Horrific as they were, the bombs appeared to do what the president and his advisors determined they would do: save more lives than they took, and hasten the end of World War II (see August 14).

★ QUOTE OF THE DAY

"The most terrible bomb in the history of the world . . ."

Harry Truman

August 7

1789: The War Department was established by Congress. President George Washington would appoint Henry Knox as its first secretary.

1792: The Badge of Military Merit was created by President George Washington. It was designed for those who performed heroically in wartime. It fell into disuse, however, and would be replaced during the Civil War by the Medal of Honor (see July 12).

1942: Operation Watchtower—the Guadalcanal Campaign—began. It was the first major offensive by Allied forces—mostly Marines—against Japan. The principal objective was to deny enemy use of Guadalcanal to threaten Allied supply and communication routes between the United States, Australia, and New Zealand, and to use it for further advances against the enemy. When the battle was deemed over (see February 9), it was regarded as a major strategic Allied victory.

1964: Congress passed the Gulf of Tonkin Resolution—giving President Lyndon Johnson the authority to use military force in Vietnam. The resolution came about after the U.S. destroyer *Maddox* (conducting electronic espionage) was purportedly fired on by North Vietnamese torpedo boats. Further attacks were later reported (the validity of which has since been questioned by some historians), prompting the president to seek military action.

1990: After Iraq's invasion of Kuwait on August 2, George H.W. Bush ordered Operation Desert Shield. Operation Desert Shield was the beginning of the U.S. military buildup that culminated in Operation Desert Storm, which freed Kuwait. The United States briefly crossed into Iraq for tactical purposes but did not consider occupying it; Defense Secretary Cheney said it wasn't worth the casualties or "getting bogged down."

"Suddenly, from the bridge, I saw a brilliant yellow-green flash of light coming from the gray shape of a cruiser on our starboard bow. I saw the red pencil-lines of the shells arching through the sky, saw flashes on the dark shore of Guadalcanal where they struck."

Richard Tregaskis, describing the early morning of August 7, 1942, from *Guadalcanal Diary* (1943)

August 8

1885: Ulysses S. Grant was laid to rest at Riverside Park, New York City. An estimated 1.5 million people witnessed the funeral, whose procession was seven miles long and included members of the surviving Grand Army of the Republic. Pallbearers were William T. Sherman, Philip Sheridan, Joseph E. Johnston, and Simon Bolivar Buckner. The construction of Grant's Tomb, paid for by volunteer subscription of 90,000 donors, was completed in 1897.

1918: The Hundred Days Offensive, World War I. The Battle of Amiens began in France and ended August 12 with an Allied victory.

1946: The Convair B-36 Peacemaker flew for the first time. It was the world's first mass-produced nuclear weapon delivery vehicle, the heaviest mass-produced piston-engine aircraft, with the longest wingspan of any military aircraft, and the first bomber with intercontinental range.

☆ QUOTE OF THE DAY

"There was hardly a sound, except the roll of drums in the distance and the tread of approaching troops, while the coffin was lowered . . ."

New York Times report on the funeral of Ulysses S. Grant

August 9

1945: A second atomic bomb was dropped on Nagasaki, Japan. Nagasaki was not the intended target, but bad visibility over Kokura forced the switch to the city of more than 250,000 people. Major Charles Sweeney was mission commander flying B-29 *Bockscar*.

The bombing, ordered by President Harry Truman, came three days after a similar bomb was dropped on Hiroshima. The obliteration of two cities in three days helped convince the Japanese to surrender on August 14, bringing World War II to an end.

1990: Operation Desert Shield, the American defense of Saudi Arabia, began, one week after Iraq invaded neighboring Kuwait. The rapid military buildup by the U.S. and its allies culminated in Operation Desert Storm, a six-week war against Iraq (see January 16).

★ QUOTE OF THE DAY

"If you suppose the Secretary of War has any personal hostility to you, or would not rejoice at your success as much as that of any other general, I think you are mistaken. I do not think he would willingly do you any injustice, but, as I have before written, neither the President nor the Secretary have been satisfied with your long delays."

General H.W. Halleck, August 9, 1863, letter to
Major-General William S. Rosecrans

August 10

1861: The second major land engagement of the Civil War—Wilson's Creek, Missouri. Union general Nathaniel Lyon was killed on Bloody Ridge as his troops repulsed rebel charges. After his death, Union troops pulled back to Rolla, Missouri, giving the Confederates their second major victory in the young war.

1949: President Truman signed an amendment to the National Security Act (see September 18), which changed the War Department to the present-day Department of Defense.

★ QUOTE OF THE DAY

"[T]hink back to the lessons of the past. Think back to what caused the disenchantment of the American public with Vietnam: they felt that they were constantly being misled with false body counts and optimistic talk about the light at the end of the tunnel."

General Norman Schwarzkopf, on preparing for press conferences during Desert Shield, 1990, *It Doesn't Take a Hero* (1992)

August 11

1943: Operation Husky in Sicily: Axis forces began to evacuate the island.

1943: The Quadrant Conference began. Meeting secretly in Quebec, President Franklin D. Roosevelt and Prime Minister Winston Churchill of Great Britain agreed, among other things, that the Allied invasion of Nazi-occupied France would occur in the spring of 1944.

1967: Previously on the prohibited list, Hanoi-Haiphong in North Vietnam was designated a bombing target for American pilots. U.S. pilots were now allowed to bomb roads and railways within 25 miles of the Chinese border and use rockets and cannon within 10 miles of the border. The original restrictions had been imposed because of President Lyndon Johnson's fear of a possible confrontation with China.

★ QUOTE OF THE DAY

"The function of the bomb used against Nagasaki made the one used against Hiroshima obsolete."

Brigadier General Thomas Farrell, August 11, 1945

August 12

1898: At the White House, the United States and Spain signed an agreement to end the Spanish-American War. Spain agreed to grant Cuba its independence and cede Puerto Rico and Guam to the United States. The fate of the Philippines, site of the U.S. victory at Manila Bay on May 1, would be determined at a later date. The Spanish-American War thrust the United States—already the world's biggest economic power—onto the global stage as a military power as well.

1941: The Atlantic Charter. Meeting on a warship off the coast of Newfoundland, Franklin D. Roosevelt and Prime Minister Winston Churchill

This Day in U.S. Military History **197**

of Great Britain established the framework for what would justify the seemingly inevitable entry of America into World War II—and the post-war order. The two leaders said that the Allies were determined to fight for, among other things, to "ensure life, liberty, independence, and religious freedom and to preserve the rights of man." Roosevelt and Churchill's Atlantic Charter was the foundation for what would become, four years later, the United Nations charter.

1950: Bloody Gulch Massacre: North Korean troops executed 75 American soldiers that they had taken prisoner near Masan, Korea.

★ QUOTE OF THE DAY

"It is my wish that throughout the [peace] negotiations entrusted to the Commission the purpose and spirit with which the United States accepted the unwelcome necessity of war should be kept constantly in view. We took up arms only in obedience to the dictates of humanity and in the fulfillment of high public and moral obligations. We had no design of aggrandizement and no ambition of conquest."

President William McKinley, September 16, 1898, private directive to peace treaty commission

August 13

1779: The Penobscot Expedition, a Continental strike force of 44 vessels sent to attack British Fort George at Penobscot Bay, Maine, were decimated by a royal relief fleet on August 13 and 14. All ships were lost and there were almost 500 American casualties. Lt. Col. Paul Revere survived, but was forced to resign his commission due to his part in the fiasco. (He was later exonerated.)

1952: The Air Force ordered full-scale production of the Boeing B-52 Stratofortress, an eight jet heavy bomber.

★ QUOTE OF THE DAY

"The B-52 warriors that rotated in and out of the Middle East absolutely crushed their mission."

Major General Thomas A. Bussiere, USAF, 2018

August 14

1900: American troops, part of an international force, relieved the Chinese capital of Peking (today Beijing) bringing the Boxer Rebellion to an end. The Boxer Rebellion was an anti-imperialist, anti-colonial, and anti-Christian uprising that took place in China between 1899 and 1901.

1945: The final B-29 combat mission against Japan occurred when the Twentieth Air Force sent 754 B-29s and 169 fighters into the sky.

1945: President Harry S. Truman announced the surrender of Japan, bringing World War II to an end. The surrender of Japan came within days of two atomic bombs being dropped on the cities of Hiroshima (see August 6) and Nagasaki (see August 9). Japanese Emperor Hirohito cited "a new and most cruel bomb" in his surrender proclamation, overriding his ministers' objections.

★ QUOTE OF THE DAY

"I'll try, Sir!"

> Corporal Calvin Titus, 14th Regiment trumpeter, volunteering and succeeding in climbing the 30-foot outer city wall of Beijing. The climb enabled his comrades to follow. Titus received the Medal of Honor for his bravery

August 15

1845: The U.S. Naval Academy was established at Annapolis, Maryland.

1895: The first American steel-hulled battleship—*Texas*—was commissioned. As part of the North Atlantic Squadron and under the command of J.W. Philip, *Texas* was part of the blockade of Cuba during the Spanish-American War. *Texas* took part in the decisive Battle of Santiago (see July 3).

1914: The Panama Canal formerly opened, and the steamship *Ancon* made the first official transit. The U.S.-built waterway connecting the Atlantic and Pacific oceans quickly became a vital military and commercial asset for the United States.

1934: The last U.S. Marines, an occupying force on Haiti since July 28, 1915, left the island nation.

1944: Operation Dragoon—the Allied invasion of Southern France—began. Allied forces went ashore on a front between Toulon and Cannes. They encountered minimal opposition, and by the end of August, the French coast from the mouth of the Rhone to Nice was in Allied hands.

1945: V-J—Victory over Japan—Day was celebrated following Japan's surrender the day before. A formal ceremony would soon take place in Tokyo (see September 2).

★ QUOTE OF THE DAY

"I am no longer a commander in the United States Army. I am commanding the Army of Panama; the enemy is Culebra Cut and the locks and the dams."

Colonel George Washington Goethals, Engineer Corps, on taking over the Panama Canal construction in 1907

August 16

1780: The Battle of Camden, South Carolina, was fought. Lord Cornwallis handed the Americans one of their worst defeats during the Revolutionary War—with nearly 1,000 Americans killed and another 1,000 captured by the British.

1812: Fort Detroit was surrendered to the British in the War of 1812. British general Isaac Brock, who moved to take the fort in Michigan, commanded 2,000 soldiers (British and Native American). William Hull, the American commander, reluctantly surrendered in the face of possible slaughter. Hull's men were taken as prisoners to Canada and the Michigan Territory was declared a part of Great Britain. In September 1813, General William Henry Harrison, the future president, recaptured Detroit. The fort was renamed Fort Shelby.

1945: Lt. Gen. Jonathan Wainwright was freed by Russian forces from a POW camp in Mukden (now Shenyang), China. Wainwright had been captured by the Japanese on the island of Corregidor, in the Philippines, in 1942. Wainwright would be present on *Missouri* for the formal

Japanese surrender that ended World War II and was later given a hero's welcome—and a Medal of Honor—upon his return to America.

⭐ QUOTE OF THE DAY

"Sir, The force at my disposal authorizes me to require of you the immediate surrender of Fort Detroit. It is far from my inclination to join in a war of extermination, but you must be aware that the numerous body of Indians, who have attached themselves to my troops, will be beyond my control the moment the contest commences."

Isaac Brook, letter to William Bull

August 17

1862: The Dakota War began when Sioux attacked white settlements in Minnesota. Union forces soon defeated them, and a military tribunal ordered 303 Sioux to be executed. President Abraham Lincoln waived most executions but did allow the military to hang 38 Sioux in December.

1863: Fort Sumter was shelled by Union troops. Getting revenge for the Confederate attack that started the Civil War (see April 12), the Union prepared to lay siege to the fort in Charleston harbor in September.

A sketch of Fort Sumter under Confederate control. Library of Congress.

This Day in U.S. Military History

1942: In the first amphibious attack made from submarines, *Nautilus* (SS-168) and *Argonaut* (SM-1) landed more than 200 Marines on Makin Island in the Gilbert Islands.

1942: The first Eighth Air Force mission occurred when Colonel Frank A. Armstrong, Jr., led 12 B-17s against Nazi targets in France. The raid demonstrated the feasibility of daylight bombing.

1943: Sicily was declared secure—just 39 days after Allied forces invaded the island during World War II.

1946: The first person to be ejected from an aircraft by ejection seat was Sgt. Lawrence Lambert, who bailed out of his P-61 while flying 302 m.p.h. at 7,800 feet in altitude over Wright Field in Ohio.

1955: The Civil Affairs/Military Government Branch of the Army Reserve Branch was established. Today called the Civil Affairs Branch, it provides guidance to commanders on a broad range of activities ranging from host-guest relationships to the assumption of executive, legislative, and judicial processes in occupied or liberated areas.

2014: In an historic first, an unmanned plane, the X-47B, took off and landed from an aircraft carrier, the *Theodore Roosevelt*.

★ QUOTE OF THE DAY

"Today we showed that the X-47B could take off, land, and fly in the carrier pattern with manned aircraft while maintaining normal flight deck operations. This is key for the future Carrier Air Wing."

Captain Beau Duarte, U.S. Navy

August 18

1965: In the first major U.S. ground battle of the Vietnam War, Marines destroyed a Viet Cong stronghold. The six-day operation began after a deserter told the Americans that an attack against them was imminent.

1965: The first successful launch of a Minuteman II from an operationally configured silo at Vandenberg AFB occurred.

1976: Two U.S. Army officers were killed in Korea's demilitarized zone when a group of North Korean soldiers wielding axes and metal pikes attacked them. The Americans, along with South Korean troops, were

Young soldiers who have just been drafted for Vietnam at Fort Jackson, Columbia, South Carolina, May 1967. Photograph by Warren K. Leffler. Library of Congress.

attempting to cut down a tree. It would lead to Operation Paul Bunyan three days later (see August 21).

★ QUOTE OF THE DAY

"A bold, vigorous assault has won many a faltering cause."

Ira C. Eaker

August 19

1812: The frigate *Constitution* defeated and burned the British warship *Guerriere* in a battle near Halifax, Nova Scotia. At one point in the battle, the two ships became entangled and slowly rotated while the crews exchanged musket fire. It was in this battle that *Constitution* earned its nickname Old Ironsides—as shots seem to slide off her sides with no discernible effect.

1940: The first flight of the B-25 Mitchell medium bomber occurred. A workhorse of World War II, some 10,000 B-25s—named in honor of

Major General William "Billy" Mitchell, a pioneer of U.S. military aviation—were produced.

1944: The Liberation of Paris was begun by Allied troops.

1981: Two Navy F-14 Tomcats, flying off *Nimitz*, shot down two Soviet-made Libyan jet fighters.

⭐ QUOTE OF THE DAY

"Huzzah! Her sides are made of iron!"

American sailor on the *Constitution*, August 19, 1812

August 20

1982: Marines arrived in Beirut, Lebanon, as part of a multinational force meant to oversee a Palestinian withdrawal from that civil war-torn country. Fifteen months later, a terror attack would devastate a barracks, killing 241 American service members (see October 23).

1998: Operation Infinite Reach: President Bill Clinton ordered cruise missile attacks on Sudan and Afghanistan, in retaliation for terror attacks on U.S. Embassy bombings in Kenya and Tanzania on August 7 that killed more than 200 people and injured more than 4,000. More than 60 Tomahawk missiles were fired at an al Qaeda camp in Khost, Afghanistan. Controversially, 13 Tomahawks destroyed the Al-Shifa pharmaceutical factory in Khartoum, Sudan—prompted by what turned out to be soft evidence that the factory was producing chemical weapons. The United States faced condemnation for attacking Al-Shifa, where a civilian employee died.

⭐ QUOTE OF THE DAY

"I could not submit to stoop before the sovereigns of Europe, so I came to hazard all for the freedom of America, and desirous of passing the rest of my life in a country truly free and settling as a citizen to fight for Liberty."

Casimir Pulaski, letter to Congress, August 1779

August 21

1918: Part of the Hundred Days Offensive, the Second Battle of the Somme began, ultimately an Allied victory led by the British Third Army. The U.S. II Corps participated. In the autumn of this Somme River offensive, Cherokee members of the 119th and 120th infantry regiments used their language for communications, one of the first uses of Native American code talking.

1976: Operation Paul Bunyan. In response to the "axe murder incident" in the Korean DMZ (see August 18), the United States and United Nations Command decided to cut down the tree that had been the focus of an attack that took the lives of two U.S. Army officers. Planning the operation in the White House, President Gerald Ford decided to make an overwhelming show of force—while trying not to provoke the North Koreans.

2017: In a policy reversal, President Donald Trump said the U.S. military commitment in Afghanistan would be open-ended. Trump originally said he would withdraw troops, but changed his mind after consulting with advisors. He added that he did not want Afghanistan to be a "vacuum for terrorists."

★ QUOTE OF THE DAY

"I would rather have a wrong decision made than no decision at all."

Robert S. McNamara, Secretary of Defense (1961-68)

August 22

1990: President George H.W. Bush signed an order calling up reservists, as the U.S. military buildup in the Persian Gulf accelerated, following the Iraqi invasion of Kuwait.

1994: The first North American ships to reach the North Pole were from the U.S. Coast Guard: icebreaker *Polar Sea* and *CCCS Louis S. Ste Laurent*.

★ QUOTE OF THE DAY

"Would not the converse be true in that we probably would have suffered fewer casualties in the South if the air campaign against the North had not been burdened with restrictions and prohibited targets?"

"It is my opinion that this is correct."

General John P. McConnell, USAF Chief of Staff, during August 1967
Senate subcommittee hearings on the air campaign in Vietnam

August 23

1864: The Battle of Mobile Bay ended with Union forces victorious and in possession of the strategic Alabama bay. Confederate brigadier-general Richard Page, in the besieged Fort Morgan, ordered gunpowder stores flooded and guns destroyed and then surrendered.

1954: The C-130 Hercules made it first flight. The four-engine turboprop, built by Lockheed, was designed to carry troops, cargo and carry out medical evacuations. It is capable of using unprepared runways for take-offs and landings. It is still in use for a variety of tasks, including airborne assault.

1958: Second Taiwan Strait Crisis. The People's Republic of China began shelling the Republic of China's (Taiwan's) islands of Kinmen and Matsu, prompting a U.S. response. President Dwight D. Eisenhower ordered the reinforcement of the navy's Seventh Fleet, which stepped up patrols near Taiwan. The battle between Taiwan—an American ally—and China lasted for a month and killed hundreds on both sides.

⭐ QUOTE OF THE DAY

"Nothing in life is more liberating than to fight for a cause larger than yourself, something that encompasses you but is not defined by your existence alone."

John McCain, U.S. senator and former Vietnam P.O.W.,
Faith of My Fathers (1999)

August 24

1814: The White House and Capitol were burned to the ground by invading British troops—a dark day for the United States in the War of 1812. President James Madison, who earlier in the day had gone to the front in Bladensburg, Maryland, returned to the White House to find it deserted.

He fled as well, never to live in the mansion again. Just before the president's retreat, First Lady Dolley Madison helped save Gilbert Stuart's famous portrait of George Washington.

1962: President John F. Kennedy amended the Bronze Star, signing an executive order to expand its awarding to include those serving with friendly forces. The Bronze Star was originally created in 1944 (see February 4).

★ QUOTE OF THE DAY

"I must leave this house, or the retreating army will make me a prisoner in it."

Dolley Madison, letter to her sister

August 25

1943: The first mass, low-level, long-range strafing raid by the United States in World War II occurred when the Twelfth Air Force sent 140 P-38s to attack enemy airfields. The P-38s flew at tree-top level to attack airfields at Foggia in southeastern Italy.

1944: Paris was liberated by Allied forces, ending four years of Nazi occupation. Adolf Hitler had ordered the destruction of Paris, but the senior German commander refused and peacefully surrendered. Among the Allied liberators was George Patton's Third Army.

1945: The first U.S. casualty of the Cold War was Army Captain John Birch. Leading a group of American, Nationalist Chinese, and Korean forces to liberate Allied prisoners of war from a Japanese POW camp, he was halted by Chinese Communist troops and ordered to surrender his revolver. He refused and was shot.

1950: President Harry Truman ordered the U.S. Army to take control of the railroads, ahead of a threatened strike by civilian workers. Because the Korean War had just broken out, the president said the railroads had to keep operating to move troops and materiel.

★ QUOTE OF THE DAY

"Who could not conquer with such troops as these?"

General Thomas "Stonewall" Jackson, to his staff, August 15, 1862

August 26

1992: A southern "no-fly zone" was created over southern Iraq by the United States, Britain, and France to protect Iraqi dissidents from regime air attacks. A northern "no-fly zone" had been in place since the end of the 1991 Gulf War. (The date in Iraq was August 27.)

⭐ QUOTE OF THE DAY

"Don't be alarmed for me. 'Whatever is to be will be and whatever is is right.' When you hear from us you will hear that I am at my post if that post be in the blazes of a thousand Yankee hells."

Captain Elijah P. Petty, Walker's Texas Division, letter to his daughter, August 1863

August 27

1861: Union ships sailed into North Carolina's Hatteras Inlet, beginning an operation to deny Confederate access to the Atlantic Ocean. Union commanders were Commodore Silas Stringham and General Benjamin Butler, who led 800 troops on eight warships. It was a two-day operation.

1945: U.S. Navy ships entered Japanese waters for the first time during World War II, to prepare for Japan's formal surrender (see September 2).

⭐ QUOTE OF THE DAY

"Above all was the relief we would not have to invade Japan. We all knew there would have been terrible casualties if we had to invade."

First Lieutenant Sally Hitchcock Pullman, Army nurse, August 1945 letter

August 28

1859: The U.S. took possession of the Midway Islands, the first offshore islands annexed by the U.S. government. In World War II, Midway was the site of a pivotal battle that turned the Pacific War in America's favor (see June 4).

1861: Confederate forces at the forts at Hatteras Inlet surrendered.

1862: The Second Battle of Bull Run began. Confederate general Thomas "Stonewall" Jackson's troops seized Manassas Junction (northern Virginia) and a key railroad line, and encircled Union forces. Union general John Pope found his communication links to President Abraham Lincoln severed, and retreated towards Washington, D.C.

1945: After Japan's surrender, the first U.S. forces set foot on Japanese soil. An advance guard of 150 technicians landed at Atsugi Airfield, near Yokohama.

☆ QUOTE OF THE DAY

"Never take counsel of your fears."

George S. Patton, quoting Stonewall Jackson

August 29

1862: The second Battle of Bull Run was a Union disaster—leaving Washington D.C. vulnerable to attack. A year after Union forces were routed at present-day Manassas, Virginia (see July 21), a second battle yielded the same result. President Abraham Lincoln was told that the capital city was exposed to possible attack. But Confederate general Robert E. Lee, leading his troops across the Potomac, would march not into Washington—but to the Maryland town of Sharpsburg, where the titanic battle of Antietam would soon occur (see September 17).

1916: The Naval Reserve and the Marine Corps Reserve was created by an act of Congress.

1945: With World War II finally over, President Harry Truman signed an order allowing for voluntary military enlistments. Some 16 million Americans—out of a population of about 130 million—had served in the African, European, and Pacific theaters. The president that day also ordered the U.S. Navy to seize control of oil refineries, to head off a planned strike by civilian workers; Truman said the oil was needed to help with the military's massive demobilization that was underway.

1945: Major Gregory "Pappy" Boyington, the "Black Sheep" squadron leader who had disappeared in January 1944 during an air battle, was reported to be alive and released from a Japanese prisoner-of-war camp on this day. The "Marine ace of the South Pacific," who downed 28 planes in World War II, received the Medal of Honor.

★ QUOTE OF THE DAY

"Major Boyington struck at the enemy with daring and courageous persistence, leading his squadron into combat with devastating results. . . his forceful leadership developed the combat readiness in his command which was a distinctive factor in the Allied aerial achievements in this vitally strategic area."

Medal of Honor citation, excerpt, for Major Gregory Boyington, 1944

August 30

1913: The General Board of the Navy asked for a naval air service to be created, with funding first budgeted in 1914.

1945: The Third Fleet established headquarters at Japan's Yokosuka Naval Base. The base had earlier surrendered to Rear Adm. Robert B. Carney and Rear Adm. Oscar C. Badger.

1995: Operation Deliberate Force began. U.S. and NATO aircraft began airstrikes on Serbian ground positions in Bosnia-Herzegovina in support of a United Nations operation. The airstrikes, along with a Bosnian-Croatian ground attack, convinced the Serbs to accept peace terms in late 1995.

★ QUOTE OF THE DAY

"And then ... came the electrifying announcement; too blessedly good to be true. We were just returning to the barracks from dinner when the official announcement of the capitulation was flashed across the nation from Washington, D.C."

Lieutenant Colonel Ben M. Snyder, bombardier, in his journal,
August 1945

August 31

1864: Union general William T. Sherman launched a siege that would capture Atlanta. It was the culmination of a four-month campaign by Sherman, who had led his troops on a 100-mile march from Chattanooga, Tennessee, against a Confederate force led by General Joseph Johnston.

1962: The last flight of a Navy airship was made at Naval Air Station, Lakehurst, New Jersey.

2010: President Barack Obama declared an end to U.S. combat operations in Iraq. He said America had "met its responsibility" after seven-and-a-half years of conflict. By October 2011 the last American troops had left Iraq.

⭑ QUOTE OF THE DAY

"Operation Iraqi Freedom is over, and the Iraqi people now have lead responsibility for the security of their country."

President Barack Obama, August 31, 2010

Fleet Admiral Chester W. Nimitz signing surrender document on board the *Missouri*. Looking on are (left to right): Gen. Douglas MacArthur, Adm. William F. Halsey, and R. Adm. Forrest P. Sherman. Library of Congress.

September

September 1

1864: William T. Sherman was victorious in the Battle of Jonesborough (part of the Atlanta Campaign). His troops defeated Confederate troops led by John B. Hood.

1942: The U.S. Naval Air Force, Pacific Fleet was established. Vice Admiral Aubrey W. Fitch assumed command. It replaced the commands Carriers, Pacific Fleet and Patrol Wings, Pacific Fleet.

1942: The first Naval Construction Battalion (better known as Seabees) to serve in a combat area arrived on Guadalcanal.

1982: The Air Force Space Command (AFSPC) was established, a branch of the U.S. Air Force. Its duties include the launch, oversight, and protection of satellites.

2008: After a transition process that began in February, U.S. forces formally returned Iraq's Anbar province to local control. The largest province in Iraq, Anbar had previously been one of the most dangerous regions in Iraq, with Islamic extremists controlling large portions of it. A quarter of all U.S. fatalities in the Iraq War occurred in Anbar, which includes the city of Fallujah.

★ QUOTE OF THE DAY

"Deterrence in the space world has got to be built on a little bit different construct. It's the ability to convince an adversary that if they attack us, they will fail."

General John E. Hyten, 2015, then head of
Air Force Space Command

September 2

General William Sherman before Atlanta, Georgia, 1864. Photo taken by George N. Barnard. Civil War photographs, 1861-1865, Library of Congress, Prints and Photographs Division.

1862: Abraham Lincoln put General George McClellan back in command of the Army of the Potomac. The president had previously demoted him for failing to capture the Confederate capital, Richmond—accusing him of having a "case of the slows."

1864: Union forces entered Atlanta. The city had been under siege for a month before surrendering to General William T. Sherman, who would soon begin his March to the Sea. Union troops would later burn virtually the entire city (see November 15) to cut off supply lines that provided Confederate troops with reinforcements, ammunition, and goods such as clothes, first-aid medicines, and equipment.

1945: Japan officially surrendered to the Allies, ending World War II. The formal ceremony on board *Missouri* in Tokyo Bay was led by General Douglas MacArthur.

★ QUOTE OF THE DAY

"We are all proud that we have been able to help win this war. Let us all hope that this will be the last time that a war has to be won."

Edward Wadington, sailor on *Missouri*, letter to family

September 3

1777: According to legend, the American flag (whose stars and stripes design was set by resolution on June 14, 1777) was flown in battle at Cooch's Bridge, near Newark, Delaware. General William Maxwell supposedly ordered it raised as his infantry and cavalry met Lt. Gen. William Howe's British and Hessian troops.

1783: The Treaty of Paris was signed, ending the American Revolution. Signed in Paris, France, at the Hotel d'York, signatories were Benjamin Franklin, John Jay, and John Adams for the United States, and David Hartley for Great Britain. In Article 1, the United States was formally acknowledged by Great Britain as a sovereign and independent nation. The remaining articles established boundaries of the United States (comprised of 13 colonies), prisoner of war releases, fishing rights, and other items.

1855: Troops under Brig. Gen. William S. Harney attacked a Sioux village in Ash Hollow, Nebraska, in revenge for the "Grattan Massacre"—killings of 31 U.S. soldiers the year before. In the attack on the Brulé Lakota Sioux village—authorized by then Secretary of War Jefferson Davis—600 troops killed 85 people (half of them women and children) and carried away 70. The attack is known as the Battle of Blue Water Creek or the Harney Massacre.

1908: Orville Wright flew the Wright Flyer on its first test flight at Fort Myer, Virginia.

1925: Naval airship *Shenandoah* (ZR-1) broke up in a thunderstorm and crashed near Caldwell, Ohio. Killed was Commander Zachary Lansdowne and 13 other crew. Col. William "Billy" Mitchell, making public complaints about the state of affairs of the airship program, was court-martialled December 17 as a consequence.

1944: As part of Operation Anvil, an old B-17 bomber, stripped down and loaded with explosives, was flown at German U-boat pens on Heligoland

Island: the pilot parachuted out of the plane and the flight was then to be radio-controlled into the pens. But the "drone"—essentially a guided missile—failed to hit its target and crashed instead at a neighboring island. Operation Anvil (U.S. Navy) and its Air Force counterpart Aphrodite, were begun in August 1944, but never successfully hit their targets.

★ QUOTE OF THE DAY

"Brave airmen are being sent to their deaths by armchair admirals who don't care about air safety."

Col. William "Billy" Mitchell

September 4

1812: The Siege of Fort Harrison began. The fort, built by William Henry Harrison on the Wabash River at Terre Haute, Indiana, was defended by General Zachary Taylor against a force of Miami Indians.

1919: The first General of the Armies of the United States was confirmed: General John J. Pershing.

1941: After the destroyer *Greer* (DD-145) was attacked by a German submarine off Iceland, Franklin D. Roosevelt issued a shoot-on-sight order. The U.S. ship, which was not damaged, launched depth charges, which damaged the German sub. Germany and the United States would declare war on each other three months later (see December 11).

1984: Rockwell International rolled out the first B-1B for the public. Commonly called the Lancer or "Bone" (from "B-One"), it is one of three strategic bombers in the U.S. Air Force fleet.

2002: George W. Bush made his case for war with Iraq. The president said that Iraqi president Saddam Hussein was a threat to America's national security, and brought up the idea of regime change. The United States would lead an invasion of Iraq six months later (see March 19).

★ QUOTE OF THE DAY

"General Pershing's fame rests largely upon his personal character. He was not a genius at strategy and his tactical experience was limited, but in his indomitable will for victory, in his implacable belief in the American soldier, in his invincible resistance to all attempts to exploit or patronize American arms, he rose to the highest flights of his profession."

Douglas MacArthur, on John J. Pershing, *Reminiscences* (1964)

September 5

1781: Although no American sailors were involved, the Battle of Chesapeake Bay was a key battle in the war for American independence. Taking place off the Virginia Capes, the French fleet defeated the Royal Navy fleet, which suffered the loss or damage of five ships. More important, the Royal Navy fleet, under the command of Rear Admiral Sir Thomas Graves, was unable to bring relief to General Cornwallis.

1812: The Siege of Fort Wayne began, conducted by Miami and Potawatomi against the Americans in Indiana.

1877: In the Plains Indian Wars, Oglala Sioux leader Crazy Horse was bayoneted by a U.S. soldier in murky circumstances while at Fort Robinson in northwest Nebraska. Crazy Horse died.

1944: Captain William H. Allen of the 55th Fighter Group, Eighth Air Force, became an ace in just a few minutes. Flying a P-51 with another ace, Capt. William H. Lewis, Allen's flight encountered and shot down 16 German fighters over enemy-held territory.

★ QUOTE OF THE DAY

"Hokahey, today is a good day to die!"

Crazy Horse, battle exhortation to his warriors

September 6

1781: Raid on New London and the Battle of Groton Heights: Connecticut militia led by Colonel William Ledyard were confronted by a large British force led by turncoat General Benedict Arnold. Arnold had raided and burned the town of New London, Connecticut, across the Thames River (part of an effort to divert George Washington's forces then in Virginia). Ledyard and his militia—numbering only around 160 men—were manning Fort Griswold at Groton Heights. Arnold's force of more than 1,500 took Fort Griswold after 40 minutes. There are conflicting accounts as to whether the British forces began massacring the fort's occupants. Eighty-three Americans were killed; Ledyard was either executed or run through with a bayonet. New London and Groton were razed. "Remember New London" became a Yorktown battle cry.

1978: The first production-model F-16 fighter landed at Edwards AFB, California, for testing, following a two-hour flight from the General Dynamics plant at Fort Worth, Texas.

⭐ QUOTE OF THE DAY

"We shall not surrender, let the consequences be what they may."

Captain Shapley, Fort Griswold, Groton Heights

September 7

1776: The first use of a submarine in warfare occurred when the American submersible craft *Turtle* tried to attach a bomb to the hull of British Admiral Richard Howe's flagship *Eagle* in New York Harbor. *Turtle*'s pilot, Ezra Lee, was unsuccessful, however. *Turtle* made other attempts during the Revolutionary War to attach bombs to unsuspecting British craft, but never succeeded.

1997: The F-22 Raptor advanced tactical fighter flew for the first time, from Dobbins Air Reserve Base near Atlanta.

⭐ QUOTE OF THE DAY

"I am Distressed my Dear Sir, to find on my Arrival, that the Supplies for the Army collectg [sic] here, are not in that desirable Train, that could be wished; they have already experienced a Want of Provisions, and are greatly apprehensive in future, particularly in the Article of Bread. . . ."

General George Washington, in a September 1781
letter to Thomas Sim Lee

September 8

1847: In the lead-up to the Battle for Mexico City, the Battle of Molino del Rey took place on this day on the outskirts of the Mexican capital. General Winfield Scott had almost 10,000 troops at his disposal, outnumbering the Mexicans two to one. Although the United States prevailed, casualties were heavy—a Pyrrhic victory.

1939: With World War II underway in Europe, President Franklin D. Roosevelt declared a limited national emergency and ordered increases of enlisted personnel in the Navy and Marine Corps. The order also authorized the recall to active duty of officers, men, and nurses on the retired lists of the Navy and Marine Corps.

1943: The surrender of Italy (on September 3) was announced by the Allies. Germany immediately launched Operation Axis: the occupation of its former ally. As German troops entered Rome, General Dwight Eisenhower, commander of Allied forces in Europe, paused the advance of American troops into the Italian capital.

1945: U.S. troops arrived in now-independent Korea to begin their post-war occupation of the southern half of that peninsula, while Soviet troops occupied the northern half. Both occupations, a result of the Potsdam Conference (see July 17), were meant to be temporary, until Koreans could determine their own political future.

1954: The United States signed the SEATO—South East Asian Treaty Organization—pact, designed to thwart communist expansion. Dwight Eisenhower had ordered Secretary of State John Foster Dulles to form an alliance to prevent aggression in Vietnam, Laos, and Cambodia, or Southeast Asia in general. Signatories, including France, Great Britain, Australia, New Zealand, the Philippines, Pakistan, Thailand, and the United States, pledged to "act to meet the common danger"; but SEATO did not contain a mutual defense clause like the better known North Atlantic Treaty Organization (NATO) pact had (see April 4).

★ QUOTE OF THE DAY

"All Italians who now act to help eject the German aggressor from Italian soil will have the assistance and support of the United Nations."

Dwight D. Eisenhower, announcing the surrender of Italy on radio

September 9

1841: Congress authorized the first iron-hulled warship. *Michigan* launched two years later was deployed in the Great Lakes.

1863: Union forces captured Chattanooga, Tennessee, when Confederate troops under General Braxton Bragg left the city, which had been undergoing shelling since August 21. The victory, led by General William Rosecrans, gave U.S. troops greater control of strategic south-central Tennessee.

1959: The first Atlas D—an intercontinental ballistic missile—was fired from Vandenberg AFB in California, after which the system was declared operational. The missile traveled 4,300 miles at 16,000 MPH.

1961: The first nuclear-power surface warship in history—*Long Beach* (CGN-9)—was commissioned and assigned to the Atlantic Fleet, based in Norfolk, Virginia.

★ QUOTE OF THE DAY

"He was the light and life of this army."

Major James Connolly, on William Rosecrans and the Army of the Cumberland, in his memoir

September 10

1813: Flying his "Don't give up the ship" flag on the *Lawrence*, Commodore Oliver H. Perry led his fleet into the Battle of Lake Erie near Put-in-Bay, Ohio, during the war of 1812. In the midst of battle, the *Lawrence* was destroyed, and Perry undertook a dangerous transfer to the *Niagara*. The British commander of Lake Erie, Robert Heriot Barclay, saw his entire squadron captured. Barclay lost a leg and the use of his right arm in the battle. The *Lawrence* suffered 22 fatalities and 55 injured—Perry forced the British to surrender on what was left of her deck. The Battle of Lake Erie forced the British to abandon Detroit, ensuring U.S. control over the lake and the territorial northwest.

2005: Operation Restoring Rights began, with U.S. and Iraqi troops entering Tal Afar. The operation tested a new American strategy of "clear, hold, build," in which areas would be rid of insurgents and then occupied and then rebuilt to win support from local people before being handed over to the Iraqi security forces. It was considered one of the first successful counterinsurgency operations in Iraq.

 **QUOTE OF THE DAY**

"We have met the enemy and they are ours…."

Oliver Hazard Perry, Battle of Lake Erie

September 11

1777: The Battle of Brandywine began—the largest engagement of the American Revolution. British troops, led by General William Howe, marched on Philadelphia; Continental forces led by General George Washington tried to stop them at the Brandywine River near Chadds Ford, Pennsylvania. The Americans were defeated and the British went on to take Philadelphia two weeks later. Washington's men began their long and insufferable winter encampment at Valley Forge, Pennsylvania.

1944: The first U.S. troops entered Nazi Germany. It was a reflection of how far and how fast Allied forces had advanced since invading Nazi-occupied France three months earlier.

2001: The United States was attacked when 19 Islamic terrorists hijacked four civilian airliners and crashed them into both World Trade Center towers in New York City and the Pentagon just outside of Washington, D.C. A fourth plane, believed headed for either the White House or the Capitol, crashed in Pennsylvania after passengers counterattacked their hijackers. The terror group al Qaeda took credit for the attack; the United States would attack Afghanistan a month later, in an effort to root out the terror group's leader, Osama bin Laden.

2001: NORAD—the North American Air Defense Command—began combat air patrols over more than 30 American cities, amid fears of new terrorist attacks on the United States.

QUOTE OF THE DAY

"Make no mistake: the United States will hunt down and punish those responsible for these cowardly acts."

George W. Bush

September 12

1775: Nathan Hale, recruited by Benjamin Tallmadge to be a Revolutionary spy (see February 4), was ferried to New York City on a volunteer mission for George Washington to report on British troop strength.

1804: The frigates *Constellation* and *President* captured two ships while attempting to enter a harbor during the blockade of Barbary ports; *Argus* and *Constellation* later captured a third vessel. The seizures occurred during the First Barbary War.

1814: The Battle of North Point was fought on this day near Baltimore between General John Stricker's Maryland Militia and Major General Robert Ross's British force. U.S. forces wound up retreating, but not before inflicting sizable casualties on the enemy and lowering their morale. General Ross, fresh from the Peninsular Wars (serving under the Duke of Wellington) and from the Burning of Washington, D.C., which he directed, was killed by an American sharpshooter.

1918: The first major U.S. offensive of World War I—the Battle of Saint-Mihiel—began, when more than 550,000 Americans (AEF), led by General John J. Pershing, as well as 100,000 French, attacked 50,000 German troops at the Saint-Mihiel Salient in northeastern France. The Allied forces pushed the Germans back after 36 hours of heavy fighting. The United States suffered 7,000 casualties, while the Germans had 22,000 casualties.

1942: The Battle of Edson's Ridge began on Guadalcanal in the Solomon Islands. The battle, also called the Battle of the Bloody Ridge, took its name from U.S. Marine Corps Lieutenant Colonel Merritt A. Edson, whose men (12,500) repulsed the nighttime attacks of Japanese commander General Kiyotake Kawaguchi's 6,000 troops. This was the second of three major Japanese ground offensives during the Guadalcanal Campaign. The Marines were under the overall command of U.S. Major General Alexander Vandegrift.

★ QUOTE OF THE DAY

"Every taxi-driver or waiter in Paris could have told one just where the Americans were concentrating for their great attack on the St. Mihiel salient. The number of guns, the number of troops and just where they were located, how many aeroplanes we had and similar topics of war interest were discussed by every man on the streets."

Captain Eddie Rickenbacker, *Fighting the Flying Circus* (1919)

September 13

1814: During the Battle of Baltimore, the British shelled Fort McHenry at Baltimore Harbor. Lawyer Francis Scott Key, on board the British ship *Tonnant* to discuss prisoner exchanges, was detained onboard during the shelling. He was so inspired by the sight of the American flag still flying after the bombardment on September 14 that he wrote "Defence of Fort M'Henry," a poem that later became "The Star-Spangled Banner"—and the U.S. national anthem.

1847: The United States prevailed in the Battle of Chapultepec, at Chapultepec Castle, Mexico City, the last major battle of the Mexican-American War. The next day, General Winfield Scott marched U.S. troops into the city and raised the American flag over the Mexican National Palace—the "Halls of Montezuma" later celebrated in the famous Marine Corps Hymn. American officers at the battle included Robert E. Lee, P. G. T.

Battle of Chapultepec, seen in a contemporary print. Library of Congress.

This Day in U.S. Military History

Beauregard, Joseph E. Johnston, Ulysses S. Grant, Stonewall Jackson, and many other now-famous men.

1847: A mass execution of 30 San Patricios took place as the American flag was raised over Chapultepec, ordered by Winfield Scott. The San Patricios, members of the Saint Patrick's Battalion, were predominately Catholic Irish U.S. Army deserters who joined the Mexican side. With 20 San Patricio executions earlier in the week, it comprised the U.S.'s largest mass execution.

1860: John Joseph "Black Jack" Pershing was born in Laclede, Missouri. He was the only American to be promoted in his own lifetime to the rank of General of the Armies—the highest possible rank in the U.S. Army. He is best known for serving as commander of the American Expeditionary Forces (AEF) on the western front in World War I from 1917 to 1918. Pershing also served as a mentor to virtually every general who led the Army during World War II, including George C. Marshall, Dwight D. Eisenhower, Omar Bradley, Lesley J. McNair, George S Patton, and Douglas MacArthur.

1862: Union troops found a copy of Confederate general Robert E. Lee's Antietam battle plan—"Special Orders, No. 191"—wrapped around three cigars and discarded in a field. Lee planned to divide up his troops and General George B. McClellan adjusted his forces accordingly, ahead of what would become the bloodiest one-day battle in American history (see September 17).

★ QUOTE OF THE DAY

"I have had a good share of what goes by [the name of luxury] in my lifetime, but I have never had since anything in that way that might be compared with the nights in the guardroom, and the routine of the sentinel's duty in weather wet or dry, and in moonlit and moonless midnights, to which I have been detailed at Fort McHenry."

John Pendleton Kennedy, Maryland Militia, journal entry 1813

September 14

1939: Aircraft innovator Igor Sikorsky made the first test flight of the VS-300, a single-engine helicopter (with protective cables). The VS-300 was the first successful single lifting rotor helicopter built in the United

States and the first successful helicopter to use a single vertical-plane-tail-rotor configuration. Sikorsky modified the VS-300 into the R-4, which was used by the U.S. Air Force, Navy, and Coast Guard.

1940: The U.S. Congress passed the Selective Training and Service Act of 1940, providing for the first peacetime draft in U.S. history.

1944: The 1st Marine Division landed on the Pacific island of Peleliu, as part of a larger operation to provide support for Gen. Douglas MacArthur's planned invasion of the Philippines. The nine-week battle would result in an American victory, its strategic value would later be questioned, particularly given the high number of casualties: 10,786 killed or wounded. The National Museum of the Marine Corps calls it "the bitterest battle of the war for the Marines."

★ QUOTE OF THE DAY

"He fought often and once bled in the cause of freedom, but his habits of war did not lessen in him the peaceful virtues which adorn private life."

Benjamin Rush, eulogizing John Barry, who had died September 13, 1803. Barry is often considered the "Father of the U.S. Navy" along with John Paul Jones

September 15

1777: Congress, noting his bravery at the Battle of Brandywine, appointed Polish noble Casimir Pulaski "Commander of the Horse with the rank of Brigadier." Pulaski is considered the "Father of the American Cavalry."

1812: U.S. forces commanded by Zachary Taylor at Fort Harrison, Indiana, successfully repelled a Native American siege. Native forces withdrew. The fort would be an important staging area for the Battle of Tippecanoe.

1950: Inchon—a daring amphibious assault on the West coast of Korea—began. In Operation Chromite the X Corps were successful and U.N. forces were able to break out of Pusan and race toward Seoul. Inchon is considered one of the boldest military operations in American history. Many had doubted Douglas MacArthur's strategy—Admiral James H. Doyle had told MacArthur a week before, "The best I can say is that Inchon is not impossible."

This Day in U.S. Military History

★ QUOTE OF THE DAY

"The amphibious landings of September 15, 1950, were MacArthur's masterstroke."

Max Hastings, *The Korean War* (1987)

September 16

1776: George Washington's first victory of the Revolutionary War occurred in the Battle of Harlem Heights, in upper Manhattan.

1940: The United States moved closer to a war footing when Franklin D. Roosevelt signed the Selective Training and Service Act—requiring men aged 21 to 35 to register for draft.

1974: Gerald Ford announced a conditional amnesty for Vietnam War deserters—if they agreed to work for up to two years in public service jobs. The president said he wanted America to move beyond Vietnam, which had seriously divided the country.

★ QUOTE OF THE DAY

"Reconciliation calls for an act of mercy to bind the nation's wounds and to heal the scars of divisiveness."

Gerald Ford

September 17

1862: The bloodiest single day in U.S. history—the Battle of Antietam. George B. McClellan's Army of the Potomac fought Robert E. Lee's Army of Northern Virginia. The clash near the Maryland town of Sharpsburg left 23,000 Union and Confederate soldiers dead, wounded, or missing in 12 hours of savage fighting. Antietam is generally regarded as a strategic victory for the Union, ending the Confederate Army's first invasion of the North. It also gave President Abraham Lincoln the confidence to issue a preliminary Emancipation Proclamation just days later.

1895: The battleship *Maine* was commissioned. In 1898 it was destroyed in Cuba's Havana Harbor after an explosion (see February 15)—a catalyst to the Spanish-American War.

1908: The world's first fatal airplane accident occurred when 28-year-old Lt Thomas E. Selfridge, flying as a passenger with Orville Wright, died when their Wright Flyer crashed at Fort Myer, Virginia. Wright was also severely injured.

1944: Operation Market Garden began, a major Allied airborne assault made to secure the Rhine River. An estimated 1,546 Allied planes and 478 gliders carried 35,000 troops for the operation, which focused on the area between Eindhoven and Arnhem in Holland.

✷ QUOTE OF THE DAY

"Now I know what to do!"

George B. McClellan, upon receipt of Lee's Antietam battle orders (see September 13)

September 18

1947: The U.S. Air Force was established as a result of the National Security Act of 1947 (see July 26). The Air Force's motto is "Uno Ab Alto" ("One over all").

2007: A C-5 fitted with Northrop-Grumann's AN/AAQ-24 Large Aircraft Infrared Countermeasure (LAIRCM) system made its inaugural flight. The system was designed to protect large transports from missile attacks by activating a high-intensity system to track and defeat the threat.

✷ QUOTE OF THE DAY

"A peculiar and lasting friendship is created between boys who fight in the air. No other fraternity upon Earth is like it."

Captain Eddie Rickenbacker, *Fighting the Flying Circus* (1919)

September 19

1777: The first battle of Saratoga ended in an American victory. With their control of Manhattan, Newport, Rhode Island, and Canada, British victory in the Revolutionary War seemed imminent—until U.S. forces stopped a British attempt to invade upstate New York. A second battle soon began (see October 17) that would convince France to enter the war on America's side.

1794: George Washington told Virginia governor Henry "Light Horse Harry" Lee that he would subdue the "Whiskey Rebellion." And the president would do just that—with force (see October 1).

1796: George Washington's Farewell Address. After nearly eight years in office, the president—who had been reluctant to take the job in the first place—decided that he would not accept a third term and would retire to Mount Vernon. In his address—never actually spoken but printed in Philadelphia's *Daily American Advertiser* and later reprinted in other newspapers—the Commander-in-Chief cautioned Americans to avoid political infighting, and advised future leaders to avoid permanent alliances with other nations.

★ QUOTE OF THE DAY

"The unity of government which constitutes you one people is also now dear to you. It is justly so; for it is a main pillar in the edifice of your real independence, the support of your tranquility at home, your peace abroad, of your safety, of your prosperity, of that very liberty which you so highly prize."

George Washington, farewell address

September 20

1776: A devastating fire broke out in New York City, then occupied by British forces. Americans blamed the British; the British blamed the Americans.

1863: The Union Army (under William Rosecrans) was defeated by the Confederates (under Braxton Bragg) in the Battle of Chickamauga, at Chickamauga Creek in northeastern Georgia, near Chattanooga, Tennessee. The battle had begun on September 18. Casualties for both sides were severe: some 25,000 killed, wounded, or missing. Union troops retreated to Chattanooga, where the Confederates laid siege.

2001: George W. Bush warned Americans to prepare for a long war against terrorism. Speaking to a joint session of Congress nine days after terrorists attacked New York City and Washington, D.C., the president outlined his administration's plans to combat global terror. He emphasized that America was not at war with Islam itself.

2011: The Don't Ask, Don't Tell Repeal Act of 2010 went into effect on this day, ending the military's 1993 directive of the same name. U.S. service members now had the right to openly declare their sexual orientation without fear of reprisal.

★ QUOTE OF THE DAY

"Harlan was severely wounded in the arm but clung to the flag, which was soon stained with his blood."

Wilbur Hinman, in *The Sherman Brigade* (1897), describes Sergeant George Harlan's heroism during the Battle of Chickamauga when ordered to "keep the flags well up"

September 21

1780: Major John André, who headed British intelligence activities in America, met disgruntled American general Benedict Arnold secretly to discuss Arnold's handing over West Point, New York, which he then commanded.

1942: The Boeing B-29 Superfortress made its debut flight. The B-29 was a four-engine heavy bomber, able to carry loads almost equal to its own weight at altitudes of 30,000 to 40,000 feet. Innovations included a rear pilot console and a radar bombing system. The B-29 would see significant action during World War II.

★ QUOTE OF THE DAY

"The inherent ardor of his warlike spirit, his habits of activity, and the desire of efficiently serving the cause, which he had so warmly embraced did not permit him to wait for the decision of Congress on his application—but he immediately joined the army."

General George Washington, General Order, September 21, 1777, announcing Casimir Pulaski's appointment to the command of the American Light Dragoons

September 22

Nathan Hale at his hanging, in a 19th-century interpretation by Alexander Hay Ritchie. Library of Congress.

1776: Continental Army spy Nathan Hale, 21 years old, was hung in New York City by the British. He had been captured the day before during investigations into the New York City fire.

1950: Joining Dwight D. Eisenhower, Douglas MacArthur, George C. Marshall, and Henry "Hap" Arnold, Omar N. Bradley was promoted to five-star general.

1950: As a result of MacArthur's successful Inchon landing (see September 15), the Eighth Army broke out from the Pusan Perimeter. North Korean troops began a wholesale withdrawal to the North.

2006: The F-14 Tomcat was officially retired, 26 years to the day after its introduction, having been supplanted by the Boeing F/A-18E and F Super Hornets. The Grumman F-14 Tomcat was a fourth-generation, super-sonic, twin-jet, two-seat, variable-sweep wing fighter aircraft that first flew December 12, 1970, and made its first deployment in 1974.

★ QUOTE OF THE DAY

"I only regret that I have but one life to lose for my country."

Nathan Hale, reported last words

September 23

1779: The Battle of Flamborough Head: In the North Sea off England's Yorkshire coast, a British convoy of 40 ships found itself challenged by the *Bonhomme Richard* and a Franco-American squadron commanded by John Paul Jones of the Continental Navy. The Royal Navy's *Serapis*, the convoy escort, engaged and severely damaged *Bonhomme Richard*, prompting Jones' famous retort to the query of whether he would surrender, "I have not yet begun to fight!" The two ships were locked together, resulting in close fire between the crews. With help from the frigate *Alliance*, Jones captured *Serapis* (as well as a second escort, *Countess of Scarborough*). Two days later, *Bonhomme Richard* sank.

1780: Major John André, traveling in civilian dress with the plans of West Point hidden on his person, was captured by American soldiers. Soon, the treachery of Benedict Arnold was exposed. André was tried and executed as a spy on October 2.

2014: The United States and its key Arab allies began air strikes against the so-called Islamic State in Syria. Assisting were Bahrain, Jordan, Qatar, Saudi Arabia, and the United Arab Emirates.

★ QUOTE OF THE DAY

"I have not yet begun to fight!"

John Paul Jones

September 24

1846: The Battle of Monterrey, in Mexico's state of Nuevo León, concluded this day. Begun on September 21, the battle pitted Mexico's Army of the North against General Zachary Taylor's Army of Occupation. Saint Patrick's Battalion (the San Patricios) fought for the Army of the North. The battle evolved into house-by-house fighting by the 24th, resulting in serious civilian casualties, and General Pedro de Ampudia decided to capitulate. A two-month armistice was arranged—to President James Polk's anger. Polk fumed in his diary: "[Taylor] had the enemy in his power & should have taken them prisoners."

1918: Lt. j.g. David S. Ingalls became the U.S. Navy's first ace. During a test flight in a Sopwith Camel, he spotted an enemy plane over Nieuport,

Belgium, and, with another Sopwith Camel, attacked and scored his fifth aerial victory.

1960: The first nuclear-powered aircraft carrier, *Enterprise*, was launched at Newport News, Virginia. In 1975 she was designated (CVN-65).

★ QUOTE OF THE DAY

"Monterrey was converted into a vast cemetery. The unburied bodies, the dead and putrid mules, the silence of the streets, all gave a fearful aspect to this city."

Contemporary account of the Battle of Monterrey, reported in *The Other Side: The Mexican View of the War* (1850), by Ramon Alvarez et al.

September 25

1950: Marines captured the South Korean capital of Seoul after a five-day battle with North Korean troops.

2007: The first operational mission for the MQ-9 Reaper occurred when the drone flew over Afghanistan during Operation Enduring Freedom. The Reaper, a larger and heavily armed version of the MQ-1 Predator, provided intelligence, surveillance, and reconnaissance capabilities and an ability to attack time-sensitive targets quickly and precisely.

★ QUOTE OF THE DAY

"The first of the gull-winged, dark blue Corsairs peeled from the circle and dove at the white smoke. Red tracers from its guns poured from the forward edges of the wings. The plane leveled off only yards above the ridgeline. We could see the pilot in the cockpit and the big, white Marine Corps emblem on the fuselage..."

Lieutenant Joseph R. Owen, 7th Marines, describing air support during the Battle for Seoul, quoted in *Battle of the Barricades*, by Colonel Joseph H. Alexander

September 26

1918: The Battle of Meuse-Argonne began a French-American effort that was part of the Hundred Days Offensive. After four weeks, U.S. troops had advanced ten miles, and the French twenty—but that was enough to rid the Argonne Forest of enemy forces. Meuse-Argonne is considered the final great battle of World War I—it was also one of the costliest in terms of casualties for the United States.

1931: The keel of the first ship designed and constructed as an aircraft carrier was laid at Newport News, Virginia: *Ranger* (CV-4).

1941: A Provost Marshal General's Office and Corps of Military Police were established. With the exceptions of the Civil War and World War I, there was no regularly appointed Provost Marshal General or regularly constituted Military Police Corps—though a "Provost Marshal" can be found as early as January 1776, and a "Provost Corps" as early as 1778.

1950: U.S. forces from the Inchon invasion (see September 15) and Pusan linked up, stepping up their offensive against retreating North Korea forces. B-29 bombers pounded enemy targets, marking the end of the first strategic bombing campaign against North Korea.

★ QUOTE OF THE DAY

"Half an hour spent with the brakeman of a freight train running into Occupied France would produce more useful information than Mata Hari could learn in a night."

William "Wild Bill" Donovan

September 27

1941: The first Liberty ship—*Patrick Henry*—was launched by President Franklin D. Roosevelt at Baltimore, Maryland. Liberty ships were cargo ships that were mass produced during World War II and came to symbolize what FDR called America's "arsenal of democracy" during the war.

1991: With the Cold War over, President George H.W. Bush ended the Strategic Air Command's alert force operation, which had been operating since October 1957. This resulted in the Pentagon taking B-52 bombers off their full-time alert. The president also ordered some 2,400 short-range land and sea-based nuclear weapons eliminated, a move he said could save $2 billion a year.

⭑ QUOTE OF THE DAY

"You're standing your watches, you're doing your job, and you're always wondering if there is somebody out there, following you."

Commander Harold Douglas Barker, Navy submariner, on the Cold War, in the Veterans History Project

September 28

1781: The final battle of the Revolutionary War—Yorktown—began. General George Washington's forces, linking up with French troops commanded by the Comte de Rochambeau, surrounded the British troops of Lieutenant General Charles Cornwallis in the Virginia city (see October 19).

1850: Congress passed a bill banning flogging on Navy and merchant marine ships.

⭑ QUOTE OF THE DAY

"A man—a human being, made in God's likeness—fastened up and flogged like a beast!"

Richard Henry Dana, Jr, merchant marine, in his memoir
Two Years before the Mast (1840)

September 29

1899: The VFW—Veterans of Foreign Wars—was established. The VFW advocates for veterans issues in Congress and around the nation and "to preserve and strengthen comradeship among its members; to foster true patriotism; and to preserve and defend the United States from all her enemies, whomsoever."

1918: The Battle of St. Quentin Canal began: U.S. and Allied forces would break through Germany's Hindenburg Line in France.

1946: A Lockheed P2V Neptune, "Truculent Turtle," left Perth, Australia, on what would be the longest non-stop, non-refueling flight ever conducted at that time. Landing on October 1 at Columbus, Ohio, the crew flew 11,235.6 miles in 55 hours and 17 minutes.

☆ QUOTE OF THE DAY

"We love you as the savior of our race!"

Korean president Syngman Rhee, to General Douglas MacArthur at the ceremony celebrating Seoul's liberation from North Korean forces

September 30

1949: The Berlin Airlift officially came to an end, after 15 months and more than 250,000 flights. It had begun in June 1948, when the Soviet Union blocked all ground traffic into West Berlin, which was located entirely within the Russian zone of occupation in Germany. It was a Soviet attempt to force the United States, Great Britain, and France (the other occupying powers in Germany) to accept Soviet demands concerning the postwar fate of Germany. But the United States defied the Soviets by beginning a round-the-clock aerial supply of West Berlin in Operation Vittles.

1954: The world's first nuclear-powered submarine, *Nautilus* (SSN-571), was commissioned at Groton, Connecticut. In 1958, she became the first U.S. vessel to transit across the geographic North Pole (see August 3).

☆ QUOTE OF THE DAY

"I'll wiggle my wings."

Lt. Gail "Hal" Halvorsen, one of the Berlin Airlift pilots, telling Berlin children how they could recognize him when he flew over to drop candy. "Uncle Wiggly Wings" solo effort to include candy in the airlift led to the bigger "Operation Little Vittles"

An 1846 Currier and Ives lithograph of the death of Tecumseh at the Battle of the Thames. Library of Congress.

October

October 1

1794: George Washington and the Whiskey Rebellion. With "the deepest regret," the president made good on a threat to order federal troops to western Pennsylvania to put down a rebellion by farmers who refused to pay a tax on whiskey. In doing so, Washington soon became the first commander-in-chief ever to lead troops into battle. He led more than 12,000 men, called the Constitutional Army, west to crush the rebellion. By the time Washington arrived, however, the rebellion had essentially collapsed. The incident showed the power and ability of the new federal government to suppress violent resistance to its laws.

1880: John Philip Sousa became leader of the Marine Corps Band—its 17th. The "March King" had earlier apprenticed with the band at age 13. Sousa led the band on its first tour and, in 1890, into recording. Sousa's baton is passed to each new conductor of the band.

1942: The first U.S. jet—the Bell P-59 Airacomet fighter—made its first (unofficial) flight, with Robert M. Stanley at the controls out of California's Muroc Army Air Field. Problems with the plane (including unsuitability for carrier use) meant that the P-59 never saw combat, but nonetheless it provided training for AAF personnel and invaluable data for subsequent development of higher performance jet airplanes.

1947: The North American F-86 Sabre (or Sabrejet) made its debut flight, also out of Muroc Army Air Field (now Edwards Air Force Base). This first swept-wing jet fighter, which broke speed and sound barriers, was a key element in the Korean War. It engaged the Soviet MiG-15 in high-speed dogfights during the conflict.

1957: SAC—the Strategic Air Command—began a round-the-clock watch for Soviet missiles. Headquartered at Offutt Air Force Base in Nebraska, SAC provided 24/7 surveillance of airspace around the United States and abroad throughout the remainder of the Cold War.

1960: The Ballistic Missile Early Warning System radar post at the 26th Air Division's Thule AB, Greenland, became operational. It was the first of three planned warning sites against enemy missile attacks on North America—designed to give 15 minutes' warning.

1961: America's first centralized military espionage organization, the Defense Intelligence Agency (DIA), was established.

⭐ QUOTE OF THE DAY

"Anthems are usually the product of some national crisis."

John Philip Sousa, 1928, entering the national debate on what should be the U.S. national anthem

October 2

1895: Born today: Ruth Cheney Streeter in Brookline, Massachusetts. Streeter was the first director of the US Marine Corps Women's Reserve in 1943. She was also the cofounder of the U.S. Air Force's Cheney Award recognizing valor in aviation (created in memory of her brother who died in WWI).

1981: Ronald Reagan's military buildup: the 40th president, who came to office promising to expand and strengthen America's defense posture, pledged that the United States would produce the B-1 bomber and MX missile. The B-1, designed to penetrate Soviet air space by flying at supersonic speeds while jamming enemy radar, was killed by President Jimmy Carter in 1977, but Reagan resurrected it. On the other hand, the MX (called the "Peacekeeper") was supported by Carter as president but criticized by Reagan. Yet when Reagan became president he changed his mind and supported it.

⭐ QUOTE OF THE DAY

"I was able to tell them about our ships being sunk in plain sight of Atlantic City. In the interior, this was not entirely realized the way we on the coast realized it. That was the first thing, that they were needed, that this was no show, that this was a vast necessity."

Ruth Cheney Streeter, recalling her tour of the U.S. to discuss the war situation, U.S. Naval Institute oral history

October 3

1862: The Battle of Corinth, in Mississippi, began. The Army of the Mississippi, commanded by General William Rosecrans, fought Confederate general Earl Van Dorn's Army of West Tennessee.

1940: The first Army airborne units were formed, and there were five divisions by the summer of 1944.

1962: With Commander Wally Schirra, Jr, piloting, Mercury 8 was launched at Cape Canaveral, Florida. Velocity was up to 17,557 miles per hour. In the nine-hour mission, Schirra orbited Earth six times, achieving an altitude of 175.8 statute miles. The carrier *Kearsarge* picked up the capsule upon reentry and splashed down in the Pacific Ocean.

1993: Two U.S. Army Black Hawk helicopters were shot down during the Battle of Mogadishu, Somalia, killing 19 American soldiers. Master Sergeant Gary Gordon and Sergeant First Class Randy Shughart, snipers who protected the surviving downed servicemen at the second crash site, were killed. They received posthumous Medals of Honor for their lifesaving actions against Somali attackers. The United States had been in Somalia since December 1992 on a peacekeeping and humanitarian mission. After the deaths of the American servicemen Bill Clinton, who became president in January 1993, ordered a withdrawal.

★ QUOTE OF THE DAY

"I don't have too much to do today, so I think I'll get in some flying time."

Commander Wally Schirra on Mercury 8, quoted on
www.WallySchirra.com

October 4

1777: George Washington's troops were repelled during an attack on British positions at Germantown, Pennsylvania. The failed attempt to retake Philadelphia forced Washington and his men to spend the winter at Valley Forge.

1862: The Battle of Corinth concluded as a Union victory. The victory gave the Union control of Corinth, an important transportation center. Union casualties were more than 2,500, while Confederate casualties were more than 4,200. Crucially, for Van Dorn's Confederates, Union general William Rosecrans rested his own men instead of immediately running down the defeated army—prompting Ulysses S. Grant's fury at the wasted opportunity.

★ QUOTE OF THE DAY

"I stand in the presence of brave men, and I take my hat off to you."

General William Rosecrans, after the Battle of Corinth

October 5

1813: The Battle of the Thames: Major general William Henry Harrison led almost 4,000 troops to a decisive victory at the village of Moraviatown in Ontario, Canada. Harrison engaged around 1,600 British-Native American troops led by the Shawnee leader Tecumseh and the inexperienced British general Henry Procter. Procter's troops fled during the battle, leaving Tecumseh's Confederacy warriors to fight alone. Tecumseh and his coleader, the Wyandot leader Roundhead, were killed—and Tecumseh's Confederacy fell apart. Harrison's victory put western Upper Canada into American control.

1937: In remarks clearly aimed at Nazi Germany and Japan, Franklin D. Roosevelt called for a "quarantine" of aggressor nations. Without mentioning them by name, the president said aggressor nations were spending up to 50 percent of their budget on the military—compared to about 11 to 12 percent for the United States.

★ QUOTE OF THE DAY

"By treating them with affection and kindness—by always recollecting that they were my fellow-citizens, whose feelings I was bound to respect, and by sharing on every occasion the hardships which they were obliged to undergo."

General William Henry Harrison, hero of the Battle of the Thames, on how he retained the good will and respect of his men

October 6

1777: British forces captured Fort Clinton and Fort Montgomery—only constructed the year before—and razed them. The forts were overseeing an enormous iron chain stretching the Hudson River as a submerged defense system. The British destroyed the chain.

1884: The Naval War College was established at Newport, Rhode Island.

1958: *Seawolf* (SSN-575) completed a record submerged run of 60 days (starting on August 7), logging more than 13,700 nautical miles.

1961: The Air Force got its first Titan I missile; it was deployed at Lowry AFB, Colorado.

⭑ QUOTE OF THE DAY

"If you're going to look at a leader, the quality of a leader is that his kids are better than he is."

Staff Sergeant David Bellavia, 2019 Medal of Honor recipient,
Eyewitness to War, Volume II

October 7

1777: The second battle of Saratoga began (the first was September 19). The battle near the Hudson River north of New York City proved to be a victory for Continental forces (on October 17).

1924: The rigid airship *Shenandoah* (ZR-1) began a round-trip transcontinental journey from NAS Lakehurst, New Jersey. It returned 18 days later, after covering 9,317 miles in 258 hours of flight. It was commanded by Lt. Cmdr. Zachary Lansdowne.

1950: U.S. and U.N. forces crossed the 38th parallel into North Korea, as the offensive that began with the amphibious landing at Inchon (see September 15) continued.

2001: The United States attacked Afghanistan—the beginning of Operation Enduring Freedom. It came three weeks after terrorists attacked New York City and Washington, D.C., with hijacked commercial airliners (see September 11). President George W. Bush said the goal of Operation Enduring Freedom was to crush the Taliban and al Qaeda, the terror group behind the 9/11 attacks. Bush warned that the United States would take the war on terrorism to any country that sponsored or harbored terrorists.

★ QUOTE OF THE DAY

"Realizing the impossibility of communicating in the extreme terrain, and in the face of almost certain death, [Lieutenant Michael Murphy] fought his way into open terrain to gain a better position to transmit a call. This deliberate, heroic act deprived him of cover, exposing him to direct enemy fire."

President George W. Bush, from Navy SEAL Michael Murphy's Medal of Honor citation. Murphy died June 28, 2005, during Operation Enduring Freedom

October 8

1842: Commodore Lawrence Kearny, who as commander of the East India Squadron had sailed to China to protect Americans during the Opium Wars, on this day sent a letter to the viceroy of China asking that American merchants be given the same privileged trading rights as the

Alvin C. York. Library of Congress.

This Day in U.S. Military History

British. The Chinese ultimately agreed and Chinese ports were opened to U.S. trade for the first time.

1890: America's "Ace of Aces," Eddie Rickenbacker, was born this day in Columbus, Ohio. Rickenbacker was race car driver before entering WWI in the 94th Aero Squadron and recording 26 victories—the most in that war.

1918: Under heavy fire and separated from his patrol in the Argonne Forest, Sgt. Alvin C. York killed 20 German soldiers and captured a hill along with 132 soldiers and 35 machine guns. York, who had unsuccessfully petitioned to be excluded from combat as a conscientious objector, engaged the enemy with only his rifle and service revolver. He received the Medal of Honor and the French Croix de Guerre.

1968: Operation Sealords began—an attack on North Vietnamese supply lines and base areas (SEALORDS was an acronym for Southeast Asia Lake, Ocean, River, and Delta Strategy). It turned into a two-year campaign.

★ QUOTE OF THE DAY

"It's over; let's forget it."

Alvin C. York's modest response to his heroic actions

October 9

1779: During the Second Battle of Savannah, Casimir Pulaski, leading French and American cavalry, was mortally wounded.

1864: The Battle of Tom's Brook resulted in a Union victory for General Philip Sheridan—and firm control of Virginia's strategically important Shenandoah Valley. Confederate general Thomas Rosser engaged his West Point roommate and friend George Armstrong Custer at Tom's Brook: Custer's cavalry chased Rosser's men for 10 miles.

1999: The SR-71 "Blackbird," created by Lockheed's "Skunk Works" division, made its last flight. It had been in service for the U.S. Air Force since 1964. The SR-71 was a Mach 3+ strategic reconnaissance aircraft whose ability to operate at high speeds and altitudes meant that it could evade surface-to-air missiles. The SR-71 never had a loss due to enemy action.

Rigid airship *Shenandoah* with its tender, the oiler *Patoka*, 1924. Library of Congress.

☆ QUOTE OF THE DAY

"You may have made me take a few steps back today, but I will be even with you tomorrow."

Thomas Rosser, to George Armstrong Custer after
the Battle of Tom's Brook

October 10

1845: The Naval School, now known as the U.S. Naval Academy, was established in Annapolis, Maryland—the second oldest service academy. The first class had 50 midshipmen and seven professors.

1923: The first American-built rigid airship, *Shenandoah* (ZR 1), powered by helium gas instead of hydrogen, was christened at NAS Lakehurst, New Jersey (see October 7).

1963: The Limited Nuclear Test Ban Treaty went into effect. The pact with Great Britain and the Soviet Union—the only other nuclear powers at that time—capped eight years of negotiations, which resulted in all three countries agreeing to ban the testing of nuclear weapons in the atmosphere, space, and underwater. Underground tests would be allowed, as no radioactive debris fell beyond the boundaries of the nation conducting the test. The United States, Britain, and Soviet Union also pledged to work towards complete nuclear disarmament, a goal that has proven to be elusive.

1985: President Ronald Reagan authorized a mission to intercept an EgyptAir flight carrying Palestinian Liberation Front terrorists. The PLF terrorists had hijacked the Italian cruise ship *Achille Lauro* on October 7 and killed an American passenger. They demanded a flight out of Egypt for what they thought would be asylum in Tunisia. Instead, Navy F-14's, flying from *Saratoga* (CV-60), intercepted the 737 airliner and forced it to land in Sigonella, Italy.

★ QUOTE OF THE DAY

"Ex Scientia Tridens (Through Knowledge, Sea Power)."

U.S. Naval Academy, motto

October 11

1776: The Battle of Valcour Island took place—one of the first naval battles of the Revolutionary War. It was a tactical British victory in that most American ships—commanded by Brigadier General Benedict Arnold—were captured or destroyed. But it was a strategic American victory in that its defense of Lake Champlain delayed British plans reaching the upper Hudson River Valley.

1779: Casimir Pulaski died of wounds received at the Second Battle of Savannah on the brig *Wasp*.

1968: The first Apollo mission—Apollo 7—blasted into space on an 11-day mission, commanded by Wally Schirra, Jr. Donn F. Eisele was the command module pilot and Marine Corps Major Ronnie Cunningham served as the lunar module pilot. Apollo 7 made 163 orbits of Earth.

1976: George Washington was appointed, posthumously, to the grade of General of the Armies by a congressional joint resolution, and signed by President Gerald R. Ford.

★ QUOTE OF THE DAY

"Whereas it is considered fitting and proper that no officer of the United States Army should outrank Lieutenant General George Washington on the Army list: Now, therefore, be it

This Day in U.S. Military History

Resolved by the Senate and House of Representatives of the United States of America in Congress assembled, That (a) for purposes of subsection (b) of this section only, the grade of General of the Armies of the United States is established, such grade to have rank and precedence over all other grades of the Army, past or present.

(b) The President is authorized and requested to appoint George Washington posthumously to the grade of General of the Armies of the United States, such appointment to take effect on July 4, 1976.

Approved October 11, 1976."

From Public Law 94-479

October 12

1800: During the Quasi-War with France, the U.S. frigate *Boston* captured the French frigate *Le Berceau,* which was later returned to her home country after the Treaty of Mortefontaine.

1914: The first U.S. Navy ship transited the Panama Canal: *Jupiter* (AC-3).

1944: U.S. Army Air Force 1st Lt. Charles E. "Chuck" Yeager became an ace in one day, when his 357th Fighter Group ambushed 22 Messerschmitt fighters over Germany. Yeager, flying a P-51D Mustang—nicknamed "Glamorous Glenn II"—scored five of the group's eight victories, two without firing a shot. Yeager finished World War II with 11.5 kills.

2000: A terror attack against the Navy destroyer, *Cole,* resulted in the deaths of 17 Americans. The ship was refueling in the Yemeni port of Aden when al Qaeda terrorists in a small boat laden with explosives ignited them against the *Cole*'s hull. Thirty-nine sailors were injured.

⭐ QUOTE OF THE DAY

"We last night advanced our second parallel within 300 yards of the Enemy's Works, without the least annoyance from them. Lord Cornwallis's conduct has hitherto been passive beyond conception; he either has not the means of defence [sic], or he intends to reserve himself untill we approach very near him. A few days must determine whether he will or will not give us much trouble."

General George Washington, in an October 12, 1781, letter to Thomas Sim Lee (see October 19)

October 13

1775: The U.S. Navy was born, when the Continental Congress voted for two vessels to be fitted out and armed. The ships had ten carriage guns, a proportional number of swivel guns, and crews of 80 men each. "Semper Fortis"— always strong!

1812: Major general Stephen Van Rensselaer, leading U.S. forces, attempted an invasion of Upper Canada near Queenston, Ontario. British defenders repulsed the Americans in this first major battle of the War of 1812, but they lost Major general Isaac Brock, who was killed.

★ QUOTE OF THE DAY

"[At sea] we possessed a small but highly effective force, the ships well built, manned by thoroughly trained men, and commanded by able and experienced officers. The deeds of our navy form a part of history over which any American can be pardoned for lingering."

Theodore Roosevelt, from *The Naval War of 1812* (1882)

October 14

1890: Dwight D. Eisenhower (as David Dwight Eisenhower) was born in Denison, Texas. The West Point graduate (from the famed class of 1915— see June 12) went on to become a five-star general during World War II. He led the Allied invasion of North Africa in 1943 and Allied invasion of Normandy (Operation Overlord) on June 6, 1944. He also became one of just five men to receive the title of General of the Army. In 1952, he was elected president of the United States and won re-election four years later.

1915: The keel for the first electrically driven battleship—*New Mexico* (BB-40)—was laid at the Brooklyn Navy Yard in New York City. She was commissioned in May 1918 and later saw significant action during World War II in the Pacific. *New Mexico* was one of the escorts to President Woodrow

Wilson when he sailed to France to sign the Treaty of Versailles, and in World War II, was in Tokyo Bay on September 2, 1945, when the formal Japanese surrender took place.

1938: The Curtiss P-40 Warhawk fighter made its first flight. The single-engine, all-metal fighter was used by most of the Allies in World War II. The Curtiss-Wright Corporation, whose main production facilities were in Buffalo, New York, built 13,738 planes. Production ceased in November 1944.

1947: Chuck Yeager became the first person to break the sound barrier—flying faster than the speed of sound—when his Bell X-1 rocket plane (named "Glamorous Glennis" after his first wife) flew over Edwards Air Force Base, Calif.

★ QUOTE OF THE DAY

"I hate war as only a soldier who has lived it can, only as one who has seen its brutality, its futility, its stupidity."

Dwight D. Eisenhower, from an address to the Canadian Club, Ottawa, Canada, January 10, 1946

October 15

1948: The first women officers on active duty were sworn in as commissioned officers in the Navy.

2014: Operation Inherent Resolve was the name given to the military campaign against the Islamic State (also known as ISIS or ISIL) that was launched August 8.

★ QUOTE OF THE DAY

"[T]he name INHERENT RESOLVE is intended to reflect the unwavering resolve and deep commitment of the U.S. and partner nations in the region and around the globe to eliminate the terrorist group ISIL and the threat they pose to Iraq, the region, and the wider international community. It also symbolizes the willingness and dedication of coalition members to work closely with our friends in the region and apply all available dimensions of national power necessary—diplomatic, informational, military, economic—to degrade and ultimately destroy ISIL."

U.S. Central Command, news release, October 15, 2014

October 16

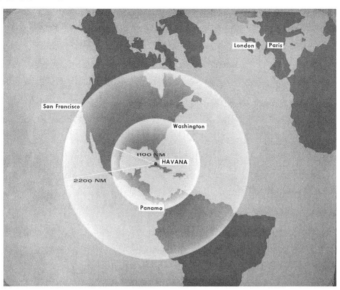

Nuclear missiles placed in Cuba by the Soviet Union sparked the most dangerous chapter of the Cold War: the Cuban Missile Crisis. United States. Department of Defense. Department of Defense Cuban Missile Crisis Briefing Materials. John F. Kennedy Presidential Library and Museum, Boston.

1943: The Navy received its first helicopter, a Sikorsky YR-4B (HNS-1) at Bridgeport, Connecticut.

1962: The Cuban Missile Crisis began. John F. Kennedy was informed that the Soviet Union was placing nuclear missiles in Cuba that were capable of destroying most of the United States. It was the beginning of a tense 13-day standoff that nearly led to nuclear war between the United States and the Soviet Union. Historians estimate that had the Cuban Missile Crisis escalated into nuclear war, 100 million Americans and 100 million Soviets would have died. The standoff gave birth to the term Mutual Assured Destruction (MAD), in which both sides understood that they would each be destroyed in a nuclear conflict.

★ QUOTE OF THE DAY

"I could see the missiles in crates. And missiles out of crates. I could see the roadwork, the missile sites being developed."

Sergeant Thomas Lax, U.S. Air Force, on the Cuban Missile Crisis, in a 2013 interview, Veterans History Project

October 17

1777: Britain surrendered at the second Battle of Saratoga. It was a turning point in the Revolutionary War, for the Continental victory helped persuade the French to recognize American independence and to openly provide military assistance.

1859: President James Buchanan ordered Colonel Robert E. Lee to retake Harper's Ferry. Abolitionist John Brown led a group of 22 who raided the town and captured the U.S. armory at Harper's Ferry, Virginia (now West Virginia) on October 16. The president ordered Marines—commanded by Lee—to regain control of the arsenal. Brown had hoped that his raid would spark a nationwide slave revolt.

1922: The first takeoff from a U.S. aircraft carrier occurred when a Vought VE-7SF, piloted by Lt. Cmdr. Virgil C. Griffin, took off from *Langley* (CV-1), anchored in York River, Virginia.

1941: Less than two months before the United States entered World War II, a German submarine attacked *Kearny* (DD-432). *U-568* torpedoed *Kearny* near Reykjavík, Iceland, after the destroyer came to the aid of British vessels under attack. Eleven sailors were killed and 22 were injured. *Kearny* was repaired and back on combat duty by April 1942. The ship would go on to serve throughout World War II, notably in the North Atlantic and Mediterranean.

★ QUOTE OF THE DAY

"*Kearny* Brought Safely to Port in Iceland by Crew's Heroic Job of Repairing Engines."

Headline, *Evening Star* of Washington, November 4, 1941

October 18

1775: British Royal Navy captain Henry Mowat burned Falmouth (now Portland, Maine) to the ground—at least 300 homes. Mowat had given notice to the Falmouth citizens, who had two days to evacuate women and children. The town was bombarded and then a landing party completed the destruction. Outraged members of the Second Continental Congress decided to confront Royal Navy dominance by forming their own Continental Navy.

1859: Under the command of Colonel Robert E. Lee, U.S. federal troops reached Harper's Ferry, Virginia. After John Brown refused to surrender the armory, Lt. Israel Greene's Marines stormed the barricades and killed or captured the "insurgents," losing one Marine in the attack. After being found guilty of treason, murder, and inciting a slave insurrection by the Commonwealth of Virginia, Brown was hung on December 2, 1859— the first person convicted of treason in U.S. history. Harper's Ferry was emblematic of the tensions leading to the Civil War, in which both Lee and Greene would later join the Confederate Army.

1867: As the United States formally took possession of the Alaska territory from Russia, the American sloop-of-war *Ossipee* carried Russian officials to the transfer ceremonies at Sitka.

1997: The Women in Military Service for America Memorial was dedicated at Arlington National Cemetery.

★ QUOTE OF THE DAY

"The summons [to surrender], as I had anticipated, was rejected. At the concerted signal the storming party moved quickly to the door and commenced the attack. . . . At the threshold one marine fell mortally wounded. The rest, led by Lieutenant Green and Major Russell, quickly ended the contest. The insurgents that resisted were bayoneted. . . . The whole was over in a few minutes."

Colonel Robert E. Lee, report on Harper's Ferry, October 19, 1859

October 19

1781: The American Revolution came to a close with the surrender of British forces at Yorktown, Virginia. British forces were led by General Charles Cornwallis, American forces were led by General George Washington, and French forces were led by Comte de Rochambeau. Cornwallis, under siege since September 28, asked for terms on October 17 sending an officer with a white handkerchief and surrendered on October 19. The Continental Army took more than 7,500 British and German troops captive. The Treaty of Paris (September 3, 1783) formally ended the war.

1915: Three submarines arrived at the navy yard (established 1868) in New London, Connecticut, giving it a new purpose and direction. The

Navy's first submarine base was renamed the Naval Submarine Base New London in June 1916. It is today known as the "Home of the Submarine Force."

1993: President Bill Clinton ordered a withdrawal of Rangers from Somalia, two weeks after 19 Americans died during the Battle of Mogadishu (see October 3).

★ QUOTE OF THE DAY

"The First and Finest."

Naval Submarine Base New London, motto

October 20

1944: U.S. forces invaded Leyte, one of the main islands in the Philippines. Japanese efforts to stop the offensive would lead to the Battle of Leyte Gulf, the largest naval battle of World War II (see October 23). General Douglas MacArthur, who had been ordered to evacuate from the Philippines in March 1942 (see March 11), waded ashore and sent a now famous radio message to the Philippine people: "I have returned."

1950: The first airborne operation of the Korean War occurred when 2,860 paratroopers jumped between Sukchon and Sunchon, 25 miles north of Pyongyang. Far East Air Force C-119s and C-47s transported the assault force and F-80 and F-51 fighters provided air cover.

★ QUOTE OF THE DAY

"I have returned."

General Douglas MacArthur

October 21

1797: The frigate *Constitution* was launched in Boston Harbor. The 44-gun, 204-foot frigate is still in active service and is now the oldest commissioned ship in the U.S. Navy. "Old Ironsides" is berthed today at Charlestown Navy Yard, Boston, Massachusetts.

1837: Despite a truce flag waved by the Seminoles, federal troops shackled Seminole chief Osceola with chains. The disrespectful move so angered the Seminoles that instead of entering into a truce with the United States, they continued to fight for another five years.

1916: The Army established the Reserve Officers Training Corps (ROTC) program, to help bolster the national defense, particularly in time of war.

1917: American troops saw combat for the first time in World War I, when members of the Army's First Division entered the front lines at Sommer-villier under French command.

⭐ QUOTE OF THE DAY

"He was a thunderbolt of war, and always sought the post of danger as the post of honor."

Dr. David Ramsay, field surgeon in the Revolutionary War,
remembering Casimir Pulaski, memorialized on this day
in 1779 in Savannah, Georgia

October 22

1918: The new Army Air Service was organized. It was the forerunner of today's Air Force.

1944: The first use of napalm in the Southwest Pacific occurred when P-38s dropping 75-gallon belly tanks on oil storage tanks at Boela, Ceram, Dutch East Indies.

1957: The first American casualties in Vietnam occurred when eight servicemen were injured in an explosion in Saigon.

1962: Going public with his knowledge of Soviet nuclear missiles in Cuba, John F. Kennedy demanded their removal and threatened war. Speaking on TV, the president announced a naval "quarantine" of Cuba and warned that any Soviet missiles fired anywhere in the Western hemisphere would be regarded as an attack on the United States, "requiring a full retaliatory response."

1972: Operation Linebacker I, the bombing of North Vietnam with B-52s, ended. President Richard Nixon called a cease fire and cessation of bombing to further peace talks then being held in Paris.

✯ QUOTE OF THE DAY

"This Government, as promised, has maintained the closest surveillance of the Soviet military buildup on the island of Cuba. Within the past week, unmistakable evidence has established the fact that a series of offensive missile sites is now in preparation on that imprisoned island. The purpose of these bases can be none other than to provide a nuclear strike capability against the Western Hemisphere."

John F. Kennedy, speech to the nation, October 22, 1962

October 23

1944: The Battle of Leyte Gulf—the largest naval battle of World War II and, according to some historians the largest naval battle in history—began. It would end four days later with a decisive U.S. and Australian victory that effectively crippled the Japanese navy for the remainder of World War II.

1983: A suicide attack destroyed a Marine barracks in Beirut, Lebanon, killing 241 U.S. servicemen. Lebanon-based Hezbollah, terrorists funded by Iran, took responsibility for the attack (and another on French troops the same day). Condemning the "despicable" attacks, President Ronald Reagan would soon order a withdrawal of American forces and would never again send ground troops there—or anywhere in the Middle East.

✯ QUOTE OF THE DAY

"CENTRAL FORCE HEAVILY DAMAGED ACCORDING TO STRIKE REPORTS. AM PROCEEDING NORTH WITH THREE GROUPS TO ATTACK CARRIER FORCES AT DAWN."

Admiral William F. "Bull" Halsey, radio message during the Battle of Leyte Gulf

October 24

1962: A naval blockade of Cuba began, designed to stop further Soviet nuclear missiles and supplies from reaching Cuba—and to force the

U.S.S.R. to agree to remove ballistic missiles and long range bombers it had already deployed there.

1973: Richard Nixon vetoed the War Powers Resolution, aimed at limiting a president's ability to wage war. The president objected to the bill, introduced by Senator Jacob K. Javits of New York, which stipulated that a commander-in-chief had to report to Congress 48 hours after sending troops into combat. The law also said that Presidents could also keep troops in combat for just 60 days (and a 30-day withdrawal period) unless they had Congressional approval for longer deployments. Congress later overrode Nixon's veto.

★ QUOTE OF THE DAY

"And our ship then went down to Cuba and were to monitor incoming freighters and ships that we thought may or may not be carrying missiles into Cuba. We would escort them as far as we could. We didn't want to go into the Cuban . . . waterways, you know, so we had to stay outside. Any ship that we thought was carrying a missile either by sight or just by intelligence, we stopped from going in there. We barricaded the line, they could not pass our line."

> Matthew F. Daulerio, U.S. Navy Sonar Technician Third Class, on *Cone* (DD-866) during the Cuban Missile Crisis, Veterans History Project

October 25

1942: John Basilone and two other Marines repelled an estimated 3,000 Japanese troops in Guadalcanal. The enemy was trying to retake Henderson Field, a key airfield, but Basilone and his fellow Leathernecks, manning three machine guns, held them off until reinforcements arrived. Basilone received the Medal of Honor for his actions; the citation read in part: "Moving an extra gun into position, he placed it in action, then, under continual fire, repaired another and personally manned it, gallantly holding his line until replacements arrived. A little later, with ammunition critically low and the supply lines cut off, Sgt. Basilone, at great risk of his life and in the face of continued enemy attack, battled his way through hostile lines with urgently needed shells for his gunners, thereby contributing in large measure to the virtual annihilation of a Japanese regiment."

1973: The Pentagon moved to DEFCON 3 worldwide for the first time. The previous defense readiness condition (DEFCON) alert was "2" during the 1962 Cuban Missile Crisis. In 1973, the alert was over concern to possible Soviet involvement in the Yom Kippur War between Egypt and Syria against Israel.

1983: President Ronald Reagan ordered U.S. Marines to invade the Caribbean island of Grenada, and rescue 600 American medical students after a coup installed a Marxist regime. Under Operation Urgent Fury, more than 7,300 troops secured the island by November 2. Sixteen U.S. servicemen were killed.

★ QUOTE OF THE DAY

"Now, for chrissakes, try and be helpful, would you? We've got a tough job to do and we don't need the Army giving us a hard time."

Admiral Wes McDonald, commander in chief of Atlantic Command, to Norman Schwarzkopf, on the eve of the Grenada invasion, quoted in Schwarzkopf's memoir *It Doesn't Take a Hero* (1992)

October 26

1774: Ready "on a minute's notice," the "Minutemen" were created within the Massachusetts militia. The tensions of the coming War of Independence prompted their creation. The Massachusetts Provincial Congress asked their militia leaders to pick one third of their members as Minutemen, who were more highly trained.

1940: The P-51 Mustang made its first flight. The North American Aviation P-51 was an iconic long-range, single-seat fighter and fighter-bomber used during World War II, the Korean War, and other conflicts. Praised in 1944 by the Truman Senate War Investigating Committee as "the most aerodynamically perfect pursuit plane in existence."

1944: The Battle of Leyte Gulf—the largest naval battle of World War II and, according to some historians the largest naval battle in history—ended with a decisive U.S. and Australian victory. The Japanese lost so many ships (including 11 destroyers and three battleships) and men in the four-day battle that it could play only a minor role during the remaining ten months of the war. Allied casualties were 3,000 while the Japanese suffered 12,500 casualties.

1956: The XH-40 Bell helicopter was flown for the first time at Fort Worth, Texas. The XH-40 later became the UH-1 Iroquois, or Huey, one of the most widely used helicopters in the Vietnam War.

★ QUOTE OF THE DAY

"The most important thing for survival [in solitary confinement] is communication with someone, even if it's only a wave or a wink, a tap on the wall, or to have a guy put his thumb up."

John McCain, U.S. senator and Navy pilot, taken prisoner by the North Vietnamese on October 26, 1967. Two of his five and a half years as a prisoner were spent in solitary.

October 27

Col. Benjamin O. Davis, in Ramitelli, Italy, March 1945. Photographed by Toni Frissell. Toni Frissell Collection, Library of Congress.

This Day in U.S. Military History

1858: Theodore Roosevelt was born in New York City. The 26th president was in office from 1901 to 1909. A former secretary of the Navy, he gained widespread fame for his leadership of the Rough Riders in the Spanish-American War.

1941: Ten days after a German U-boat torpedoed the U.S. destroyer *Kearny*, Franklin D. Roosevelt told Americans that "America has been attacked, the shooting has started." The president stopped short of declaring war on Germany, though, given that many Americans remained reluctant to get into another European conflict. Another U.S. destroyer, the *Reuben James*, was torpedoed by a German U-boat on October 31, killing 100 Americans. The United States and Germany would declare war on each other in December (see December 11).

1954: Benjamin O. Davis, Jr., became the first African-American general in the Air Force. Davis had been commander of the Tuskegee Airmen in World War II.

1962: Air Force Major Rudolf Anderson, Jr., was shot down by two Soviet missiles over Cuba, becoming the only known casualty of the Cuban Missile Crisis. Anderson's U-2 reconnaissance plane was tasked with taking photographs of Soviet missile installations. He received the first Air Force Cross posthumously.

★ QUOTE OF THE DAY

"[He] was looking far into the future and, seeing airplanes in that future, realized in some mysterious way that I would benefit from the experience."

Benjamin O. Davis, Jr, in his memoir *Benjamin O. Davis, Jr.: American* (1991), on his father purchasing a ride for him with a barnstormer in 1926

October 28

1918: The third phase of the Meuse-Argonne Offensive began, led by U.S. forces.

1962: The Cuban Missile Crisis ended when the Soviet Union agreed to remove nuclear missiles from Cuba. President John F. Kennedy, hours from ordering an attack on Cuba, accepted the Soviet offer and ended the U.S. naval quarantine (blockade). Easily the most dangerous chapter of the Cold War, the Cuban Missile Crisis nearly led to nuclear war between the United States and Soviet Union. Analysts estimate a nuclear exchange between the two nations would have killed 100 million Americans and 100 million Soviets.

★ QUOTE OF THE DAY

"We was cold without blankets and not enough to eat. We had left our mess kits behind so had to eat out of tin cans and some of the boys got sick, but you had to be half dead to get to a hospital."

Private Hubert Joseph Wesselman, 89th Division, AEF, WWI journal entry, Veterans History Project

October 29

1863: The Battle of Wauhatchie (Brown's Ferry) ended with a Union victory, when general Ulysses S. Grant's forces repelled a Confederate attack. The victory gave the Union a key supply line into Chattanooga, Tennessee.

1814: The first steam-powered U.S. Navy warship was launched. The *Demologos* (later renamed *Fulton)* would be commissioned in June 1816 but was never in combat. Uniquely, the *Demologos* was a catamaran, with the steam engine supported between two keels.

1940: As Franklin D. Roosevelt looked on, the first peacetime draft in American history was held. Five weeks earlier on September 14, the president had signed the Selective Training and Service Act of 1940, requiring men aged 21 to 35 to register.

2015: President Barack Obama ordered U.S. ground troops to Syria, to combat the Islamic State (also known as ISIS or ISIL). It marked the first open-ended U.S. military mission in that war-torn country. It was a reversal of his 2013 pledge not to put "American boots on the ground" there.

★ QUOTE OF THE DAY

"Our intensified counter-ISIL campaign will support those efforts by continuing to strengthen opposition partners on the ground, while also coordinating the efforts of our coalition partners."

Secretary of State John Kerry, 2015

This Day in U.S. Military History

October 30

1882: William F. Halsey Jr.—"Bull Halsey"—was born at Elizabeth, New Jersey. An admiral during World War II, he is one of just four individuals to have attained the rank of fleet admiral of the United States Navy. The others were Ernest King, William Leahy, and Chester W. Nimitz.

1953: Dwight Eisenhower signed a National Security Council document stating the U.S. nuclear arsenal must be expanded to meet the growing Soviet threat. The president saw atomic weapons as the best deterrent to Soviet power, but feared the U.S. economy couldn't support both military and domestic spending.

 QUOTE OF THE DAY

"Hit hard, hit fast, hit often."

William F. Halsey

October 31

1959: The first Atlas missile equipped with a nuclear warhead went on alert at Vandenberg AFB, California.

1968: President Lyndon Johnson announced a halt to the bombing of North Vietnam. Speaking five days before the 1968 presidential election, Johnson said the halt was justified because of progress in peace talks with North Vietnam.

 QUOTE OF THE DAY

"All you are suggesting is that we keep on fighting and having our men killed indefinitely."

Secretary of Defense Clark Clifford, to Secretary of State Dean Rusk, 1968

Grumman TBF-1 "Avenger" torpedo bomber being hoisted aboard *Santee* (ACV-29) at Norfolk, Virginia, just before the *Santee* sailed to take part in Operation Torch. Photographed by Lieutenant Horace Bristol, USNR. National Archives.

November

November 1

1861: President Abraham Lincoln appointed George B. McClellan as general-in-chief of the Union army, replacing Winfield Scott. It was Lincoln's *first* appointment of McClellan.

1941: In an uncommon move, President Franklin D. Roosevelt transferred authority of the Coast Guard to the Navy.

1943: The 15th Air Force was established as part of the USAAF in Tunis, Tunisia. General Jimmy Doolittle was its first commander.

1950: The first major ground combat between American and Chinese troops occurred during the Korean War near Unsan.

1952: The United States tested the world's first hydrogen bomb, "Mike," on tiny Elugelab Island at the Enewetak Atoll in the Marshall Islands. Designed by American physicist Richard Garwin, the bomb was a thousand times more powerful than the bombs dropped on Hiroshima and Nagasaki. Detonated at 7:15 a.m., the blast left a crater where Elugelab had been.

★ QUOTE OF THE DAY

"The first lesson is that you can't lose a war if you have command of the air, and you can't win a war if you haven't."

Jimmy Doolittle

November 2

1943: The newly formed 15th Air Force completed its first mission: bombing the Messerschmitt aircraft manufacturers at Wiener Neustadt, Austria. The mission involved 74 B-17 and 38 B-24 bombers in a 1,600-mile round-trip.

1983: The Grenada invasion was declared a success. American troops had invaded a week before (see October 25) after communist forces overthrew the government on that Caribbean island.

★ QUOTE OF THE DAY

"So valiantly did our small party fight that, to the memory of those who unfortunately fell in the battle, enough of honour cannot be paid."

Daniel Boone, born today in 1734, commemorating those who fought in what was perhaps the last engagement of the Revolutionary War: the Battle of Blue Licks (1782). Famed woodsman Boone was a veteran of the French and Indian War as well as of the Revolutionary War

November 3

1813: In the War of 1812, the Battle of Tallasseehatchee took place in the Mississippi Territory near Alexandria, Alabama. An aspect of that war was the battles with Native American tribes. Nine hundred U.S. troops (including legendary frontiersman Davy Crockett) under General John Coffee attacked Red Stick Creek warriors near their village of Tallasseehatchee. The troops routed them, killing women and children as well. An estimated 186 Red Sticks died. Overall commander Andrew Jackson would engage the Red Sticks again at Talladega less than a week later.

1967: Part of the Vietnam War "border battles," the Battle of Dak To began, a three-week battle in the small village of Dak To in the Kon Tum Province of South Vietnam. The Kon Tum Province is bordered by Laos and Cambodia. The People's Army of Vietnam (PAVN) battled the 4th Infantry and 173rd Airborne Brigade—the PAVN hoping to "deplete and destroy" American troops in the highlands. Although the PAVN ultimately withdrew, the United States and South Vietnamese incurred heavy losses. The United States suffered 361 killed and 1,441 wounded. Forty helicopters were lost as well. The North Vietnamese retreated to Laos and Cambodia.

★ QUOTE OF THE DAY

"You just knew the area was crawling with North Vietnamese and that they were there not to avoid contact with us, but to have contact with us."

First Lieutenant Matthew Harrison, 173rd Airborne, quoted in *The Vietnam War* (2017), by Geoffrey C. Ward

November 4

1791: The Western Confederacy, led by Little Turtle, Blue Jacket, and Buckongahelas, surprised and routed the U.S. Army commanded by General Arthur St. Clair in the Battle of Wabash in the Northwest Territory near Fort Recovery, Ohio. The Native American confederation of Miami, Lenape, Shawnee, Potawatomi, and other tribes sprang at dawn. Of the 1,000 American forces, 623 soldiers were killed and 258 wounded. It was the biggest victory by Native Americans over U.S. forces.

1939: Congress agreed to President Franklin D. Roosevelt's proposal to let Allied nations buy American weapons. Roosevelt's changes to the Neutrality Act were clearly aimed at benefitting Britain and France, which had just declared war on Nazi Germany. Roosevelt successfully argued that U.S. neutrality laws prior to the war may have given passive "aid to an aggressor" because it denied aid to victimized nations.

1971: *Nathanael Greene* (SSBN-636) launched a Poseidon C-3 Missile—the first surface launch of the weapon.

 QUOTE OF THE DAY

"November the fourth in the year of ninety-one,
we had a sore engagement near to Fort Jefferson;
Sinclair was our commander, which may remembered be,
for there we left nine hundred men in the Western Territory."

> "Sinclair's Defeat," American folksong first published in 1836

November 5

1862: Abraham Lincoln fired, for the second time, General George McClellan as commander of the Union Army. Lincoln was frustrated that McClellan seemed unable to engage Confederate general Robert E. Lee's Army of Northern Virginia. Lincoln gave McClellan two chances, and the general capitalized on neither of them. It was the second instance that particularly infuriated Lincoln. At Antietam (see September 17)—still the single bloodiest day in American history—McClellan, despite knowing Lee's plan in advance and having a superior force at his disposal, fought Lee to a standstill but failed to defeat him. He also failed to pursue Lee's forces as they withdrew across the Potomac River to Virginia. McClellan, Lincoln famously said, has a "case of the slows."

1915: The first underway catapult launch from a ship occurred when Lt. Cmdr. Henry C. Mustin, in an AB-2 flying boat, took off from *North Carolina* (ACR-12) at Pensacola Bay, Florida. The successful launch led to the use of catapults on battleships and cruisers through World War II and to the present-day steam catapult system.

1945: The first jet landing on an aircraft carrier occurred when Ensign Jake C. West landed his FR-1 Fireball on board *Wake Island* (CVE-65). West made the landing despite losing power on his forward radial engine shortly after taking off, forcing him to start his rear engine.

★ QUOTE OF THE DAY

"[No] victory is assured until the man on the ground takes possession by his physical presence on the enemy's soil."

General Omar Bradley, November 1949

November 6

1854: "The March King," John Philip Sousa was born in Washington, D.C. He followed his father into the Marine Corps Band at age 13, eventually becoming its commander. Among scores of other marches, he composed "Semper Fidelis" (1888), the official Marine Corps march, and "The Stars and Stripes Forever" (1896), the official national march of the United States (per Congress, 1987).

1865: Confederate raider *Shenandoah* sailed to Liverpool, England, and on this day surrendered—making this the last surrender of the Civil War. The *Shenandoah* sailors knew the Civil War was over, but wanted to avoid possible piracy charges in the United States.

1976: Patrick "Pat" Tillman was born at Fremont, California. A professional football player, he enlisted in the army in 2002 after the terror attacks of 9/11. The Army Ranger was killed by friendly fire at Spera, Afghanistan, on April 22, 2004, a fact that was initially—and controversially—kept secret. Tillman was awarded the Purple Heart, Silver Star, Meritorious Service Medal, and many other posthumous honors.

☆ QUOTE OF THE DAY

"Hurrah for the flag of the free.
May it wave as our standard forever
The gem of the land and the sea,
The banner of the right."

> Some of the lyrics to "The Stars and Stripes Forever," written and
> composed by John Philip Sousa

November 7

1811: Battle of Tippecanoe: General William Henry Harrison routed the Shawnee at the Tippecanoe and Wabash Rivers near Battle Ground, Indiana. Harrison commanded 1,000 troops to Tenskwatawa's estimated 700 (or fewer) warriors. Tenskwatawa, or The Prophet, was the brother of Shawnee leader Tecumseh, and the federal victory put an end to Techumseh's dream of a pan-Indian confederation. The battle also provided a campaign slogan for Harrison's successful presidential bid in 1840.

1861: As part of the Union's blockade strategy, a U.S. Naval force under Samuel Francis Du Pont captured Port Royal Sound, South Carolina. Du

General William Henry Harrison. Library of Congress.

This Day in U.S. Military History

The Union frigate *Wabash*, part of the South Atlantic Blockading Squadron.

Pont, on the *Wabash*, was the commander of the South Atlantic Blockading Squadron and oversaw a fleet of 77 vessels. On this day, 14 gunboats—arranged in an oval—fired on the Confederate positions. The harbor remained in Union control for the rest of the war. Du Pont was made a rear admiral for the success. He mused on the victory: "It is not my temper to rejoice over fallen foes, but this must be a gloomy night in Charleston."

1881: Secretary of Navy William H. Hunt, seeking $30 million in Congressional appropriations for 21 armored and 70 unarmored vessels, included in his report a recommendation that these new armored ships be constructed of steel instead of iron. Hunt had formed the Naval Advisory Board in June 29, 1881. He worried that the navy was languishing after the Civil War. In the Naval Appropriations Act of 1883, Congress gave Hunt four steel-hulled ships.

1973: Vetoed by President Richard Nixon on October 24, the War Powers Resolution (or War Powers Act of 1973) became law when the House and Senate overrode Nixon's veto. The law requires a president to notify Congress within 48 hours of committing armed forces to military action and forbids those forces from remaining for more than 60 days without Congressional authorization or a formal declaration of war.

2004: The bloodiest battle of the Iraq War—Operation Phantom Fury—began, when U.S., British and Iraqi forces attacked Iraqi insurgents in

Fallujah. It was the biggest urban combat fighting the Marines had been engaged in since the Vietnam War. The battle would last for six weeks, ending on December 23.

★ QUOTE OF THE DAY

"The condition of the Navy imperatively demands the prompt and earnest attention of Congress. Unless some action be had in its behalf it must soon dwindle into insignificance."

Secretary of the Navy, William H. Hunt, 1881

November 8

1942: Operation Torch—the Allied invasion of North Africa—began. Its objectives were to ease Nazi Germany's pressure on Allied forces in Egypt, while laying the groundwork for a subsequent invasion of Southern Europe. Torch—a three-pronged attack on Casablanca, Oran, and Algiers—also provided the second front that the Soviet Union had asked for after it was invaded by the Germans in June 1941. General Dwight D. Eisenhower had been named commander of Torch in July 1942. The operation ended eight days later in an Allied victory.

1990: President George H.W. Bush announced that he planned to add more than 200,000 U.S. troops to those already deployed in Operation Desert Shield in the Persian Gulf region. The number of Marines in the area would be doubled by the addition of II MEF units from the Corps' east coast bases, and the 5th MEB from California. Within the next two months, Marine strength in the objective area would increase to nearly 90,000 Marines.

★ QUOTE OF THE DAY

"The fact that land resistance was not great anywhere testifies to the success of [General Mark] Clark's mission."

General Dwight D. Eisenhower, on General Mark Clark's secret mission to gather intelligence before Operation Torch

November 9

1861: Samuel Francis Du Pont's gunboats seized control of Beaufort, South Carolina—cutting off communications between Charleston and Savannah, Georgia.

1862: General Ambrose Burnside assumed command of the Union Army of the Potomac, following the removal by President Abraham Lincoln of General George B. McClellan.

1901: Worried about Japan's growing power, President Theodore Roosevelt established a U.S. naval base in the Philippines. The base at Subic Bay was on territory the United States had won from Spain during the Spanish-American War of 1898. Roosevelt wanted to move the Navy's entire base of Pacific operations to Subic Bay, but encountered intense political opposition. Instead the headquarters of the U.S. Pacific Fleet was established in Pearl Harbor, on the Hawaiian island of Oahu.

1950: In the first engagement between MiG-15 and F9F jets, Lt. Cmdr. William T. Amen shot down a MiG, becoming the first Navy pilot to shoot down a jet aircraft. Aircraft based on *Philippine Sea* (CV-47) also made their first attack on bridges over the Yalu River, which connected North Korea and China.

★ QUOTE OF THE DAY

"The enemy having complete possession of the water and inland navigation, commands all the islands on the coast and threatens both Savannah and Charleston, and can come in his boats, within 4 miles of this place [Lee's headquarters]… We have no guns that can resist their batteries, and have no resources to meet them in the field."

Robert E. Lee, reacting to the capture of Beaufort

November 10

1775: The U.S. Marine Corps was born, when the Continental Congress approved the creation of two battalions of Continental Marines. Its motto is "Semper fidelis," a Latin phrase that means "always faithful" or "always loyal."

F-117 Nighthawk in 2002.

1988: The existence of the Lockheed F-117A Stealth Fighter, which had made its first flight on June 18, 1981, was confirmed by the Pentagon in a press conference.

1954: President Dwight D. Eisenhower dedicated the Marine Corps War Memorial in Arlington, Virginia, on the Corps' birthday.

2001: George W. Bush said the United States would, if needed, attack any nation that presented a threat to American security. As proof, Bush cited Operation Enduring Freedom, the American-led invasion of Afghanistan, which he launched the previous month (see October 7). The president's speech at the United Nations came two months after 9/11.

★ QUOTE OF THE DAY

"If I do my full duty, the rest will take care of itself."

General George S. Patton, diary entry during Operation Torch,
November 1942

November 11

1861: Chief Aeronaut of the Union Army Balloon Corps, Thaddeus S. C. Lowe, ascended in the balloon *Washington* to conduct aerial observation of Confederate positions. The balloon was towed from the coal barge *George Washington Parke Custis* on the Potomac River.

1885: George S. Patton was born at San Gabriel, California. Known as "Old Blood and Guts," he was a World War II general who commanded the Seventh Army in the Mediterranean and the Third Army in France and Germany following D-Day. Earlier in his career he was attached to the newly formed United States Tank Corps of the American Expeditionary Forces and saw action during World War I. Between the wars, he played a central figure in the development of the Army's doctrine of armored warfare and commanded its Second Armored Division.

1918: On the eleventh hour of the eleventh day of the eleventh month of the year, World War I ended, as an armistice was signed between Germany and the Allied nations.

1919: Woodrow Wilson proclaimed the first Armistice Day, to honor the nation's veterans one year to the day after the end of World War I—"the war to end all wars." Armistice Day is now known in the United States, of course, as Veterans Day. Wilson: "Armistice Day will be filled with lots of pride in the heroism of those who died in the country's service and with gratitude for the victory, both because of the thing from which it has freed us and because of the opportunity it has given America to show her sympathy with peace and justice in the councils of the nations."

1921: Warren Harding dedicated the Tomb of the Unknowns at Arlington National Cemetery. Holding unidentified remains of U.S. soldiers, the Tomb is inscribed, "Here Rests in Honored Glory an American Soldier Known but to God." Guarded solemnly around the clock, the Tomb of the Unknowns is an important pilgrimage for any visitor to Washington, D.C. Of Arlington National Cemetery, it is said to be "Where valor proudly sleeps."

★ QUOTE OF THE DAY

"I was reading a book at the time and at 10.59 the guns all quit at once. It was to [sic] good to be true. I didn't cheer as I cheered myself hoarse while at Souilly and it was a false report so I didn't want to do it again."

Private Hubert Joseph Wesselman, 89th Division, AEF,
journal entry for November 11, 1918

November 12

1921: The first air-to-air refueling occurred when Wesley May, with a 5-gallon can of gasoline strapped to his back, stepped from the wing of a Lincoln Standard to the wing skid of a JN-4 and climbed to the engine to pour gas into the tank. Frank Hawks flew the Lincoln and Earl S. Daugherty the JN-4.

1942: The Naval Battle of Guadalcanal (or the Battle of the Solomons) began and lasted through November 15. Operation Watchtower—the Guadalcanal Campaign—had begun August 7, 1942. In this phase of the campaign, the Imperial Japanese Navy attacked during an effort to bring reinforcements.

☆ QUOTE OF THE DAY

"You look out, you get on deck and look around and it's just hundreds of ships, all over the place, and it's all ours, you know."

William T. Burrows, Seaman First Class on the *Drexler*, describing arriving at Guadalcanal, Veterans History Project

November 13

1942: The five Sullivan brothers—George, Frank, Joe, Matt, and Al, of Waterloo, Iowa—were killed when *Juneau* (CL-52) was destroyed during the Naval Battle of Guadalcanal. In the wake of their deaths, the War Department adopted its Sole Survivor Policy, designed to protect members of a family from the draft or combat duty if they have already lost family members in military service.

1982: The Vietnam Veterans Memorial was dedicated on the National Mall in Washington, D.C. The Memorial Wall, designed by architect Maya Lin, is comprised of polished black granite panels upon which are inscribed (to date) 58,220 names of those who have been declared dead in the conflict. The other parts of the memorial, added later, are the Vietnam Women's Memorial (dedicated November 11, 1993) and the statue *The Three Soldiers* (dedicated November 11, 1984).

2001: The Afghan capital, Kabul, fell. Taliban forces, who had controlled the city since 1996, fled the night before, leaving the city to American, NATO, and Northern Alliance forces.

The Sullivan Brothers on board the *Juneau* during its christening in the New York Navy Yard on February 14, 1942. NH 52362 courtesy of Naval History & Heritage Command.

★ QUOTE OF THE DAY

"We do not seek to make any statement about the correctness of the war. Rather, by honoring those who sacrificed, we hope to provide a symbol of national unity and reconciliation."

Jan C. Scruggs, Vietnam War veteran and founder of the Vietnam Veterans Memorial Fund, on his drive to create the Vietnam Veterans Memorial

November 14

1862: Abraham Lincoln approved a plan by General Ambrose Burnside to capture the Confederate capital of Richmond, Virginia. It would be a mistake. It led to the disastrous Battle of Fredericksburg on December 13, in which the Army of the Potomac was dealt one of its worst defeats at the hands of General Robert E. Lee's Army of Northern Virginia.

1910: The birth of U.S. Navy aviation: 24-year-old civilian Eugene Ely piloted the first aircraft to take off from a ship. It was the cruiser *Birmingham*

(CL-2) at Hampton Roads, Virginia. Ely's plane was Glenn Curtiss's Curtiss Model D biplane, constructed of spruce, bamboo, and linen, with a tricycle undercarriage and the propeller mounted behind the pilot.

1965: U.S. and North Vietnamese forces clashed in a major engagement for the first time at Ia Drang Valley. U.S. forces included the 3rd Brigade, 1st Cavalry Division (Airmobile). In a strategy they used for the remainder of the war, the North Vietnamese countered superior U.S. air power and artillery by instigating close combat—such physical proximity meant that U.S. air strikes could not be used without endangering American lives.

★ QUOTE OF THE DAY

"An alert soldier is an alive soldier."

General Mark W. Clark

November 15

1864: Union troops set Atlanta, Georgia, ablaze. The city had surrendered two months earlier (see September 2) but now General William T. Sherman ordered it destroyed, to deprive Confederate forces of key supply lines. Captain O.M. Poe, chief engineer, oversaw preliminary razing of buildings such as railroad roundhouses, smokestacks, and warehouses. Then the city was torched (Sherman attempted to exempt private homes with moderate success). The port city of Savannah would soon be the next target of Sherman's scorched earth policy (see December 21).

★ QUOTE OF THE DAY

"On the morning of the 16th, nothing was left of Atlanta except its churches, the City Hall and private dwellings."

Lt. Col. Charles Morse, Union soldier with Sherman

November 16

1776: The American flag was first saluted by a foreign power on this day. As the Continental ship *Andrew Doria* made its salute, it was returned by the

Dutch at St. Eustatius, West Indies. The flag was the "Grand Union Flag," adopted on December 3, 1775. The "Stars and Stripes" wasn't adopted until June 14, 1777.

1776: Twenty-five-year-old Margaret Corbin, who had accompanied her husband John to war in the American cause as a nurse, entered the battle on this day during the defense of Fort Washington. She took over a cannon along with 600 other defenders when her husband was killed. Corbin was herself seriously wounded, and later became the first woman to receive a military pension.

1961: John F. Kennedy ordered an increase in military aid to South Vietnam, but did not commit U.S. combat troops. The president was concerned at the advances being made by the communist Viet Cong, but did not want to become involved in a land war in Vietnam.

★ QUOTE OF THE DAY

"Reward and punish every man according to his merit, without partiality or prejudice; hear his complaints; if well founded, redress them; if otherwise, discourage them, in order to prevent frivolous ones."

General George Washington, November 10, 1775, letter to Colonel
William Woodford, who had asked for advice

November 17

1917: The first German submarine sunk by the United States during World War I occurred when *Fanning* (DD-37) and *Nicholson* (DD-52) sank *U-58* off Milford Haven, Wales.

1924: The Navy's first aircraft carrier—*Langley*—began fleet operations. The 11,500-ton flat top, commissioned in 1922, had been converted from the collier *Jupiter.*

2008: The United States and Iraq signed an accord that mandated a full withdrawal of American troops by the end of 2011. The so-called Status of Forces Agreement (SOFA) said that U.S. combat operations would be limited beginning January 1, 2009, and that American troops would be withdrawn from urban areas by June 30, 2009.

⭐ QUOTE OF THE DAY

"I dove off of Charleston, South Carolina, and surfaced off of Rota, Spain, three months later. We never came up for three months. We stayed under for three months."

Jack Blank, U.S. Navy submarine chief, Veterans History Project

November 18

1890: The first American battleship—*Maine*—was launched. In 1898 it would be destroyed in an explosion at Havana, Cuba (see February 15). The United States would use that disaster as an excuse to declare war on Spain.

1961: 18,000 American military advisors were sent to South Vietnam by President John F. Kennedy.

⭐ QUOTE OF THE DAY

"There was an awful moment of trembling and roar, then a tearing, wrenching, crunching sound of immense volume, so great that you cannot conceive it: then falling metal, a great wrench and twist and a heeling subsidence of the Vessel. There was instantaneous darkness and smoke filled my cabin. There was no mistaking it. I knew in the instant that my vessel had been destroyed."

Captain Charles D. Sigsbee, commander of the *Maine*, letter to his wife, February 17, 1898

November 19

1863: A somber President Abraham Lincoln dedicated the Gettysburg National Cemetery in Gettysburg, Pennsylvania, site of the bloody July battle that took the lives of an estimated 8,000 soldiers. His 272-word address is considered among the greatest of all presidential speeches.

1969: Two American astronauts walked on the moon. The second moon landing—Apollo 12—occurred when astronauts Charles (Pete) Conrad,

Jr., and Alan L. Bean, flew their command module to the lunar surface and landed at the Ocean of Storms. A third astronaut, Richard F. Gordon Jr., orbited in the command module during the lunar mission.

★ QUOTE OF THE DAY

"But in a larger sense, we can not dedicate, we can not consecrate, we can not hallow this ground. The brave men, living and dead, who struggled here, have consecrated it, far above our poor power to add or detract."

Abraham Lincoln, from the "Gettysburg Address"

November 20

1856: Diplomatic relations between China and the United States began after the navy ships *Levant, Portsmouth*, and *San Jacinto* landed at Canton, under the command of Cmdr. Andrew Foote.

1943: The U.S. invasion of Betio Island, Tarawa Atoll, Gilbert Islands, began. It was the first American offensive in the central Pacific region. It was also the first time in the Pacific War that the United States had faced serious Japanese opposition to an amphibious landing. Some 4,500 Japanese defenders, heavily armed, fought nearly to the last man—taking a heavy toll on U.S. Marines. After 76 hours of bitter fighting, during which nearly 1,000 Marines were killed and more than 2,000 wounded, Betio Island was declared the island secure.

★ QUOTE OF THE DAY

"The island [Tarawa] was the most heavily defended atoll that ever would be invaded by Allied forces in the Pacific."

Joseph Alexander, historian and former U.S. Marine amphibious officer.

November 21

1817: 250 U.S. soldiers from Fort Scott under Major Twiggs attacked a Miccosukee Seminole encampment at Fowlton (now present-day Bainbridge,

Georgia) in an attempt to capture Chief Neamathia. The Miccosukees were able to resist, but another attack on November 23 forced the tribe to abandon their village. These events are considered the beginning of the First Seminole War (1817-19) in which General Andrew Jackson ultimately defeated the Seminoles and helped push Florida out of Spanish hands into American control.

1944: *Sealion,* a *Balao*-class submarine, sank the Japanese battlecruiser *Kongō* and the destroyer *Urakaze* in the Taiwan Strait.

1970: In Operation Ivory Coast, a joint military operation, U.S. Army Special Forces landed by helicopter to raid a North Vietnamese prisoner-of-war camp near Hanoi. They discovered no Americans to rescue—they had been moved.

1994: A post-Cold War drama—Project Sapphire—occurred when three C-5 aircraft secretly transported nuclear technicians, equipment, and 1,300 pounds of highly enriched uranium (HEU) from the former Soviet republic of Kazakhstan to the United States to keep it from potentially falling into the hands of terrorists, smugglers, or hostile governments. The HEU was converted into commercial nuclear fuel.

★ QUOTE OF THE DAY

"I fought in three wars and three more wouldn't be too many to defend my country."

General Daniel "Chappie" James

November 22

1988: Its creation and development kept in secrecy for years, on this day the B-2 Spirit "stealth" bomber was unveiled to the public in Palmdale, California. Designed by Northrop Grumman, the B-2 high subsonic aircraft has a wingspan of 172 feet (more than half a football field), yet its radar signal is the size of a bird. The unusual batwing-shaped, two-pilot craft could carry a large payload and operate long range (6,000 miles without refueling). It was painted dark grey to disappear against a night sky. The B-2 made decisive strikes against the Taliban in Operation Enduring Freedom.

This Day in U.S. Military History

★ QUOTE OF THE DAY

"[The] B-2 became a poster child for excessive Pentagon spending due to its $2 billion price tag . . ."

Sandra Erwin, *National Defense* magazine, 2015

November 23

1878: Ernest J. King was born in Lorain, Ohio. At 19 years of age—and still attending the Naval Academy—King served on the cruiser *San Francisco* (C-5) during the Spanish-American War. *San Francisco* was patrolling the waters off Florida and Cuba. King's first command came in 1914 on the destroyer *Terry*. An admiral during World War II, he was one of just four individuals to have attained the rank of fleet admiral of the U.S. Navy. The others were William Halsey, William Leahy, and Chester W. Nimitz. King served in the U.S. Navy for 55 years.

1943: The Battle of Tarawa ended with an American victory. It took place at the Tarawa Atoll in the Gilbert Islands, and was part of Operation Galvanic. Tarawa was the first American offensive in the critical central Pacific region. American casualties were horrific: in three days of battle, an estimated 1,009 Marines were killed and 2,101 wounded; the *Liscome Bay*, an escort carrier, was also sunk, with the loss of 644 lives. (Among *Liscome Bay* deaths was that of Doris Miller, first African American to receive the Navy Cross.)

★ QUOTE OF THE DAY

"No fighter ever won his fight by covering up—by merely fending off the other fellow's blows. The winner hits and keeps on hitting even though he has to take some stiff blows in order to be able to keep on hitting."

Ernest J. King

November 24

1794: Twelfth U.S. president Zachary Taylor was born in Barboursville, Virginia. His illustrious military career of 41 years propelled him into the presidency. "Old Rough and Ready" was a hero of the Mexican-American War of 1846 to 1848, winning the battles of Palo Alto, Monterrey, Buena Vista, among others.

1863: The "battle above the clouds": the Battle of Lookout Mountain saw 10,000 Union troops under Major general Joseph Hooker climb and capture Lookout Mountain near Chattanooga. They faced the Army of Tennessee (more than 8,700 troops) commanded by General Carter L. Stevenson. The Union was beginning to break the Confederate siege of the Tennessee city.

1944: For the first time since Captain Jimmy Doolittle's daring raid in 1942 (see April 18), U.S. bombers attacked the city of Tokyo, Japan. The raid's 111 B-29 Superfortresses targeted the Nakajima aircraft engine works. Bombing of Japanese cities would intensify in the months to come.

1991: After nearly a century, the United States gave up control of Subic Bay Naval Base in the Philippines (see November 9).

★ QUOTE OF THE DAY

"Captain Bragg, it is better to lose a battery than a battle."

> General Zachary Taylor, reported comment to Braxton Bragg during the Battle of Buena Vista (1847) when Bragg wanted to pull his battery back

November 25

1863: In the Battle Missionary Ridge, the Military Division of the Mississippi commanded by General Ulysses S. Grant defeated General Braxton Bragg's Confederate Army of Tennessee, thus finally capturing Chattanooga, Tennessee. Bragg's forces retreated to Georgia, later pursued by Union general William T. Sherman the following spring.

1864: Colonel Kit Carson, in command of the 1st Regiment New Mexico Volunteer Cavalry (335 soldiers), attacked a 1,400-strong confederation of Kiowa, Comanche, and Plains Apache in the First Battle of Adobe Walls in the Texas Panhandle. Carson's remit was to stop Native American attacks on Anglo settlers in the area. The Native Americans were able to force the expeditionary troops from the field.

1950: In the Korean War, the Eighth Army launched the "Home-by-Christmas" offensive.

1961: The world's first nuclear-powered aircraft carrier—the *Enterprise*—was commissioned. It was the eighth United States naval vessel to bear that name. The "Big E" was 1,123 feet long with a displacement of 93,284-long-tons. *Enterprise* was decommissioned in 2017, but the name has been adopted for a future Gerald R. Ford aircraft carrier.

2001: The first American combat death in Afghanistan occurred when CIA officer Johnny "Mike" Spann was attacked during an uprising by Taliban captives at the Gala Jangi prisoner-of-war camp in Mazar-i-Sharif.

★ QUOTE OF THE DAY

"We are Legend;
Ready on Arrival;
The First, the Finest;
Eight Reactors, None Faster."

Enterprise, motto

November 26

1946: The battleship *Oklahoma* (BB-37) was auctioned for scrap. The battleship, sunk during the Japanese attack on Pearl Harbor, had been retrieved from the harbor to prevent navigation hazards and was decommissioned September 1, 1944. After the sale, while being towed to California, *Oklahoma* sank in a storm in the Pacific Ocean.

1969: Richard Nixon amended the draft, establishing conscription based on a lottery. The first draft lottery was held on December 1, and determined the 1970 draft order for registrants born between January 1, 1944, and December 31, 1950.

1950: A massive surprise attack by communist Chinese troops on November 25 at the Ch'ongch'on River in North Korea drove U.S. and U.N. forces (the Eighth Army) back, ending any American hopes for a quick end to the Korean War (see November 25). The Battle of Ch'ongch'on River lasted through December 2 and was a Chinese victory that saw U.N. forces retreat to the 38th Parallel. The war would become a grinding, bloody stalemate until a truce was signed July 27, 1953.

2002: George W. Bush signed a bill creating the Department of Homeland Security. Citing "the dangers of a new era," the president said the cabinet-level department would integrate and oversee 22 existing federal security agencies, such as the Immigration and Naturalization Service, Coast Guard, and Border Patrol.

★ **QUOTE OF THE DAY**

"We were pushing ahead of everybody when we ran smack into what seemed like most of the Chinese from China."

Captain Elmer Dodson, X Corps, Korean War

November 27

1901: The Army War College was founded at Washington, D.C. Its founding statement from Secretary of War Elihu Root: "Not to promote war, but to preserve peace by intelligent and adequate preparation to repel aggression...."

1950: The Battle of Chosin Reservoir began in temperatures of minus 20 to 30 degrees Fahrenheit. An important Korean War battle, it began after a surprise Chinese attack (see November 26) that pushed U.S. and U.N. forces out of North Korea.

1965: With 120,000 troops in Vietnam, the Pentagon asked Lyndon Johnson for 280,000 more. The president agreed. At the height of the Vietnam War (1968), U.S. troop strength peaked at 538,000. More than 58,000 Americans were killed during the war.

★ **QUOTE OF THE DAY**

"SURRENDER YOU ARE SAFE."

North Korean message scrawled on a hut in an abandoned village, seen in an Associated Press photo

November 28

1929: Polar explorer and naval aviator Richard E. Byrd, during his first Antarctic expedition (1928-30), concluded the first flight to the South

Pole and back in the *Floyd Bennett* trimotor transport plane with Bernt Balchen (pilot), Harold June (copilot), and Ashley McKinley (photographer). Byrd was commander and navigator. The journey from his base camp Little America took more than 18 hours. All four men were fêted on their return home to the United States in the summer of 1930.

1941: The aircraft carrier *Enterprise* (CV-6) left Pearl Harbor to deliver Marine aircraft to Wake Island—a routine mission in the Pacific Ocean. By December 5—two days before the attack on Pearl Harbor—there would be no carriers left at the Pacific base. *Enterprise* returned to Pearl Harbor on December 8.

1943: In Iran, Franklin D. Roosevelt attended the Tehran Conference to plot World War II strategy with British prime minister Winston Churchill and Soviet premier Joseph Stalin—the first meeting of the "Big Three." One of the main goals of the conference was to agree on a timetable for a second front in Europe against Nazi Germany. It was decided that "Operation Overlord," as the invasion of France would be called, would begin in May 1944 and coincide with a Soviet attack on Germany's eastern border. Stalin also agreed to enter the Pacific war against Japan.

★ QUOTE OF THE DAY

"My calculations indicate that we have reached the vicinity of the South Pole . . . Will soon turn north. We can see an almost limitless polar plateau."

Commander Richard E. Byrd, first message ever sent from the South Pole, sent by wireless "aboard airplane Floyd Bennett"

November 29

1863: The Battle of Fort Sanders, Knoxville, Tennessee, ended in Confederate withdrawal. The Union victory, plus the loss of Chattanooga (see November 25), put much of eastern Tennessee in Union control.

1864: Tensions between immigrant white settlers and nomadic Native American tribes in Colorado sparked the Sand Creek Massacre. Former preacher Colonel John Chivington, who had unapologetically vowed to exterminate Native western peoples and to "wade in gore," led his troops (including civilian volunteers) out of Fort Lyon on the night of November 28 to arrive at dawn at a peaceful Cheyenne encampment at Sand Creek. Despite Cheyennes waving white or American flags, the Chivington forces slaughtered an estimated 148 people—more than half of them women and children—and took 100 scalps as well as mutilating corpses. Some U.S. soldiers refused to participate. There were some Cheyenne survivors, whose accounts led to retaliation against U.S. soldiers and white settlers.

⭐ QUOTE OF THE DAY

"[The Sand Creek attack was a] cowardly and cold-blooded slaughter, sufficient to cover its perpetrators with indelible infamy and the face of every American with shame and indignation."

Conclusion of a Congressionally ordered Army court of inquiry into the Sand Creek Massacre

November 30

1950: Harry Truman said if necessary, he would use atomic weapons to end the Korean War. The president's threat came days after China entered the war, joining North Korea in attacks on American and United Nations troops. The top Allied commander in Korea, General Douglas MacArthur, also advocated bombing China, but his disagreements with the president led to his firing in 1951 (see April 11).

1951: In one of the largest aerial battles of the Korean War, F-86 pilots engaged 44 enemy aircraft over the island of Taehwa-do. The Sabre pilots destroyed 12 and damaged three others.

1993: A ban on women serving aboard combat ships was lifted, when Bill Clinton signed legislation ending the restriction.

⭐ QUOTE OF THE DAY

"There is no substitute for victory."

General Douglas MacArthur, 1951 letter on the Korean War

General George S. Patton in Sicily, 1943. Library of Congress.

December

December 1

1921: The first flight ever of an airship filled with helium: the C-7 left Norfolk, Virginia, and arrived later that day in Washington, D.C. It was commanded by Lt. Cmdr. Zachary Lansdowne and piloted by Lt. Cmdr. Ralph F. Wood.

1945: Captain Sue S. Dauser, Navy Nurse Corps, was the recipient of the first Navy Distinguished Service Medal awarded to a nurse. As superintendent of the Navy Nurse Corps beginning in 1939, she oversaw its growth to more than 11,000 nurses in 1945 from fewer than 500. Dauser was also the first woman to attain the rank of captain in the Navy.

2009: President Barack Obama announced a troop surge in Afghanistan. An additional 30,000 personnel would be deployed, joining 68,000 service members who were already there.

★ QUOTE OF THE DAY

"It is not enough to fight. It is the spirit which we bring to the fight that decides the issue. It is morale that wins the victory."

General George C. Marshall, 1948

December 2

1936: Boeing's B-17 Flying Fortress made a test flight for the first time. During World War II, it would be so critical to the war effort that General Carl Spaatz, the American air commander in Europe, said, "Without the B-17 we may have lost the war."

1954: President Dwight Eisenhower signed a defense pact with Taiwan, the Mutual Defense Treaty, after Communist China bombed the Taiwanese islands of Quemoy and Matsu. In 1960, he cemented his support for Taiwan by becoming the only president to visit the nation.

1965: *Enterprise* (CVAN-65) and *Bainbridge* (DLGN-25) became the first nuclear-powered task unit used in combat operations. They launched air strikes on enemy targets near Bien Hoa, Vietnam.

★ QUOTE OF THE DAY

"But all history has taught us the grim lesson that no nation has ever been successful in avoiding the terrors of war by refusing to defend its rights—by attempting to placate aggression."

Dwight Eisenhower, 1959

December 3

1775: The *Alfred* was commissioned on this day in Philadelphia, Pennsylvania—a former merchant vessel (as *Black Prince*) that had been purchased by the Continental Navy and refitted as a man-of-war. Either on this date or shortly after, *Alfred* became the first ship to raise the American flag. Commander Lt. John Paul Jones hoisted the "Grand Union Flag."

1826: George B. McClellan was born in Philadelphia, Pennsylvania. Best known as the Civil War general twice put in command of the Union Army and twice fired from that command by President Abraham Lincoln. McClellan had previously fought in the Mexican-American War and was made a captain after the Battle of Chapultepec. He pursued without enthusiasm the "Anaconda Plan" that sought to encircle and blockade the Confederacy—a plan that was first envisioned by his old commander, General Winfield Scott. McClellan's methodical ways (he was called the "Mud Mole" by the *New York Herald Tribune*) and failure to pursue Robert E. Lee after Antietam ultimately ended his Civil War command. After a failed run at the presidency (the 1864 election against incumbent Lincoln), McClellan was elected governor of New Jersey (1878-81).

★ QUOTE OF THE DAY

"Will you pardon me for asking what the horses of your army have done since the Battle of Antietam that would fatigue anything?"

Abraham Lincoln, letter to George B. McClellan

December 4

1942: U.S. forces attacked Italy for the first time, when 24 B-24s of the Ninth Air Force attacked ships docked at Naples.

1944: *Flasher* (SS-249), the only American submarine to sink more than 100,000 tons of enemy shipping in World War II (21 ships), sank Japanese destroyer *Kishinami* in the South China Sea. Lieutenant Commander Reuben T. Whitaker was at the helm. *Flasher* would receive the Presidential Unit Citation for its service.

1992: George H.W. Bush ordered 28,000 Marines to Somalia, to be sent in four stages. The East African country was being torn apart by civil war; the outgoing president wanted to help with the distribution of humanitarian aid. He called the military mission "God's work." But the Americans soon found themselves drawn into the conflict—with disastrous results (see October 3).

★ QUOTE OF THE DAY

"Only the United States has the global reach to place a large security force on the ground in such a distant place quickly and efficiently and, thus, save thousands of innocents from death."

George H.W. Bush

December 5

1941: *Lexington* (CV-2) left Pearl Harbor to deliver Marine aircraft to Wake Island. Its sailing meant that there were no aircraft carriers at Pearl Harbor, which would be attacked two days later by Japan.

1994: The Strategic Arms Reduction Treaty (START I) entered into force on this day with the aim of reducing warhead arsenals by 35 percent. The pact, signed on July 31, 1991, by President George H.W. Bush and Soviet general secretary Mikhail Gorbachev (and later carried over to the former Soviet socialist republics after the U.S.S.R. was dissolved), had been initiated by U.S. president Ronald Reagan. It limited the parties to 1,600 deployed missiles and 6,000 "accountable" warheads.

★ QUOTE OF THE DAY

"I felt as if I had been hit in the face with a pound of red pepper. It burned my eyes, nose, and throat, and I could not breathe. The pain was so intense."

> Lau Sing Kee, 77th Infantry, describing running messages through German gas attacks during World War I, in a 1919 interview with *The San Jose Mercury Herald.* Kee won the Distinguished Service Cross for his valor, the first Chinese-American to be awarded a combat medal

December 6

1904: Theodore Roosevelt made the case for U.S. military intervention abroad. In his State of the Union, the president, building upon the Monroe Doctrine, said America was obliged to be an "international police power" in the Western hemisphere as needed in flagrant cases of wrongdoing or impotence."

1959: Piloting a McDonnell F4H-1 Phantom II, Cmdr. Lawrence E. Flint, Jr., set a new world altitude record by reaching 98,560 feet above Edwards Air Force Base, California.

2001: The Battle of Tora Bora began, an 11-day engagement in eastern Afghanistan within a system of natural caves. The objective was to capture or kill Osama bin Laden, the leader of al Qaeda, the terrorist group responsible for the 9/11 attacks on America. By December 17, the last cave complex had been captured, and U.S forces continued searching the area for weeks, but did not find any signs of bin Laden or the al Qaeda leadership. It is believed that bin Laden escaped into Pakistan, where he would be killed nearly ten years later (see May 1).

★ QUOTE OF THE DAY

"We in the military missed the opportunity [capturing bin Laden], not the president, who properly deferred to his senior military commander on how to carry out the mission."

> James Mattis, *Call Sign Chaos* (2019)

December 7

1941: A surprise attack by Japan on the U.S. naval base at Pearl Harbor, Hawaii, thrust the United States into World War II. The attack at 7:48 a.m. killed 2,459 Americans—the third-single bloodiest day in American history. Franklin D. Roosevelt would ask Congress the next day to declare war. America would soon declare war on two of Japan's allies—Germany and Italy—after those countries declared war on the United States first (see December 11).

2001: U.S. forces took Kandahar, marking what was said to be the collapse of the Taliban regime in Afghanistan. The last major city in Afghanistan controlled by the Taliban, Kandahar was also the birthplace of the Taliban itself.

★ QUOTE OF THE DAY

"It is no joke. It is a real war."

KTU radio reporter covering the attack from
the roof of a Honolulu building

December 8

1941: The United States formally entered World War II, when Congress declared war on Japan. The House vote was 388-1 and the Senate vote was 82-0. The votes came after a dramatic speech by Franklin D. Roosevelt, in which the president called "yesterday, December 7, 1941, a date which will live in infamy" after "the United States of America was suddenly and deliberately attacked by naval and air forces of the Empire of Japan."

1941: Japanese bombers from the Marshall Islands attacked the isolated USMC base at Wake Island, destroying 12 aircraft. The attack came only hours after Pearl Harbor. The Marine 1st Defense Battalion, Marine Fighter Attack Squadron 211, some Navy and Army personnel, and civilian construction workers repulsed the Japanese with heavy casualties before surrendering on December 23.

1965: Operation Tiger Hound began, an Air Force and Navy campaign to sever the Ho Chi Minh Trail in Laos—the North Vietnamese supply route. The campaign would extend into 1968.

★ QUOTE OF THE DAY

"No matter how long it may take us to overcome this premeditated invasion, the American people in their righteous might will win through to absolute victory."

Franklin D Roosevelt, asking Congress for a declaration
of war against Japan

December 9

1775: The Battle of Great Bridge: Lord Dunmore, royal governor of Virginia, with 700 troops attacked Virginia militiamen under Colonel William Woodford, but the colonial troops were triumphant. The battle took place on the Elizabeth River near Great Bridge, Virginia. The victory denied British access to the major seaport of Norfolk. Dunmore later burned Norfolk on January 1, 1776, and then left America the following summer.

1906: Grace (Murray) Hopper was born at New York City. The mathematician joined the Navy in 1943 and served in the Bureau of Ordnance Computation Project. When she retired from the U.S. Navy at the age of 79, she was the oldest naval officer ever on active duty. She attained the rank of rear admiral and was a leader in the computer revolution, having developed the computer language COBOL. She also aided in the development of the Univac I computer. Hopper coined the word "bug" to describe a computer or technical glitch.

★ QUOTE OF THE DAY

"Things were going badly, there was something wrong in one of the circuits of the long, glass-enclosed computer. Finally, someone located the trouble spot and, using ordinary tweezers, removed the problem, a two-inch moth. From then on, when anything went wrong with a computer, we said it had bugs in it."

Admiral Grace Hopper, describing the 1945 origin
of the word "bug"

December 10

1864: Troops led by Union general William T. Sherman arrived outside Savannah, Georgia, completing their March to the Sea. Since November 15, Sherman's forces had swept across Georgia, starting with the burning of Atlanta to the ground and then leaving a trail of destruction behind them. It was the culmination of a plan, approved by President Lincoln and Ulysses S. Grant, general-in-chief of the Union armies, to—in Sherman's words—"make Georgia howl." Sherman was confronted by Confederate commander William J. Hardee and 10,000 defenders. Sherman prepared to siege.

1898: The Treaty of Paris was signed between the United States and Spain, formally ending the Spanish-American War. Under the terms of this treaty, Spain granted the United States the Philippine Islands and the islands of Guam and Puerto Rico and agreed to withdraw from Cuba. The war effectively made the United States, for the first time, a global military power. The treaty went into effect April 11, 1899.

1941: U.S. warplanes, operating from the aircraft carrier *Enterprise* (CV-6), sank a Japanese submarine off Hawaii. "The Big E" was the first American ship to sink a Japanese warship.

★ QUOTE OF THE DAY

"Until we can repopulate Georgia, it is useless to occupy it, but the utter destruction of its roads, houses, and people will cripple their military resources. . . . I can make the march, and make Georgia howl..."

General William T. Sherman, letter to General Ulysses S. Grant in October 1864

December 11

1862: The Battle of Fredericksburg, Virginia began. The clash between Union major general Ambrose's Army of the Potomac and Confederate general Robert E. Lee's Army of Northern Virginia would turn into a rout of northern forces (see December 13). A visitor to the front described the battle to President Lincoln as a "butchery." The North would get revenge a month later, when Union forces captured Arkansas Post, a Confederate stronghold on the Arkansas River (see January 11).

1862: After reviewing a military commission's judgment that 303 Dakota warriors be executed for their purported involvement in a massacre (see August 17), President Lincoln announced to the U.S. Senate his decision on the matter. In his December 11, 1862, message, he explained that he approved the execution of 39 warriors but commuted the death sentences of the other 264. One of the 39 was later spared. The remaining 38 were executed December 26, 1862, at Mankato, Minnesota.

1941: Germany and Italy—allies of Japan in the Axis—declared war on the United States—and the United States responded in kind. The United States was now engaged in a two-front war—in Europe and the Pacific.

1954: The first supercarrier was launched at Newport News, Virginia: *Forrestal* (CV-59). At that time, it was the largest vessel ever constructed, with a height (keel to mast) the equivalent of a 25-story building and a length of 1,039 feet. An innovative feature among many was the angled flight deck.

1969: U.S. paratroopers left Vietnam. Troops from the U.S. Third Brigade, 82nd Airborne Division, had been deployed in February 1968 to assist the 101st Airborne in the wake of the Tet Offensive (see January 31). The withdrawal was part of the Nixon administration's "Vietnamization" program, designed to gradually turn over control of the war to South Vietnam.

★ QUOTE OF THE DAY

"Anxious to not act with so much clemency as to encourage another outbreak on the one hand, nor with so much severity as to be real cruelty on the other, I caused a careful examination of the records of trials to be made, in view of first ordering the execution of such as had been proved guilty of violating females. Contrary to my expectations, only two of this class were found. I then directed a further examination, and a classification of all who were proven to have participated in *massacres*, as distinguished from participation in *battles*."

Abraham Lincoln, December 11, 1862, message to the U.S. Senate. Lincoln was under intense political and military pressure to approve the execution of 303 Dakota warriors

December 12

1776: The Continental Congress authorized the formation of a cavalry unit. The first cavalry unit to be formed for continuous service was the United States Regiment of Dragoons, organized in 1833. This in turn, would be the precursor to the tank service (see March 5).

1799: In his last letter, George Washington urged the creation of a U.S. military academy. Written to Alexander Hamilton, an aide during the Revolutionary War and later his treasury secretary, Washington soon fell ill and would pass away two days later (see December 14).

1937: Japan sank an American warship in China's Yangtze River. The U.S. gunboat *Panay* was escorting U.S. evacuees away from Nanking, which the Japanese had invaded and ravaged during the Sino-Japanese war. After the *Panay* was sunk, Japanese troops machine-gunned life-boats and survivors, killing two American sailors and a civilian passenger. The incident sparked a crisis in U.S.-Japanese relations. Japan claimed the attack was unintentional, and agreed to pay $2 million in reparations.

1941: The Naval Air Transport Service (NATS) was established. A branch of the Navy from 1941 to 1948, it operated at its peak some 540 aircraft with 26,000 personnel assigned.

1950: The 1st Marine Division closed in on Hungnam—North Korea's third-largest city—after fighting its way through six Chinese divisions. The leathernecks killed 20,000 enemy troops. Marine Major General Oliver P. Smith allegedly barked, "Retreat? Hell, we're just attacking in a different direction!"

1985: 248 American soldiers and eight crew members were killed when their charter crashed after takeoff from Gander, Newfoundland.

★ QUOTE OF THE DAY

"So the Chinese are to our east. They're to our west. They're to our north. And to our south. Well, that simplifies things. They can't get away from us now!"

> Colonel Lewis B. "Chesty" Puller, 1st Marine Regiment

December 13

1862: A disastrous defeat for the Union army, when a series of attacks by General Ambrose Burnside's Army of the Potomac was thwarted by Confederate general Robert E. Lee's Army of Northern Virginia. The fighting at Fredericksburg, Virginia—just north of the Confederate capital of Richmond—was one of the worst Union losses during the entire Civil War. There were more than 13,000 Union losses to about 5,000 Confederate casualties.

2001: George W. Bush told Russia the United States would pull out of a key arms control pact. The president said the United States would withdraw from the 1972 Anti-Ballistic Missile Treaty, allowing it to conduct anti-missile defense tests.

2003: Operation Red Dawn: the capture of Saddam Hussein. The former Iraqi leader was found by the U.S. 4th Infantry Division in a small "spider-hole" in the ground at ad-Dawr, Iraq. He would be tried and convicted of crimes against humanity by an Iraqi Special Tribunal and, on December 30, 2006, executed.

★ QUOTE OF THE DAY

"The nervous strain was simply awful. It can be appreciated only by those who have experienced it. The atmosphere seemed surcharged with the most startling and frightful things. Deaths, wounds and appalling destruction everywhere."

Lt. Frederick L. Hitchcock, 132nd Pennsylvania Infantry,
Battle of Fredericksburg

December 14

1799: The first president—the commander-in-chief—died. George Washington, who commanded the Continental Army during the Revolutionary War before being elected president in 1789, was 67.

1911: The armored cruiser *California* (ACR-6) became the first U.S. naval vessel to enter the new naval base at Pearl Harbor, Honolulu, Hawaii. Pearl Harbor had been under U.S. control since 1887—prized for its natural deep harbor. After the Spanish-American War put the Philippines in U.S. control, Pearl Harbor became a strategic way station in the Pacific. The harbor was dredged, its reef destroyed in several years' preparation for this day in 1911.

1944: The rank of General of Army—a five-star general— was established by Congress in Public Law 78-482. Only five men have earned this honor: George Marshall, Douglas MacArthur, Dwight D. Eisenhower, Henry H. Arnold, and Omar Bradley. Marshall, MacArthur, Eisenhower, and Arnold were appointed in December 1944; Bradley was appointed in September 1950.

1944: The rank of Fleet Admiral, U.S. Navy—a five-star admiral was established by Congress (also in Public Law 78-482). Only four men have earned this honor: William D. Leahy, Ernest King, Chester Nimitz, and William Halsey, Jr.

1960: Record flight: a U.S. B-52 bomber flew 10,000 miles without refueling, averaging around 511 mph. This record stood until January 11, 1962.

1964: Operation Barrel Roll began. It was the first in a series of bombings of targets in northern Laos. The operation was aimed at supporting forces of the Royal Lao government, who were fighting rebel forces—the Pathet Lao. Parts of the Ho Chi Minh trail—the North Vietnamese supply line— also ran through parts of Laos. By 1973, when Barrel Roll and two other operations—Steel Tiger and Tiger Hound—were terminated, Laos had become the most heavily bombed country in the world; it was hit by an estimated three million tons of bombs, more than three times the amount dropped on North Vietnam itself.

☆ QUOTE OF THE DAY

"First in war, first in peace, and first in the hearts of his countrymen."

Henry "Light-Horse Harry" Lee, on George Washington

December 15

1864: The Battle of Nashville began, and, when it ended on December 16, the once powerful Confederate Army of Tennessee was nearly destroyed. Union forces under General George H. Thomas swarmed Rebel trenches near Nashville. Confederate general John Bell Hood suffered 6,000 casualties—of those, 1,500 were killed—while the Union Army of the Cumberland endured an estimated 3,000 casualties.

1890: When native officers from Fort Yates, Sioux County, North Dakota, attempted to arrest Lakota leader Sitting Bull, a skirmish broke out and Sitting Bull was shot and killed. Tensions were high—leading to the Wounded Knee Massacre on December 29.

1948: The Marine Security Guard program at U.S. embassies throughout the world was established.

1950: F-86 Sabrejets flew their first missions of the Korean War; they were attached to the Air Force's Fourth Flight Interceptor Wing.

1997: The last Minuteman II missile silo was destroyed in Missouri; the result of the START I arms reduction treaty signed with Russia.

2006: The Lockheed Martin F-35 Lightning II made its first flight. The F-35 Lightning II is single-seat, single-engine, all-weather stealth multi-role fighter.

2011: The U.S. flag was lowered in Baghdad marking the end of U.S. military operations in Iraq, more than eight years after the United States invaded (see March 19).

★ QUOTE OF THE DAY

"We were like zombies. We were so dead on our feet that whenever we got still for a few seconds, we just automatically went to sleep. I got to the point where I could sleep right through a bombing raid."

Marine private first class Wiley Sloman, on Wake Island, December 1941, quoted in *Given Up for Dead* (2003), by Bill Sloan

December 16

1907: Theodore Roosevelt's Great White Fleet. As the 20th century dawned, the United States found itself a world power. The president, eager to display America's might—and its desire for peace—dispatched a U.S. Navy fleet consisting of 16 battleships and various escorts on a goodwill trip around the world. The ships, painted white, were welcomed at many ports; their journey, which ended two weeks before

President Theodore Roosevelt shakes hands with Lieutenant Walter R. Gherardi, commanding officer of *Yankton,* **December 16, 1907, as the Atlantic Fleet departed Hampton Roads, Virginia.** NH 106193 courtesy of Naval History & Heritage Command.

Roosevelt left office in 1909, was one of the president's proudest accomplishments.

1944: The Battle of the Bulge began with a surprise German attack on allied forces in Belgium. Punching a triangular bulge in allied lines, the Germans caused massive casualties. Massive allied air power and a three-pronged offensive by American generals Omar Bradley and George Patton and British general Bernard Montgomery turned the tide. It was Germany's last major offensive in the West during World War II.

1950: Harry Truman declared a national emergency, following the entry of Communist China into the Korean War. The president was so worried that he considered using atomic weapons. Nine were sent to the region.

1965: General William Westmoreland requested more troops for South Vietnam. There were some 200,000 U.S. military personnel there already, but Westmoreland wanted nearly a quarter-million more. By 1968, there would be some 538,000 Americans in South Vietnam.

1998: Operation Desert Fox began, with cruise missiles fired at various Iraqi military sites. The strikes were in response to Saddam Hussein's continued defiance of UN weapons inspectors.

This Day in U.S. Military History

⭐ QUOTE OF THE DAY

"[I feel] sort of like a Rat without a tail just now running tanks there are none. I don't know where to go to what to do yet feel that I should be doing something fast and furious."

George Patton, letter to his aunt, December 14, 1917, as he took charge of the AEF Light Tank School, quoted in *Patton: A Genius for War* (1995), by Carlo d'Este

December 17

1925: Colonel William "Billy" Mitchell—regarded today as the "Father of the United States Air Force"—was convicted of insubordination at his court-martial. Mitchell was found guilty of conduct prejudicial to the good of the armed services. Mitchell had earned the ire of his superiors by attacking them and the White House publicly for what he saw as their lack of interest in developing air capabilities for the military. He was awarded the Medal of Honor 20 years after his death.

1944: The Malmedy Massacre occurred when, during the Battle of the Bulge, 84 American POWs of the 285th Field Artillery Observation Battalion were murdered by Nazi troops.

1947: The Boeing B-47 Stratojet strategic bomber made its first flight. The B-47 was a long-range, six-engine, jet-powered strategic bomber designed to fly at subsonic speed and at high altitude to avoid enemy interception. Its primary mission was to drop nuclear bombs on the Soviet Union.

1950: During the Korean War, the first dogfight between jet aircraft occurred as USAF F-86 Sabres of the Fourth Flight Interceptor Wing engaged Soviet-built MiG-15s at the Yalu River bordering North Korea and China. Four MiGs were shot down.

1994: North Korea shot down an Army helicopter which had strayed north of the demilitarized zone. Chief Warrant Officer David Hilemon, copilot, was killed; the pilot, Chief Warrant Officer Bobby Hall, was captured and held for nearly two weeks.

2001: In Afghanistan, the last cave complex at Tora Bora and its defenders were seized. U.S. and British forces killed some 200 al Qaeda fighters, but their leader, Osama bin Laden, was not found. No American or British deaths were reported.

★ QUOTE OF THE DAY

"Nothing can stop the attack of aircraft except other aircraft."

Colonel William "Billy" Mitchell

December 18

1941: Guam fell. Despite the best efforts of 610 American troops, the Pacific outpost was overrun by 5,000 Japanese invaders in a three-hour battle.

1944: B-29 Superfortress bombers hit Nagoya, an important Japanese aircraft manufacturing city.

1944: In the Philippine Sea, Admiral William "Bull" Halsey's Third Fleet sailed into the teeth of Typhoon Cobra (also known as Halsey's Typhoon) and suffered profound loss of life: 790 men died. Destroyers *Hull* (DD-350), *Spence* (DD-512), and *Monaghan* (DD-354) sank in the storm whose wind gusts reached 185 miles per hour. Nine other vessels were significantly damaged along with 100 airplanes (lost or damaged). Lt. Commander Henry Lee Plage and *Tabberer* were able to rescue 55 men; Plage received the Legion of Merit. On board the *Monterey*, which survived a fire during the storm, was young Lt. Gerald R. Ford, future president of the United States.

1972: Richard Nixon announced the "Christmas bombing" of North Vietnam, a massive campaign designed to bring the North Vietnamese to the negotiating table. Secret peace talks had collapsed on December 13, with each side blaming the other. A furious Nixon unleashed Operation Linebacker II, in which B-52 bombers and fighter-bombers dropped over 20,000 tons of bombs on Hanoi and Haiphong—the most concentrated air offensive of the entire Vietnamese war. The bombings continued until December 29, when the North Vietnamese agreed to resume peace talks, leading to a peace treaty six weeks later (see January 27). The United States lost 15 of its B-52s and 11 other aircraft during the 11-day onslaught. North Vietnam said that over 1,600 civilians were killed.

2011: The last U.S. troops withdrew from Iraq, marking the end of a nine-year U.S. war. The withdrawal was mandated by a 2008 agreement between then-president George W. Bush and the Iraqi government (see November 17).

★ QUOTE OF THE DAY

"[The typhoon] represented a more crippling blow to the 3rd Fleet than it might be expected to suffer in anything less than a major action."

Admiral Chester Nimitz, on "Halsey's Typhoon"

December 19

1777: Led by George Washington, the Continental Army established its winter camp at Valley Forge, Pennsylvania, just 22 miles from British-occupied Philadelphia. The severe winter of 1777-78 took a toll on Washington's troops. Of the 12,000 men stationed at Valley Forge, almost 2,000 died from typhus, influenza, cholera, and malnutrition. Washington stayed with his men, inspiring loyalty to him and their cause.

1950: The North Atlantic Council named General Dwight Eisenhower supreme commander, putting the World War II hero and soon-to-be president in charge of the defense of Western Europe.

1998: A four-day U.S. and British attack on Iraq—Operation Desert Fox—ended. The air strikes were in response to Baghdad's failure to comply with United Nations Security Council resolutions concerning Iraq's ability to produce, store, maintain, and deliver weapons of mass destruction.

★ QUOTE OF THE DAY

"[We] march'd to the Valley Forge in order to take up Winter Quarters. Here we built huts in the following manner: the huts are built in three lines . . . eighteen by sixteen feet long, six feet to the eves built of logs and covered with staves—the chimney in the east end the door in the South side."

George Ewing, Colonial soldier at Valley Forge,
journal entry December 1777

December 20

1862: Rear Admiral D. D. Porter in his flagship *Black Hawk* joined General William T. Sherman at Helena, Arkansas, and prepared for the joint assault on Vicksburg. The fleet under Admiral Porter's command for the Vicksburg campaign was the largest ever placed under one officer up to that time, equal in number to all the vessels composing the U.S. Navy at the outbreak of war.

1941: The Flying Tigers entered combat against the Japanese over China. The Flying Tigers were comprised of pilots from the Army Air Corps, Navy, and Marine Corps, recruited under presidential authority and commanded by Claire Lee Chennault.

1941: Admiral Ernest J. King was designated Commander-in-Chief, United States Fleet in charge of all operating naval fleets and coastal frontier forces, reporting directly to President Franklin D. Roosevelt.

1989: Operation Just Cause began—the invasion of Panama. President George H.W. Bush ordered the arrest of that country's military dictator, Manuel Noriega, who had been indicted in the United States on drug-trafficking charges. Noriega surrendered on January 3, 1990. He was convicted and sent to prison in the United States. The invasion took the lives of 23 American soldiers.

★ QUOTE OF THE DAY

"[He] shaves every morning with a blowtorch."

President Franklin D. Roosevelt, describing Ernest J. King

December 21

1861: Congress authorized the Medal of Honor to be awarded to Navy personnel who had distinguished themselves by their gallantry in action.

1866: U.S. Army troops were massacred in Wyoming. A decade before the better known Battle of Little Bighorn (see June 25), Army Lieutenant Colonel William Fetterman and his men from Fort Phil Kearny were lured into an ambush by Lakota, Cheyenne, and Arapaho warriors. Some 40,000 arrows rained down on Fetterman and his men—all 81 of whom were killed. It was one of the most decisive Native American victories against U.S. troops.

1944: Gen Henry H. "Hap" Arnold became a five-star General of the Army and the first airman to hold that rank (see December 14).

1945: General George S. Patton died at Heidelberg, Germany, from injuries sustained December 8 in an automobile accident.

1964: The General Dynamics F-111A supersonic fighter jet with "swing wings" made its maiden flight from Carswell AFB. On its second flight, January 6, 1965, it showed its ability to fly with its wings swept back 72 degrees.

2003: *Time* magazine named the American soldier as Person of the Year. It said U.S. troops had the duty of "living with and dying for a country's most fateful decisions."

★ QUOTE OF THE DAY

"The plane, so awkward on the ground, suddenly became as graceful as a swan in its natural element—the air."

Review of the F-111 in *Popular Mechanics* (May 1968)

December 22

1775: The first U.S. naval officers were commissioned. They were Commander-in-Chief of the Fleet Esek Hopkins; captains Dudley Saltonstall, Abraham Whipple, Nicolas Biddle, and John Hopkins; and 13 lieutenants, including John Paul Jones.

1807: Thomas Jefferson signed the Embargo Act—aimed at ending British and French harassment of American merchant ships. Britain and France were at war, and the United States was neutral—but that didn't stop either British or French forces from seizing American ships and plundering their goods for wartime use. The Embargo Act was meant to hurt both Britain and France by cutting off trade, but historians say it wound up hurting the U.S. economy itself.

1841: On this day, the commissioning ceremony for the *Mississippi* took place at Philadelphia, Pennsylvania. *Mississippi* was the Navy's first ocean-going side-wheel steamship.

1864: General Sherman presented the city of Savannah, Georgia, to President Lincoln. The Union general seized the important Georgia port—and its largest city—after his famous March to the Sea from Atlanta. Sherman would present it to President Lincoln for Christmas, wiring him: "I beg to present you, as a Christmas gift, the city of Savannah, with 150 heavy guns and plenty of ammunition, and also about 25,000 bales of cotton."

1941: The Arcadia Conference began, the first meeting between President Roosevelt and Prime Minister Winston Churchill after Pearl Harbor. The two leaders and their staffs coordinated plans for their fight against the Axis powers including a future invasion of Nazi-controlled Western Europe. It was decided that defeating Germany would be their top priority. Roosevelt also laid out huge increases in U.S. weapons production, including 45,000 warplanes, 45,000 tanks, and 500,000 machine guns by the end of 1943.

1944: U.S. troops defied German forces at Bastogne. Trapped during the Battle the Bulge, the Americans were told to surrender, to which U.S. Brigadier General Anthony McAuliffe reportedly replied: "Nuts!"

1950: The biggest air battle of the Korean War occurred when U.S. Air Force F-86 Sabres shot down six MiG-15s over North Korea with the loss of just one American plane. At that time, the F-86 was the fastest plane on Earth, attaining speeds of 685 miles per hour.

1964: The SR-71 (Blackbird) made its first test flight at Palmdale, California, reaching an altitude of 45,000 feet and a speed of 1,000 mph.

2010: The repeal of "Don't ask, don't tell" was signed into law by Barack Obama. It overturned a 17-year-old policy banning homosexuals from serving openly in the military.

⋆ QUOTE OF THE DAY

"To the German Commander.
NUTS!
The American Commander."

> Brigadier General Anthony McAuliffe

December 23

1783: George Washington resigned as commander-in-chief of the Continental Army, preferring to retire to his home at Mount Vernon,

Virginia. Some members of the Continental Congress wanted the 51-year old Washington to become head of state—the presidency would not be created until 1789—and the first president would, of course, be Washington himself.

1907: The Army sought bids for its first aircraft. Specifications called for an aircraft that could carry two people, fly at 40 miles per hour for 125 miles without stopping, with controllable flight in any direction, and able to land at its takeoff point without damage.

1919: The first hospital ship built to move wounded naval personnel was put into service.

1941: U.S. forces surrendered Wake Island to the Japanese. The enemy attacked the day after its attack on Pearl Harbor (see December 7) and the Americans were eventually overwhelmed by large Japanese air and naval forces. Wake was held by the Japanese for the duration of the Pacific War; the U.S. reclaimed it two days after the Japanese surrendered on September 2, 1945.

1950: Lt. Gen. Walton Walker, commander of the Eighth Army in Korea, died in a jeep accident. His replacement would be Lt. Gen. Matthew Ridgway (see December 27).

1968: After being held for 11 months, the crew of the *Pueblo* was freed by North Korea. The crew crossed the so-called "bridge of no return" leading from North Korea to the truce village of Panmunjom in the demilitarized zone, where they were greeted by American and South Korean troops. The *Pueblo*, an intelligence-gathering ship, had been seized earlier that year (see January 23). The 83-man crew was regularly beaten and tortured; one American died during the ordeal.

2004: Operation Phantom Fury, begun on November 7 in Fallujah, came to an end.

★ QUOTE OF THE DAY

"There was fighting from street to street and house to house and clearing from room to room."

Sergeant Major Peter Smith, recalling the Second Battle of Fallujah in 2006, *Eyewitness to War, Volume II*

December 24

1814: The Treaty of Ghent was signed, ending the War of 1812. Often called America's second war of independence, the conflict confirmed, once and for all, the nation's status as a foreign power. Great Britain agreed to relinquish claims to the Northwest Territory, and both countries pledged to work toward ending the slave trade.

1943: General Dwight D. Eisenhower was appointed supreme commander of Allied forces for Operation Overlord—the invasion of Nazi-occupied western Europe. The invasion would occur six months later (see June 6).

1950: "Inchon in Reverse": U.S. amphibious fleet Task Force 90, commanded by Rear Admiral James H. Doyle, completed the evacuation of X Corps from Hungnam. Supported by the Seventh Fleet, commanded by Vice Admiral Arthur D. Struble aboard the battleship *Missouri*, it evacuated 105,000 U.S. and Republic of Korea Marines and soldiers, 17,500 vehicles, 350,000 tons of cargo and 91,000 Korean civilians in just over 190 ships.

★ QUOTE OF THE DAY

"I guess the youth is only in my heart."

> Karl Christianson, 69 years old and a survivor of the 1898 *Maine* explosion, after trying unsuccessfully to reenlist on December 24, 1941, as reported in the *New York Times*

December 25

1776: General George Washington crossed the Delaware River with 5,400 troops, hoping to surprise a Hessian force celebrating Christmas at their quarters in Trenton, New Jersey. At about 11 p.m., his forces began crossing the river despite a fierce winter storm; at approximately 8 a.m. on the morning of December 26, troops split into two columns, reached the outskirts of Trenton and descended on the unsuspecting Hessians. Trenton's 1,400 Hessian defenders were groggy from the previous evening's festivities and underestimated the American threat after months of decisive British victories throughout New York. Washington's men quickly overwhelmed the Germans' defenses, and by 9:30 a.m. the town was sur-rounded. Although several hundred Hessians escaped, nearly 1,000 were captured at the cost of only four American lives. The news was a huge morale boost for American colonists.

1837: General Zachary Taylor led troops in the Battle of Lake Okeechobee. It was one of the major battles of the Second Seminole War. Though both the Seminoles and Taylor's troops emerged from the Florida battle claim-ing victory, Taylor was promoted to the rank of Brigadier General as a result, and he earned here his nickname of "Old Rough and Ready."

1846: En route to Chihuahua, Colonel Alexander W. Doniphan's First Reg-iment Mounted Missouri Volunteers were attacked by Mexican troops in the Battle of El Brazito near Las Cruces, New Mexico. Doniphan was victorious and the Mexicans retreated, with 43 soldiers killed.

1944: Allied forces began counterattacking German forces in the Battle of the Bulge. The U.S. 4th Armored Division, an element of the Third Army, raced to relieve Americans surrounded in Bastogne.

★ QUOTE OF THE DAY

"That there be organized now in the United States a guerrilla corps, independent and separate from the Army and Navy and imbued with a maximum of the offensive and imaginative spirit."

William "Wild Bill" Donovan, memo to President Franklin D. Roosevelt, December 22, 1941, regarding North Africa

December 26

1861: A possible war between the United States and Great Britain was avoided after the Lincoln administration freed two Confederate envoys. Envoys James Mason and John Slidell had been aboard a British mail steamer when the ship was intercepted by *San Jacinto*. News of the interception fueled anti-American sentiment in Britain, and it began preparing for war—until President Abraham Lincoln moved to ease tensions with London.

1862: Four nuns—sisters of the Order of the Holy Cross—became the first female nurses on a U.S. Navy ship—the seed of the Navy Nurse Corps. The nuns had volunteered for service aboard the *Red Rover*, a Confed-erate side-wheel steamship that had been captured and turned into the Navy's first hospital ship.

1862: The Battle of Chickasaw Bayou (also called Battle of Walnut Hills) began. It was the opening engagement of the Vicksburg campaign during the Civil War. Confederate forces under Lt. Gen. John C. Pemberton repulsed an advance by Union general William T. Sherman that was intended to lead to the capture of Vicksburg, Mississippi. This Confederate victory frustrated Ulysses S. Grant's attempts to take Vicksburg by a direct approach.

1972: Operation Linebacker II continued, with bombers attacking Hanoi, in the largest single combat launch in Strategic Air Command history.

✰ QUOTE OF THE DAY

"The enemy say that Americans are good at a long shot; but cannot stand the cold iron. I call upon you instantly to give a lie to the slander. Charge!"

General Winfield Scott, to the 11th Infantry Regiment, during the War of 1812

December 27

Lt. Commander Darlene Iskra addressing the crew of *Opportune*. National Archives.

This Day in U.S. Military History

1846: Fresh from the Christmas-Day victory at El Brazito, Colonel Alexander W. Doniphan's troops (Doniphan's Thousand) captured El Paso, Texas.

1950: Lieutenant General Matthew B. Ridgway took command of the Eighth Army in Korea after Walton Walker's death four days previous. During World War II, Ridgway had commanded the 82nd Airborne Division and XVIII Airborne Corps in Europe.

1990: Darlene Iskra became the first female commanding officer of an active U.S. Navy vessel, reporting for duty on board *Opportune* (ARS-41). Iskra had enlisted in the Navy in 1979 and was one of the first women Navy divers.

2001: The Bush administration said it would hold Taliban and al Qaeda prisoners at the U.S. Navy base at Guantánamo Bay, Cuba. The first 20 captives arrived on January 11, 2002. Guantanamo—an American base since 1903—was considered outside U.S. legal jurisdiction, and the Bush administration asserted that detainees were not entitled to any protections of the Geneva Conventions. But the Supreme Court ruled (in *Hamdan v. Rumsfeld* on June 29, 2006) that they were entitled to the minimal protections listed under Common Article 3 of the Geneva Conventions.

☆ QUOTE OF THE DAY

"Don't treat me any differently; I am the commanding officer and that's it."

Commander Darlene Iskra

December 28

1872: During the Yavapai War, seeking reprisals for attacks against white settlers, U.S. Army troops under Lieutenant George R. Crook attacked a Yavapai encampment at Skeleton Cave, Salt River Canyon, Arizona Territory. The 5th Cavalry Regiment killed 76 Yavapai, including women and children.

2014: The United States and NATO formally ended their war in Afghanistan with a ceremony at their military headquarters in Kabul. At this time, however, troops still remain to fight the Taliban, remnants of al Qaeda, and, more recently, ISIS.

★ **QUOTE OF THE DAY**

"Eighth Army is yours, Matt. Do what you think best."

> General Douglas MacArthur, to Lieutenant General Matthew B. Ridgway, after Ridgway took command of the Eighth Army, quoted in *The Korean War: The Chinese Intervention* by Richard W. Stewart

December 29

1798: The Navy should be strengthened "to make the most powerful nation desire our friendship—the most unprincipled respect our neutrality," said Secretary of Navy Benjamin Stoddert in his first annual report to Congress.

1890: The Massacre at Wounded Knee, South Dakota: When the US Seventh Cavalry were disarming Lakota Sioux at the Wounded Knee Creek encampment, a rifle went off, prompting the U.S. soldiers to fire at and kill an estimated 200 men, women, and children and wound 51. Twenty-five U.S. troops were killed; another six would die later from injuries. On the 100th anniversary of Wounded Knee, both the House of Representatives and Senate passed a resolution formally expressing "deep regret" for the massacre.

1862: General William T. Sherman was thwarted in his attempt to capture Vicksburg, Mississippi, the last Confederate stronghold on the Mississippi River.

1939: First flight of the Consolidated B-24 Liberator. Used in World War II by several Allied air forces and navies and by every branch of the American armed forces, the B-24 saw action in almost every theater of the war—Western Europe, Pacific, Mediterranean, and China-Burma-India. Often compared with the better-known Boeing B-17 Flying Fortress, the B-24 was a more modern design with a higher top speed, greater range, and a heavier bomb load.

★ **QUOTE OF THE DAY**

"A people's dream died there. It was a beautiful dream. . . . There is no center anymore and the sacred dream is dead."

> Black Elk, on the Massacre at Wounded Knee

December 30

1776: General George Washington appealed to his men. After his smashing surprise attack on Trenton, the general turned to a new challenge. Many of his troops were free to leave at the end of the year. He offered a bounty to anyone who agreed to serve for another six months. But no one stepped forward. But Washington, recalled one of his men, then made another impassioned appeal, asking for "service to the cause of liberty." Most stepped forward.

1944: Atomic bombs would be ready by August 1945, reported General Leslie Groves, head of the Manhattan Project—the federal government's crash program to develop the bomb.

★ QUOTE OF THE DAY

"My brave fellows, you have done all I asked you to do, and more than could be reasonably expected, but your country is at stake, your wives, your houses, and all that you hold dear. You have worn yourselves out with fatigues and hardships, but we know not how to spare you. If you will consent to stay one month longer, you will render that service to the cause of liberty, and to your country, which you probably never can do under any other circumstance."

General George Washington

December 31

1880: George C. Marshall was born at Uniontown, Pennsylvania. A graduate of the Virginia Military Institute and a former aide-de-camp to John J. Pershing, he went on to become a five-star general during World War II, and one of just five men to receive the title of General of the Army. Marshall also served as secretary of defense and secretary of state under President Harry S. Truman. He created the postwar recovery plan for Europe that bears his name, which earned him the Nobel Peace Prize in 1953.

1941: Fleet Admiral Chester Nimitz assumed command of the U.S. Pacific Fleet, replacing Husband E. Kimmell, 24 days after Japan's surprise attack on Pearl Harbor (see December 7).

1961: As the year drew to a close, the United States said its military forces in South Vietnam had increased to 3,200. Army helicopter units were flying combat missions, commandos were advising South Vietnamese forces, U.S. naval ships were patrolling coastal areas and Navy and Marine Corps air raft were flying reconnaissance missions.

1968: The worst year of Vietnam War came to an end. An estimated 536,040 American servicemen were stationed in Vietnam, an increase of 10 percent from 1967. U.S. losses that year totaled 14,584 killed, bringing the total since January 1961 to more than 31,000—with another 200,000 wounded.

1995: U.S. tanks entered Bosnia. It was the beginning of a deployment of some 20,000 American troops as part of a NATO force that was attempting to keep the peace between warring ethnic factions.

 QUOTE OF THE DAY

"I have just assumed a great responsibility and obligation which I shall do my utmost to discharge."

Admiral Chester Nimitz, December 31, 1941

U.S. Marine Corps glider detachment training camp: ground crew handling a barrage balloon, Parris Island, South Carolina, 1942. Farm Security Administration—Office of War Information photograph collection (Library of Congress).

Index

Note: Page numbers in *italics* refer to illustrations.

Names of ships are prefixed and filed under HMS, USCGC, USS, etc., as the case may be.

Headings of military divisions begin with numerals and spelled out forms, e.g., 1st Aero Squadron; First Marine Battalion; 3rd Bombardment Group; Third Fleet, etc.

Index

Battle of Summit Springs, 172;
Battle of the Little Bighorn, 303–4;
"Dull Knife Outbreak," 23;
Sand Creek Massacre, 8, 284–5.
See also Native Americans
Chief of Naval Operations (CNO):
Ernest J. King named, 72;
first, 65;
Japanese radio traffic analysis report, 152
Chief Petty Officer, 89
China:
Battle of Ch'ongch'on River, 282;
Boxer Rebellion, 136, 199;
Chosin Reservoir Campaign, 283;
Kearny's Mission, 242–3;
Korean War, 263, 285, 299;
Second Taiwan Strait Crisis, 206;
and U.S. diplomatic relations, 278
Chivington, John 284–5
Ch'ongch'on River, Battle of, 282
Chosin Reservoir, Battle of, 283
Churchill, Winston:
Arcadia Conference, 305;
Atlantic Charter, 197–8;
Casablanca Conference, 16, 25;
D-Day, 128;
Declaration of the United Nations, 1;
Potsdam Conference, 175–6;
Quadrant Conference, 197;
Teheran Conference, 284;
Yalta Agreement, 44.
See also Great Britain
Civil Affairs, 202
Civil Air Patrol (CAP), 133
Civil Rights:
Selma to Montgomery march, 79
Civil War:
Alabama sunk, 151;
Andersonville prison camp, 59;
Arkansas Post, 13;
Atlanta, 179, 211, 213, 214, 275;
"The Battle Hymn of the Republic," 35;
Battle of Chickasaw Bayou, 309;
Battle of Cold Harbor, 140;
Battle of Hampton Roads, 69–70;
Battle of Missionary Ridge, 281;
Battle of Seven Pines (Fair Oaks), 136, 139;
Battle of Wauhatchie, 259;
Battle of Yellow Tavern, 122;
Beaufort seized, 270;
Bentonville, 79;
Champion Hill, 126;
Chancellorsville, 26, 111, 114;
Chattanooga, 220;
Chickamauga, 228;
Columbia (South Carolina) captured, 49;
Corinth, 239–40;
"eye-for-an-eye" order, 185;
final campaign, 84;
final week, 90;
First Battle of Bull Run, 178;
first general killed, 173;
first naval officer killed, 158;

first shots fired, 99;
first Union combat fatality, 131;
first Union offensive, 127;
Five Forks, 89;
Florida, 51–2;
Fort Donelson, 49;
Fort Hindman, 13;
Fort Pillow massacre, 99;
Fort Sanders, 284;
Fort Sumter, 10, 50, 99, 100, 201;
Fort Wagner, 130, 171, 176;
Fredericksburg, 274, 293–4, 296;
General War Order No. 1, 28;
Georgia, 293;
Gettysburg, 163, 164, 165;
Glorieta Pass, 83;
Grand Army of the Republic, 135, 195;
Hatteras Inlet, 208, 209;
Housatonic sunk, 50;
Jackson, Mississippi, 124;
Jefferson Davis and wife captured, 121;
last Confederate unit surrenders, 133, 140;
last surrender, 266;
Lee surrender (end of war), 89, 95, 96;
Lee troops move to Pennsylvania, 149;
Lincoln call for volunteers to join Union Army,
   101, 115;
Lincoln directs Peninsular Campaign, 117;
Lookout Mountain captured, 281;
Marks Mill, 108;
Memphis surrenders, 142;
Meridian campaign, 47;
Mobile Bay, 192, 206;
Nashville, 297–8;
New Bern captured, 74;
New Orleans, 108, 110;
Northern Army Company, 1;
Olustee, 51–2;
Overland (Wilderness) Campaign, 115–16;
Pea Ridge, 68;
Port Hudson siege, 148;
Potomac emplacements attacked, 1;
Red River campaign, 95;
Resaca, 124;
Richmond captured, 91;
Rich Mountain Battle, 171;
Roanoke, 41;
Savannah, 305;
Second Battle of Bull Run, 209;
Shenandoah Valley, 189, 243;
Shiloh, 93, 94;
Star of the West attacked, 10;
Stones River, 3;
Union first major victory, 40;
Union naval blockade, 17, 69–70, 104–5, 267–8;
Vicksburg Campaign. *See* Vicksburg campaign;
Waynesboro, 64;
western Virginia, 173;
Wilson's Creek, 196;
women nurses, 308
Clark, Mark W., 113, 114, 123, 141, 183
Cleveland, Grover, 165
Clinton, Bill:

Index

Index

This Day in U.S. Military History

This Day in U.S. Military History

Index

Operation Zapata. *See* Bay of Pigs invasion
Ordnance Department, 124
Osceola (Seminole chief), 253
OSS. *See* Office of Strategic Services
Ovnand, Charles, 169–70

Pacific Fleet, 21, 35, 213, 312.
  See also Atlantic Fleet
Pacific Squadron, 168, 179
Page, Richard, 206
Palestinian Liberation Front (PLF), 245
Panama:
  Canal, 116, 199;
  Canal Zone, 55;
  first Navy ship transit, 246;
  invasion, 5, 303
parachute jump:
  first, 62;
  first free fall, 110
Paris Peace Accords (1973), 28
Parmalee, Phillip O., 22
Patton, George S.:
  Bastogne, 5;
  Battle of the Bulge, 299;
  bio, 272;
  death, 304;
  Frankfurt captured, 84;
  Paris liberation, 207;
  Sicily, *286*;
  WW I veteran protestors' eviction, 184
Pearl Harbor attack:
  culpable persons, 24–5;
  Doolittle raid, 104;
  Enterprise, 284;
  first witnesses, 79;
  Japanese forces used, 141;
  Lexington, 289;
  Nevada, 71;
  Oklahoma, 282;
  U.S. enters WW II, 21, 291
Peary, Robert E., 93
Pemberton, John C., 126, 127, 309
Peninsular Campaign. *See* Civil War
Penobscot Expedition, 198
pensions:
  disabled servicemen, 175;
  first women, 276
Pentagon:
  B-52 bombers, 234;
  construction, 17;
  DEFCON, 256;
  F-117 Nighthawk, 271;
  Iran Air flight 655 accident review, 165;
  new guidelines on women in combat, 42;
  Sept. 11, 2001 attacks, 221;
  Vietnam War, 283
Perry, Matthew, 85, 169
Perry, Oliver Hazard, 83, 220
Pershing, John J.:
  AEF commander, 121, 222;
  award recommendations, 14;
  bio, 224;
  first General of the Army, 216;

Lafayette grave, 166;
  Pancho Villa Expedition, 74, 120
Persian Gulf War. *See* Operation Desert Storm
  (1991 Gulf War)
Petraeus, David, 6
Philip, J.W., 199
Philippine-American War:
  Battle of Malolos, 85
Philippines:
  Battle of Bataan, 8, 49, 71–2, 91, 96–7, 118;
  combating terrorism, 18;
  First Battle of Bud Dajo, 66–7;
  MacArthur, 71–2, 91, 252;
  Manila captured (1945), 65;
  Spanish-American War, 197, 293;
  Subic Bay Naval Base, 270, 281
Philippine Sea, Battle of the, 151–2
Pickett, George, 165
Picquet de la Motte, Toussaint-Guillaume, 47
Pike, Zebulon M., 109
Poe, Orlando M., 275
Polaris missile, 9, 100, 105, 177
Poling, Clark V., 36–7
Polk, James:
  displeased with Taylor, 231;
  telegraph, 131;
  troops dispatched to Mexican border, 15, 157;
  war declared against Mexico, 124
Pope, John, 209
Porter, David Dixon, 13, 303
Potomac Flotilla, 1
Potsdam Conference, 175–6, 177, 219
Powell, Colin, 24, 44
Power, Frederic, 43
Powers, Francis Gary, 43, 113
POWs. *See* prisoners of war
Preble, Edward, 125
Prescott, William, 150
Presidential Mansion. *See* White House
Price, John D., 95
prisoner exchange:
  Cold War, 43
prisoners of war (POWs):
  Abu Gharib Prison, 16, 17;
  Bloody Gulch Massacre, 198;
  Confederate, *162*;
  first German prisoners taken in WW II, 120;
  Great Raid (1945), 31;
  Gregory Boyington freed, 210;
  highest ranking WW II POW, 118;
  Jonathan Wainwright freed, 200–1;
  Lincoln's "eye-for-an-eye" order, 185;
  longest-held, 82;
  Malmedy massacre, 300;
  Operation Homecoming, 45–6, 76, 84;
  Operation Ivory Coast, 279;
  Qala-i-Jangi uprising, 282;
  Union prisoners, 59;
  Vietnam War, 193
Project B (1921), 173, 178
Project Bullet (1957), 175
Project Kayo (1951), 64
Project Sapphire (1994), 279

This Day in U.S. Military History

Index

Index

This Day in U.S. Military History

Index

Task Force 58 (Fast Carrier Task Force), 49
Taylor, Zachary:
  Battle of Buena Vista, *54*, 55;
  Battle of Lake Okeechobee, 308;
  Battle of Monterrey, 231;
  Battle of Palo Alto, 119;
  bio, 280–1;
  crosses Rio Grande, 83;
  death, 170;
  Fort Harrison siege, 216, 225;
  Mexican border, 157
Tecumseh (Shawnee warrior), 236, 240, 267
Teheran Conference, 284
telegraph:
  first air-to-ground radio message, 22;
  first line, 131;
  Morse code, 8.
  See also communication
Tepuni, William, 62
terrorism:
  "Axis of Evil," 30;
  Beirut Marine barracks bombings, 254;
  Cole bombing, 246;
  EgyptAir flight interception, 245;
  Sept. 11, 2001 attacks, 62, 221.
  See also al Qaeda; Taliban
Texas:
  U.S. annexation, 67
thermohydrogen bomb. *See* hydrogen bomb
Third Cavalry Division, 64
Third Fleet, 210, 301
Third United States Army, 5, 84, 98, 207
Thomas, George H., 297–8
Thompson, Floyd James "Jim," 45–6, 76, 82, 193
Thompson, Stephen W., 39
Tibbets, Paul, 193
Tillman, Patrick "Pat," 266
Time (periodical), 304
Tinian Island, 180, 181–2, 186, 189, 193
Tippecanoe, Battle of, 267
Tokyo War Crimes Tribunal, 20–1
Tomahawk missiles, 95, 204
Tora Bora, Battle of, 290, 300–1
transatlantic flight:
  first, 136;
  first, by non-rigid lighter-than-air aircraft, 139;
  first nonstop, 136
transcontinental flight:
  first, carrier to carrier, 143;
  supersonic, 175
Transit 1B (satellite), 100
transport aircraft:
  C-5 Galaxy, 227, 279;
  C-47 Skytrain, 44, 115, 252;
  C-119 Flying Boxcar, 252;
  C-123 Providers, 36;
  C-130 Hercules, 107, 206;
  Ford Trimotor *Floyd Bennett*, 283–4;
  XC-142A V/STOL, 13.
  See also aircraft; helicopters
Transportation Corps, 186
transport ships:
  Dorchester torpedoed, 36–7

Treaty of Ghent (1814), 307
Treaty of Guadalupe Hidalgo, 35–6, 70
Treaty of Kanagawa, 85
Treaty of Paris (1783), 215, 251
Treaty of Paris (1898), 293
Treaty of Versailles (1919), 159
Treaty on Open Skies (1992), 2
trench warfare, 76
Trieste (bathyscaphe), 24
Trinity (nuclear test), 175
Truman, Harry:
  atomic bombing of Japan, 193–4, 196;
  atomic bomb threat, 285;
  Berlin Airlift, 123, 157–8;
  communism threat, 11;
  Executive Order No. 9981, 36, 182;
  hydrogen bomb, 9, 32;
  informed of invasion of South Korea, 156;
  invasion of Japan, 159–60;
  Japanese surrender, 199;
  MacArthur, 11, 48, 98, 169;
  military assistance to South Korea, 158, 160;
  national emergency declared, 299;
  National Security Act of 1947, 181;
  National Security Act amendment (1949), 196;
  North Atlantic Pact, 92;
  Potsdam Conference, 175–6;
  railroads seized, 207;
  steel industry seizure, 95;
  Trinity test, 176;
  VE Day, 119;
  voluntary enlistments, 209;
  Women's Armed Services Integration Act, 147
Trump, Donald:
  Afghanistan military commitment, 205
Truxtun, Thomas, 42, 91, 142
Turtle (submersible), 218
Tuskegee Airmen, 80, 177, 258
Twelfth Air Force, 207
Two-Ocean Navy Act, 29
Tyler, John, 60
Typhoon Cobra (Halsey's Typhoon), 301

U-2 spy plane incident, 113
U-boats:
  first sunk, 276;
  first U.S. warship to fire torpedo at, 128;
  Greer attacked, 216;
  Kearny attacked, 250, 258;
  Reuben James attacked, 258;
  U-52, 97;
  U-352, 120;
  U-505, 141;
  U-656, 62.
  See also submarines
U.N. *See* United Nations
Uncle Sam:
  cartoon, 73
Underwater Demolition Teams, 2
Uniform Code of Military Justice, 117
Uniform Monday Holiday Act, 135
Union Army. *See* Army of the Potomac; Civil War

Index

Index

Index

Women's Auxiliary Ferry Squadron (WAFS), 79, 125

Woodford, William, 292

Wood, Ralph F., 287

World War I:
  armistice, 272;
  combat for first time, 253;
  conscription, 127, 142;
  first AEF troops arrive in France, 158;
  first major victory, 134;
  first U-boat sunk, 276;
  flying aces, 101;
  Hundred Days Offensive, 195, 205, 233;
  Meuse-Argonne, 233, 243;
  Saint-Mihiel Salient, 222, 258;
  St. Quentin Canal, 235;
  trench warfare, 76;
  U.S. formally enters, 90, 93;
  Versailles Peace Treaty, 159;
  veterans, 74;
  Zimmermann Note, 56, 62, 90

World War II:
  aerial mining begins, 83;
  Arcadia Conference, 305;
  Atlantic Charter, 197–8;
  atomic bombing of Hiroshima and Nagasaki, 189, 193–4, 195–6, 199;
  automated radar-guided missile, 107;
  Bataan siege, 8, 49, 71–2, 91, 96–7, 118;
  Battle of Leyte Gulf, 252, 254, 256–7;
  Battle of Midway, 141, 143, 208–9;
  Battle of the Bismarck Sea, 64;
  Battle of the Bulge, 38, 299, 300, 305, 308;
  Battle of the Coral Sea, 116;
  Battle of the Java Sea, 59;
  Battle of the Philippine Sea, 151–2;
  battle on U.S. soil, 135;
  Berlin bombing, 37, 58, 65–6;
  Casablanca Conference, 16, 25;
  Casablanca Directive, 22;
  Cassino invasion, 19, 127;
  Central Pacific region, 278, 280;
  Doolittle Raid, 104;
  Dresden bombing, 46;
  Elbe Day, 108;
  first enemy bomb to fall on U.S. mainland, 55;
  first German prisoners, 120;
  first German submarine sunk, 62;
  first mass, low-level, long-range air strikes, 207;
  first meeting of "Big Three," 284;
  first troops enter Germany, 221;
  Frankfurt captured, 84;
  German surrender, 118, 119;
  Guadalcanal campaign, 12, 42, 194, 213, 222, 255, 273;
  Guam invasion, 178, 301;
  Hamburg bombing, 180;
  Hungary bombing, 140;
  Japanese surrender, 4, 56, 118, 196, 199, 200–1, 208, *212*, 214;
  Kwajalein Atoll, 31, 37;
  Manila captured, 65;
  Montgomery Ward seized, 109;
  Mulberry harbors' construction begins, 143;
  napalm use, 253;
  Nazi troops move to Eastern Front, 5;
  Nazi troops trapped in Ruhr, 89;
  North Africa invasion, 269;
  Okinawa invasion, 89, 154;
  Operation Anvil, 215–16;
  Operation Axis, 219;
  Operation Brewer, 61;
  Operation Detachment, 51, 82;
  Operation Dragoon, 200;
  Operation Hailstone, 50;
  Operation Meetinghouse, 70;
  Operation Olympic, 132, 159–60;
  Operation Overlord (D-Day), 18, 128, 142–3, 284, 307;
  Operation Tidal Wave, 189;
  operations in Burma launched, 56;
  Oschersleben raid, 13;
  Paris, 204, 207;
  Pearl Harbor attack. *See* Pearl Harbor attack;
  Peleliu Island, 225;
  Poltava attacked by Luftwaffe, 153;
  Potsdam Conference, 175–6, 177, 219;
  Quadrant Conference, 197;
  Rhine River, 227;
  rockets used against shore positions, 164;
  Rome bombed, 177;
  Rome liberated, 141;
  Saipan seized, 149;
  saturation bombing, 135;
  Sicily invasion, 170, 179, 197, 202;
  Tinian captured, 180;
  V-J Day, 200;
  Wake Island, 291, 306;
  war crimes tribunal, 20–1;
  war declared, 291;
  Wiener Neustadt bombing, 263;
  Wilhelmshaven bombing, 28;
  Yalta Agreement, 44

Wounded Knee Massacre, 16, 298, 311

Wright, Orville, 176, 183, 215, 227

X Corps, 225, 307

Yalta Agreement, 44

Yamamoto, Isoroku, 104

Yavapai War, 310

Yeager, Charles E. "Chuck":
  ace, 246;
  Bell XS-1, 6;
  bio, 46;
  breaks sound barrier, 248;
  record ascent, 7

Yeager, Laura, 144, 145

Yeltsin, Boris, 5

York, Alvin C., 74, 242, 243

Young, Edna E., 169

Young, John W., 81

Yugoslavia, 102.
  See also Serbia

Zimmermann, Arthur, 56

About the Author

A frequent speaker at presidential libraries around the United States, social media innovator, columnist, and longtime White House correspondent, **Paul Brandus** is the author of ***Under This Roof: A History of the White House and Presidency*** and ***This Day in Presidential History***. An award-winning member of the White House press corps since 2008, he is the founder of *West Wing Reports*® (Twitter: @WestWingReport), and provides reports for television and radio outlets around the United States and overseas. He is also a columnist for *USA Today* and *MarketWatch/Dow Jones*. His work has appeared in media publications and outlets such as CNN, *The Guardian, Real Clear Politics, National Review,* and *The Week*.

Brandus's Twitter account is the largest among all accredited members of the White House press corps. In 2011, he won the Shorty Award for "Best Journalist on Twitter," sponsored by the Knight Foundation. His career spans network television, Wall Street, and several years as a correspondent based in Moscow, where he covered the collapse of the Soviet Union for NBC Radio and the award-winning business and economics program "Marketplace" on NPR. He has traveled to 53 countries and has reported from, among other places, Iraq, Chechnya, China, and Guantánamo Bay, Cuba. Brandus has served on the Board of Governors of the Overseas Press Club of America, serving as its Washington, D.C., representative.

Also by Paul Brandus:

Under This Roof: The White House and the Presidency—21 Presidents, 21 Rooms, 21 Inside Stores

This Day in Presidential History